A gong shivers... the mists part to reveal a grisly visage ly:
dead but for one glowing, malefic e
It speaks, in a voice of cold command: *Silence, mortal*

Tales From The MAGICIA... SKULL

GOODMAN PUBLICATIONS

NO. 1

— CONTENTS —

— AND —

INTERIOR ILLUSTRATIONS: Jennell Jaquays, Doug Kovacs, William McAusland, Brad McDevitt, Ian Miller, Russ Nicholson, Stefan Poag, and Chuck Whelon

JOSEPH GOODMAN, Publisher
HOWARD ANDREW JONES, Editor

JIM PAVELEC, Cover Illustration
LESTER B. PORTLY, Design & Layout

THE MASTER'S SKULL
speaks

Tower of the Elephant
By Robert E. Howard

Tales of Horror & The Macabre
By H.P. Lovecraft

A Princess of Mars
by E.R. Burroughs

Swords Against Death
By Fritz Leiber

DCC RPG

HEAR this, mortal dogs. You hold in your hands a magazine the likes of which has not been seen for many suns. Once there were magicians whose weird tales could change the wormy earth. They infiltrated your waking world, bringing wonder and glory and imagination. Fantastic visions you dogs could barely grasp. But mortals they were, all of them. They're dust now. With their passing a Thing was gone, a Secret passed. Well, no more. Magicians of the word, the weird tale-tellers: they may be gone, but their vision lives on. I am the skull and soul of one such word-wizard, and I'll bring you Secrets that haven't walked the earth in this century. Stories they'll be, stories that make you bolt up and hunger for adventure. You'll remember what glory could be, you'll realize how you worms have lost sight of the sun.

I am the Magician's Skull. Which magician? One you've never heard of: a peer of Howard and Lovecraft, Burroughs and Derleth, Dunsany and Leiber. A wizard who knew Merritt and St. Clair and Vance and Brackett and Wellman and Weinbaum, and Clark Ashton Smith and even grand Gygax himself. All the word-wizards wove wonder, and it matters not whose bones I rot with today. All you need to know is: I bring tales of great fantasy and wondrous adventure. Get ready, mortal dogs. Enjoy this first issue. Enjoy the adventure!

BKM·2017

TALES FROM THE MAGICIAN'S SKULL

EDITOR'S INTRODUCTION

STRANGE but true: this project didn't begin life as a magazine, and I didn't plan to be its editor. It happened like this. In 2015 Joseph asked if I'd be interested in contributing some fiction to the *2016 Goodman Games GenCon Program Guide*. I naturally said yes, just as I said yes when he asked last year if I wanted to write a story for the 2017 Program Guide.

After I turned it over he wondered if I knew any other authors who wrote in a similar vein, because he'd decided to add more stories. Once again I naturally told him yes. I've been published with a lot of writers over the years who like to craft the same sort of fiction, so it was actually harder to narrow down their numbers rather than to hunt them up.

Once Joseph had more stories it wasn't long before he proposed publishing them all in a separate magazine, along with a final few to round things out. When he mentioned he'd need an editor I don't think he realized just how hard he was about to be lobbied.

You see, I've long had two editorial daydreams. The first was to travel back in time and become a story editor for the original *Star Trek*. The second, and slightly more plausible, was to edit a magazine publishing great adventure and horror stories that wouldn't have been out of place in some of the grand old magazines of the past.

I've briefly had an opportunity to do that before, first with a little e-zine titled *Flashing Swords*, and later when John O'Neill brought me aboard to help with the final issues of *Black Gate*.

This time, though, if I could convince Joseph to let me aboard, I'd be helping to shape the voice of a print magazine from the very first issue! It was an amazing opportunity, and I didn't just throw my hat in the ring, I somersaulted into the center myself. I must have been convincing, because here I am.

As for what we're publishing here and going forward, it has a lot to do with Appendix N, the recommended reading list near the back of the original *Dungeon Master's Guide*. It wasn't just a list, it was a touchstone for a lot of young fantasy readers back in the '70s and '80s, me included. Some time late in the 1970s I copied down that appendix and rode my bicycle to the library, the bookstore, and the used bookstore and discovered a world of adventure.

I'd be lying if I said Appendix N fired my desire to write, because I'd already dreamed of becoming a professional writer and even scribbled some fiction. But Appendix N changed the kinds of stories I wanted to tell. Before it, I was pasticheing *Star Wars* and *Star Trek*. The first books I found from the list blew the doors off my imagination, starting with *Leiber's Swords Against Death* (which I still consider the best collection of Lankhmar stories) and Zelazny's original *Chronicles of Amber*.

After those, the way was opened and I've never really looked back. I still love some good space opera, but I fell in love with heroic adventure and I've been writing in some related flavor of it ever since.

What Joseph and I hope to do with *Tales from the Magician's Skull* is blow the doors off of someone else's imagination by publishing stories rooted in that same rich fictive soil that produce different and delicious flavors of thrill. Tales with the drive and color and vivid originality from days of yore that feel familiar without being derivative, and new without breaking with the past. We fervently hope to provide these tales for many issues to come, and we sincerely hope you'll join us for the ride.

Swords Together!

– Howard Andrew Jones

CHAPTERS OF THE SKULL
A DIRECTORY OF KINDRED SOULS

Australia
Canberra
Canberra (Australia) Chapter, GPO Box 1209 Canberra ACT 2601, Australia. An informal and casual group for S&S enthusiasts and fans.

Brazil
Rio de Janeiro
Chapel of Skulls – diogoarte@gmail.com. Join the ranks of our order and explores the mysteries of new pulp masters!

Santa Catarina
Ordem da Caveira – ordemdacaveira@gmail.com. Infamous readers and gamers who love to adventure in S&S worlds in the most old-school way. Let's gather to condemn the souls of the weak ones! Contact in formation with Simone (a south Brazilian gamer addict) at ordemdacaveira@gmail.com.

Canada
Alberta
Legion of the Skull Calgary – LegionoftheSkullCalgary@D0kt0rd.ca. Calgary, Alberta based fans of Old School appendix N style swords and sorcery fiction and gaming. Open to new and long time readers and gamers of all things dark and dangerous.

Tower of the Elephant – jeffrey.bdm.robertson@gmail.com, phone: (403) 400-3086, Calgary, AB, Canada. A writer of words and a reader of books, Jeff Robertson seeks others to share in his quest for High Adventure! Whether you be an author yourself, or simply a devoted fan to fiction, I want to hear from you!

The Twilight Lodge of Winter – Jkinwa@hotmail.com. A couture of like minds, hale companions and afficianados of the esoteric, exaggerated and the abysmal. Appropriate hats encouraged but not required.

New Brunswick
DragonSlayers – will@dragonslayers.ca. In Atlantic Canada, here there be dragons.

Ontario
Chapter of the Crowking

Esoteric Order of The Legion of the Skull – vdal1812@gmail.com. For the pursuit, understanding and enjoyment of Sword and Sorcery fiction.

The Penitent Hairfooters Chapter – Hairfooters@gmail.com. Halflings have a word for humans who besmirch them bodily to satisfy their baser urges - they're called "Hairfooters". Some people try to make amends.

Ottawa Chapter of the Skull – Legionoftheskullottawa@gmail.com.

France
The Order of the Fire Goose – orderofthefiregoose@gmail.com. Created after witnessing the birth of the Fire Goose, the chaotic god of the Geese, the french Order of the Fire Goose would love discussing the matters of ancient RPGs (or playing them) with anyone interested.

Germany
Hamburg
Hamma Skulls – info@hamma-skulls.de. The Legions local chapter in Hamburg, Germany. All Hail to the Magician's Skull!

Wiesbaden
Die Eisentotenkopf Gruppe – tim.danger.hall@gmail.com. Address subject to change to keep the augurs on their toes.

Japan
Tokyo
Friendly Moons Chapter sis Sempervirent Palace of Lawful Aneran Mythoi, Eastern Capital, Land of the Rising Sun.

Saudi Arabia
Al Khobar
Bone Mohawks – bone.mohawks@gmail.com. The premier Legion of the Skull chapter in the Kingdom of Saudi Arabia.

Sweden
The Silent Chanters – duckett.bill@gmail.com. For the quiet contemplation of the dread wisdom of the Skull.

United Kingdom
England
The Spa of Questionable Delights – mark@deeparcade.com. Formed in Royal Leamington Spa in the UK, this chapter is open to all who wish to discourse on the delights of Leiber, Howard, Dunsany, et al. Or indeed those whose tastes are of the more gamey variety and wish to speak of Kojima, Newell, Miyamoto, Rosenberg, Borg, Wrede and others.

The NoGarys Chapter – garypen@gmail.com. Dedicated to spreading the message of the skull via the agency of no more than one Gary.

Thame Tyrants – TT@Hogwartscastle.co.uk

USA
Alaska
Aurora Borealis Chapter - Jeff Crews, Anchorage Alaska.

Kenai Peninsula Scions of the Skull – kenaiscions@gmail.com. The Kenai Peninsula Scions are centrally located on the Kenai Peninsula in Alaska. Join your brothers and sisters in servitude of the Skull.

Arizona
Incendium – donharrington@msn.com. Hailing from the Arizona desert, we love sword & sorcery and all pulps, classic monsters, and gaming. Dark rites are performed as necessary.

The Cohort of the Phoenix Blade. Contact Colin Anders Brodd at colin.anders.brodd@gmail.com. Chapter currently based in Phoenix, AZ

Eyes of the Skull – ebatten2@cox.net, Ernie Batten; Chief Head Banger. Group in search of the Dark and Mysterious ways of Dis-enlightenment.

Mighty Thor JRS chapter. James R. Schmidt – mightythorjrs@gmail.com. Anyone who follows my blog or in the Phoenix, AZ area who would like to be a part of the group is welcome. Excited to find more people who love S&S.

Arkansas
Shadow Legion - 1soni@comcast.net. Located in the Little Rock, Ar area roaming to Memphis Tn.

Magicians of Time and Space. Contact us through the Parliment of Voices. We sit by the river of dreams while Morpheus plays all possibilities into being. Any are welcome to join the exploration of the rivulets of potentiality.

California

Knights of the Black Diamond. Can be found at Black Diamond Games in Concord Ca.

Moldering Sanctum – ericmiles42@gmail.com. 36 Cedar Crest Ct. Thousand Oaks, CA 91320.

Order of the Purple Hand. Asher Green – coachasher@gmail.com. Encouraging Sword and Sorcery fandom in Northern California's Wine Country.

Pacifica Crawlers – iamtyrael@gmail.com. We have a weekly game in the Bay Area (San Francisco) of California, let me know if you're interested!

Skullery Society of San Francisco – flyaturtle@me.com. Seance readings of swords and sorcery. OSR gaming meetups and adventures in the city paved in gold and dreams.

The Libromancers of the Dale of Glen – christian.lindke@gmail.com. Glendale, CA. The Libromancers of the Dale of Glen are a secret group coterie of academics and entertainers who share a love for swords and sorcery. We meet to discuss films and books of the genre as well as to play games inspired by the literature of the past.

Zenopus, Leiber and Lovecraft, Socercers LLP, 371 La Perle Lane, Costa Mesa, CA 92627.

Malachite Skull – malachiteskull@aspenconsult.net.

The House of the Skull – calvariamdomus@outlook.com. The House of the Skull is seeking any brave souls who wish to discuss S&S fiction. The focus is on writers who want to talk about the art form and critique each other's work.

Chapter of Mulnd – templeofmulnd@gmail.com. Your soul is trapped in the cage that is life. Only through death will you truly be free.

Chapter Of The Wolf – wolfknight75@yahoo.com. Wolf Brothers and Sisters, Let us run ahead and explore the exciting and mysterious pages of the Tales from the Magician's Skull together.

Chapter of Torchbearers – chapterofthetorch@gmail.com. To look beyond the texts of mortal men.

Corpses of Santa Venetia – jcox@sonic.net.

Gray Matters – cerebellum@brain.organ. Dealing with all issues related to squishy part of the magician's skull.

League of the Shattered Tankard – altdsrobin@hotmail.com. Devoted to discussions of epic deeds and eldritch lore from the golden age of adventure.

Lost Souls of Lankhmar – soulsoflankhmar@gmail.com. I would be interested in talking with others who enjoy writing and reading S&S and Fantasy both old and new.

Special Task Force Unicorn.

The Naris Lords - send postcard to Castle Naris begging for mercy.

Tom Naughty's Trust.

Colorado

Denver Legion – zvanstanley@gmail.com.

Esoteric Order of the Black Scroll – ajgrotjohn@gmail.com. Adam "Grotonomus" Grotjohn, 637 East Tomahawk Circle, Grand Junction, CO. 81504. The Order is a group for like minded individuals of discerning taste to converse about classic pulp adventure fiction and participate in conventions and in-person or online role playing games.

aewestenbarger@gmail.com.

The Brothers – mtapia@TheBrothers,com. Dedicated to playing classic-style RPG and reading the Appendix N literature that inspired them.

Green Gables Chapter: 303-989-1765.

The Company of the Crow – Mark_hughes1@mac.com. An irregular DCC campaign run in my home, with hope for expanding to road crew games and open table convention games.

The Deadly Shadowz – ravenshadowz@aol.com.

Delaware

Scribes of the Inward Eye, William Craig – scribesoftheinwardeye@gmail.com. We who excogitate lucubrations fantastic... or, folks that love to read a wopper of a tale.

Florida

Terrible Tomes of Tampa, Matt Caulder – matt@mattcaulder.com.

The Sanctum Secorum (Sanctum.media / TheHub@Sanctum.media / https://plus.google.com/+SanctumMediaDCC). The library doors of the Sanctum Secorum are open for all who wish to enter and discuss the fantastic tales found within the covers of the Magician's Skull or the other, classic works, of pulps of a bygone age.

Revenants – Contact information: Deposit two gold coins into the hands of an urchin and mention that you wish to speak to The Darkness. Then goto the nearest merchant house and ask to buy something in lavender to wear. You will be met by a representative in good time.

The Horde of the Golden Skull – theprisoner1942@gmail.com. Michael Lingefelt, Brandon Florida. Supporting the golden age classics from the past and future writers

Georgia

Robin's Enclave, Ethan Burke etburketx@verizon.net.

The Lords of Sarcasm – thelordsofsarcasm@gmail.com. "This requires a special blend of psychology and extreme violence."

Idaho

Bunnies of Chaos.

Illinois

Looking to be part of a book club in the Chicagoland western suburbs. Contact info: akomins@pobox.com, or via Facebook or twitter: akomins.

Chicago - NW burbs, MickGall.com.

Tower of the City Beautiful, Joshua Rose – shooaaah@gmail.com. Facebook: https://www.facebook.com/TowerOfTheCityBeautiful/ Traipse across far away and fantastic realms of horror and magic. Talk of great Sword and Sorcery tales in Chicago face to face.

Adventure Pulp Chapter, pulpvault@msn.com.

De Bookvermis Mysteriis, Facebook group for sharing all things printed and bound.

Meat Grinder Maniacs, Slaughterhouse rules applied to the RPG universes.

Secret Legion Sect.

Zenzizenzizenzic of Ys.

Indiana

Indiana Bones and Bards of the Ancients – bmarchetti76@yahoo.com.

Keepers of the Lost Bookmark, PO Box 39113 Indianapolis, IN 46239-0113. A secretive order of scholars tasked with gathering the missing Placeholders of Knowledge, and delivering them to those in need. Send a Self-Addressed-Stamped Envelope to join.

Calumet Region Skull Legion – https://www.facebook.com/Calumet-Region-Skull-Legion-857859214395601/.

Secret Citadel, John DeCocq – j_decocq@yahoo.com. From deep inside the bowels of his secret Citadel in a forgotten corner of the Astral Plane, the Netherworlder hordes forgotten knowledge and coaxes long-buried mystical treasures from the crania of his former enemies. Join him in his quest to extract these Tales from the Magician's Skull!

Inzeladun Chapter – vincentdarlage@gmail.com.

The Owlbear Watching Society.

Iowa

Chroniclers of Cayearth – tirionalexander@hotmail.com. A Facebook group for discussing fantasy adventure literature and games.

Cutter's Irregulars.

Kentucky

Central Kentucky Bluegrass Cohort – kydungeonmaster@gmail.com. Call or Text: (859)967-7515

Greater Louisville Chapter – Lanebowen@yahoo.com.

Adepts of the Chrystal Skull – dac1981.bghs@gmail.com. Seeking truth in the fog-shrouded citadels of the abyss.

The Lost at River's Edge.

Louisiana

The SMURSH http://smursh.net/dcc-ref.

Maryland

Chapter of the Stone God – Twitter: andrian6, Web: biomechanoidblues.wordpress.com. Tread carefully or the great stone god, the Daimajin, will awake.

The Unbeholden.

Massachusetts

The Song of the Pit. Contact: Michael at mgl61@hotmail.com. Hear now the Song, ye dungeon delvers, for the awful poem of the mad poet Rinaldo has been recovered, and in its verses the monstrosities of the Pit shall soon be revealed.

Hold The Rope LLC, Western Mass, themobos.com. Imagine a 1983 GMC Vandura cargo van with a Frank Frazetta mural painted on its side, blasting The Sword's "Apocryphon" and driven by your best friend. We are Hold The Rope LLC, available for all OSR campaigns.

Michigan

Skulls of Ann Arbor. – Brisco420@msn.com. Meet ups with local Skull fans at area coffeehouse's, to expound on mystic topics.

Grym Corps, Macomb County, Michigan – grymcorps@comcast.net. Collecting Magikal Skulls from around the known dimensions for eons.

Michigan Cohort, Ann Arbor Century, Centurion: Chris Henry – chrishen@umich.edu. Looking to meet up with fellow fans of pulpy Science Fiction and Fantasy to discuss fiction, play tabletop RPGs, and/or drink strange and exotic beverages. If you like the Monster Hunter International series, run DCC games, or have somehow managed to get your hands on some authentic Mongol arkhi and bring it back to the States, drop me a line.

The Free Flying Skulls – fritz@acm.org. http://fritzfreiheit.com/wiki/The_Free_Flying_Skulls

Minnesota

The Minneapolis DCC RPG Society, Contact: Julian Bernick, 612 751 3139, Julian_bernick@yahoo.com. A benevolent association committed to the betterment of fictive worlds via mayhem.

r/Fantasy Chapter – www.reddit.com/r/fantasy. Gathering place for those who love and support speculative fiction.

The Hand and Eye Society.

Winona Skullskalds – mooreeffoceditor@hotmail.com. Gather 'round with us in a mead hall where the Mississippi does flow / To hear and recite tales of wonder, tales of woe.

Missouri

Ghost Corps – ghostcorps011@gmail.com. Southwest Missouri's official Chapter of the Legion of the Skull. "Put the mask on... now!"

Independence Skulls for Life – cotterbob1955@yahoo.com. Open to anyone who wants to promote skullduggery, good fun and fair play.

Tempest Wisdom & Insight.

Thou Who Shall Submit – brybiek@gmailcom. Rise Tall. Stand Above All

Nebraska

The Crew.

Nevada

Vegas Steel. – Kerstanszczepanski@gmail.com. Strange worlds, the stranger the better; a sharp blade, and eldritch magic is all else I ask.

Reno Dungeon Crawler's Guild, Randy Andrews, PO Box 21192 Reno NV 89515. We are a guild of Dungeon Crawler's who have fallen in league with the Legion of the Skull. If you'd like to join us on an adventure drop me a line!

Wasteland Degenerates – Nevadaknight@ymail.com. We are a group of radioactive fantasy/Sci Fi enthusiasts. Living in and around the nuclear test sites of Nevada.

The Cursed of Midian! – Midianranch@yahoo.com. "Here in the heart of the vast Black Rock Desert lies the degenerate coven of the doomed and mad known as Midian!"

New Hampshire

Ian McGarty – silverbulette@gmail.com. The rumble below, toothsome ground rises.

New Jersey

Hillsborough Chapter, 1324 Orchard Drive, Hillsborough, NJ 08844.

New Mexico

We are Chapter Lurid. You may attempt to summon us at ChapterLurid@gmail.com but it will cost one portion of your soul. We hold many secrets beyond mortal understanding, to include [REDACTED] and [TRANSMISSION ENDED].

New York

Azure Jack Chapter – eddyspaghetti8@yahoo.com. The Azure House gives us the jobs the Azure Knight isn't right for. We get them done.

Zombies Need Brains – contact@zombiesneedbrains.com. Zombies Need Brains is a small press focused on supporting SF&F short fiction, including sword & sorcery.

Devotees of Clark Action Smith.

Harbingers of Doom – ianspeaks@gmail.com. 382 13th St. Brooklyn, NY 11215. Appendix N, M, and the tangents in between.

The Radiant Eye of F'av Chapter: a place for many things of a thaumaturgical nature – fletchav@gmail.com, http://swordssorcery.blogspot.com/

NYC Appendix N Book Club – We're an offshoot of Dungeon Crawl Classics NYC that meets regularly in Brooklyn for coffee, pastry, and Appendix N book discussion. Please visit our Meetup group (https://www.meetup.com/DCCNYC) or drop us a note at AppendixNBookClub@gmail.com for more information.

North Carolina

Asheville Legion of the Skull – 828skulls@gmail.com. Seeking like minded Appendix N aficionados to discuss sword and sorcery novels, movies, games, and things of that sort. Check out the Asheville DC-CRPG Facebook page for more information.

Traveling Crowns – travelingcrowns@gmail.com. We are a currently based out of Eastern North Carolina, traveling coast to coast.

Weird Taletellers – paulke.go+wt@gmail.com. Davidson, NC.

Greenshirts – jim.niemira@gmail.com. Long-time group of gamers, now spread across Buffalo, Charlotte, and other cities, play most games from OSR to PbtA to small indie press.

The Crimson Flame – thorinthompson@gmail.com. Beware, beware, that fair and gentle stare with a beckoning flicker through yonder passage there...

The Legion of Archon – archon-gaming@googlegroups.com. Adventurer, Conqueror, and King!

Ohio

Cincinnati 158th, Making the enemies of the Emperor quake in their boots since 2002.

Tao Ludi – aelfwin.herumuzu@gmail.com. Dayton, Ohio, USA.

The Lich's Tontine – brammere@gmail.com. Gamers in central Ohio who also like to read.

Dyscrasiac Victims (Chapter of) – www.selindberg.com. Dyscrasia is a disease, an imbalance of the four medicinal humors professed by the ancient Greeks to sustain life. This Chapter of weird fiction enthusiasts collects those who study the alchemical bonds between readers and horrific scripts – a cause of dyscrasia.

Illuminated Seers of Forest Park – pjarman@ebay.com. Wisdom without a tongue. Knowledge forbidden learnt before its nature is known.

Oklahoma

Kings of Oblivion – barkingdogsstudio74@gmail.com.

Tornado Alley Game Guild. Find us on Google+, and let's see if we can generate some meet-ups in Flyover Country!

Oregon

Gary's Basement RPG Consortium – gdmcbride@hotmail.com. Beaverton OR – A weekly conclave of only the finest gaming weirdoes.

3rd Cohort, Legion of the Skull – pquixano@gmail.com.

Dark Regions Press – Independent Specialty Publisher of Horror, Fantasy and Science Fiction Since 1985. Visit on DarkRegions.com.

House of Frankenstein.

Pennsylvania

Greater Harrisburg Order of the Umber Labyrinth – forcecommander@comcast.net

Legion of the Skull, Pittsburgh East – legionoftheskullpgheast@gmail.com. For Legion of the Skull members in the Pittsburgh and east of Pittsburgh region.

Skullkateers Pittsburgh – Mike Bolam – mbolam@gmail.com. Looking to establish a Skullkateers reading group in the Pittsburgh area. Appendix N and adjacent literature welcomed.

Rhode Island

Church of Starry Wisdom – celestialprovidence13@gmail.com. Looking for cultists in the greater Providence, RI area who are interested in gaming and discussing Appendix N.

The Lost Legion. This once mighty company disappeared 50 years ago. Rumor says that only the most depraved are admitted.

South Carolina

Chapter of the Missing Eye, Rob, Greenville, SC – bloodyharbinger@hotmail.com. "In secret and darkness we watch"

Servants of the Secret Fire, Serving Greyhawk, Lankhmar, Upstate South Carolina, @rrhodeswriter (Robert Rhodes).

The Lost Riddle of Steel, Bret Hammitt – bret_hammitt@icloud.com

South Dakota

Screw The Pen I Want A Sword – stpiwas@williamdegeest.com. Twitter: @STPIWAS. Central S.D. somewhere between the Mighty Mo and the Big Jim. Infrequent meetings.

Tennessee

Legion of the Skull: Memphis, Tennessee Chapter, Jeff Scifert – jscifert@bellsouth.net. Looking to meet RPG and Sword & Sorcery enthusiasts in the Memphis, TN area for discussions and roleplaying opportunities.

Nashville Dungeoneers. Travelers through a weird land. Hack and slash, then speak with dead.

Texas

Chris James, Kilgore, TX

Descendants of Poseidonis, Houston/Katy – PoseidonisHouston@Yahoo.com Retro-RPG/WeirdTales Group

Legion of the Bloody Skulls Chapter – tallknight@gmail.com Currently based in San Antonio, Texas

Voyagers From the Outer Dark – daniel.robichaud@gmail.com. A Houston, TX chapter of Readers dedicated to sharing fabulous fiction.

D&D Geeks – havoc@boldo.com. Games, both board & RPG in Cedar Park, TX.

Empryean Diet of Dagon, Steve Muchow – merchantsteve@mythmerchant.com A council dedicated to games, literature and more covering weird fiction.

Funambulous Evangels – pockyhoodoo@gmail.com

Oath Sworn of the Skull – To summon us, you must first carve a ritualistic summoning rune of David on a two foot by two foot slab of obsidian. Then arrange 13 black candles. Ring the bell of Aphos 3 times and chant the incantation of Morgal in the celestial song of Angelic to activate the portal. We take no responsibility for the loss of flammable Grimoire.

The Bayou Barbarians. We are fans of swords & sorcery literature and gaming. Find us at https://www.facebook.com/groups/bayoubarbarians/.

The Very Most Secret Chapter – gibbsbenj@gmail.com. Meets Thursdays.

Virginia

Order of the Void – kabor6@aol.com. Sword and Sorcery cult in Tidewater, Virginia.

The Crypt of the Squamous Necromancers, P.O. Box 3221 Manassas, VA 20108 United States of America.

Lords of Madness – illithid@lordofmadness.com.

The Order of the Thousand Hammers.

Washington

Cracked Skull NW, Skeeter Green – skeetyrbug@gmail.com. Cracked up in the Northwest.

Haunting the game shops of Vancouver, WA, these numbskulls have a bone to pick with you. Any bodies dying for a lively time may find themselves in grave danger.

Keepers of the Azure Flame, Seattle, Washington https://groups.google.com/forum/#!forum/kotaf.

Luminaries of the Dark, Eric K. Rodriguez, 413 Prospect Ave. North #4 Kent, WA 98030. "Let the dark be revealed and let us be the bringer of that light."

Dreamweaver's Delight.

Runehammer Chapter – hankerin.ferinale@gmail.com. We are the many who dwell in the pine ocean of Nordheim, Thushum raiders, Iradrum smiths, and pike men of Grey. Death must wait, for we have much to do.

Skull Collector's of Camano Island, Andrew Hintz (Adotlin) – andrew.hintz@live.com Looking to become the founding chapter of Camano Island. Local or not we can play in person or online, so reach out and join the Legion!

West Virginia

Each One Teach One, Ryan – xmiyux@gmail.com. Gaming is real life but better. Spread the love of the hobby and the classic fiction that inspires it.

Wisconsin

Thulaen Lands Chapter – nolabert@gmail.com. The people of the frozen tundra along the old Ouisconsin.

Blood Kings – afrielink@dlainc.com. Gamers extraordinaire and victors of many tourneys. We look forward to any challenge.

Fealty to the Fez Society – andy@raprojectsolutions.com - Waukesha, WI. You can't judge a book by its cover, but you can judge a hat by its tassel - or lack thereof!

Skulls of the North Woods – epiclotus@gmail.com. Looking for fellow weird fiction fans in the northern Wisconsin area.

The East Side Militia – dvgrim6actual@gmail.com. Southeast Wi.

The Eville Armory – Evansville, WI – romprecentor@yahoo.com.

Golden Skulls, Chris Zank – chriszank2@gmail.com.

The Dungeon of the Barbarian Horde – trkhellian@comcast.net. The horde of barbarians issued from the dungeon crypt. Really, it's just my gaming group coming out of my basement for coffee.

The d30's - DCC MKE, Judge Jik – cubecrazy2@yahoo.com. Sculpting nubile peasants into soul fodder for thou most unholy. On top of that we run 0 level funnels, higher level modules, or just sit around rolling funky dice.

THE LEGION OF THE SKULL

1soni; A Mutated Puma Named Grrr; A. Walter Abrao ; Adam "Grotonomus the Gruesome" Grotjohn; Adam Alexander; Alan J Clark; Alexander Macris; Allen Denison; Allen Westenbarger; Alvin Helms; Andrew "The Black Hood" Thompson; Andrew Hintz; Andrew James McDole; Andrew Kluessendorf; Andrew M. Morris; Andrew O. Johnson; Andrija Popovic; Andy Action; Andy Frielink; Arbogast von Frankenstein; Arin Komins; Asher Green, Warlord; Banks Wilson; Baragoon; Baron Von Swodeck; Bart Scott; Ben Rosenberg; Bob & Jen Brinkman; BoBwire Fouts; Brad L. Kicklighter; Brandish Gilhelm; Brent Tomlonovic; Bret D. Hammitt; Breton Kabor Winters; Brian Marchetti; Bruce Wesley; Bryan Chamchoum; Bryant T. S. Biek; C. C. Scales; Casey Hendley; Cato Vandrare; Chainsaw; Charles Helm; Chris Ellis; Chris FitzPatrick; Chris Henry; Chris Ronnfeldt; Chris Wilson; Chris Zank; Christian Lindke; Christian Oliver; Christian Ovsenik; Christian Torstensson; Christopher Anderson; Christopher Avery; Christopher Ham; Christopher Hill; Christopher James; Christopher Kearney; Christopher Lee; Clément Debaecker; Colin Anders Brodd, Master of the Runes; D. Christopher Dodd; Dan Alban; Dan Domme; Daniel J. Bishop; Daniel, Trista, and Eleanor Robichaud; Darin Kerr; Dark Regions Press (DarkRegions.com); Darren Pawluk - Cat Wrangler; David Bessenhoffer; David Bresson; David Christopher Lee; David Crabtree; David Dierks; David Donohoo; David Fort; David Hoskins; David J. West; David Johnston; David Lars Chamberlain; David S. Robinson; Der Gotten Zorn; Diogo "Old Skull" Nogueira; Don Harrington; Doug Ellis; Douglas J Waltman, Esq.; Dr. Donald A. Turner; Dread Emperor; Dustin Manning; Dwayne Boothe; Echo and Ryan Full; Ed Kowalczewski; Eric D Reynolds; Eric D. Miles; Eric K. Rodriguez; Eric Neal Samuels; Eric S. Betts; Erik Brammer; Erik Gradine; Erik T Johnson; Erik Talvola; Ernie Batten ; Ethan Burke; Ethan Schoonover; Eugene V. O'Dea; Fenric Cayne; Fletcher A. Vredenburgh; flyaturtle; Fnord Prefect; Franz Georg Rösel; Fred Herman; Fritz Freiheit; G. Hartman; Gadhra the Arbiter; Gary McBride; Gary Pennington; General Lopez; Geoff Knox; Hector Cruz; Ian McGarty; Ian S. Burgess; Iro; J. Mowers; J. Stuart Pate; J.M. Sunden; James Niemira; James R. Schmidt - Mighty Thor JRS Fantasy/Sword and Sorcery blog.; James Van Horn; Jan Schattling; Jared Friant; Jason "DM Morgal" Scranton; Jason C. Penney; Jason E. Thummel; Jason Ezra (Australia); Jason S. Walters; Jason Woods; Jay Jurczynski; Jeff Crews; Jeff Robertson; Jeff Scifert; Jeff Vandine; Jeff Wright; Jen Hocking; Jeremy 'Black' Coffey ; Jeremy Harper; Jik Wreath; Jim Cox; Jim Dovey; Jim Grob; Jim Kitchen; Jim McLaughlin; Joe "Big Nasty Ceech" DiCicco; Joe Abboreno; John "Netherworlder" DeCocq; John Anthony; John Bullard; John C. Lemay; Johnny F. Normal; Jon Kimmich; Jonathan Perkel; Jonathan Pickens; Joseph Hoopman; Josh 'Tallknight' Higgins; Josh King; Joshua Cooper; Joshua Madara; Joshua Palmatier (Zombies Need Brains); Joshua Rose; Judge Joe Kilmartin; Karl Andrew Stevens; Keith Nelson; Keith West, Future Potentate of the Solar System; Kerstan Szczepanski ; Kese Chartier; Kevin "Doktor Grym" Wojciechowski; Kevin Scully; Kraken; Kyle Thorson; L.A.James (Weisenwolf); Lane Bowen ; Laura Lundy; Lawrence Ore, Adjunct History Professor, Miskatonic University; Le galopin de Coëtcandec; Lee Joseph Fulton; Lee Murphy; Lenurd the Joke Gnome; Leopold Goldimire; Loren B. Dean; Luigi McMinn; M.L. Nusbaum; Manicial Matt Caulder; Marc the Maugifer; Mark A. Woolsey; Mark AC Green; Mark Hughes; Mark Tygart; Martin of the Vale, American Antiquarian and Sub-Sub-Librarian of Mundane Magic ; Marzio Muscedere; Matt "Killer GM" Varden; Matt Couch; Matthew "Derleth" Franklin; Matthew Renfro; Matthias Weeks; Mazandus; Michael Jones; Michael Lingefelt; Michael Little; Michael P. Wolfson; Michael T. Tapia; Mick Gall; Mikayla Anya G. Cahiwat; Mike Bolam; Mike Bunch; Mike Shema; Morgan Hazel; Mr. Charles J. Erickson III; Nathan Housley; Nathaniel "Spartacusblb" Bowers ; Ngo Vinh-Hoi; Nicholas "Oz" Ozment; Pat Ludwig; Paul "TrKhellian" Morgan; Paul Bachleda; Paul Dieken; Paul Friswold; Paul Go; Paul Niedernhofer; Paul y cod asyn Jarman; Peter Sotos; Quazniak; Randy Andrews; Randy Smith; Rashad Wareh; Raven Shadowz; Raymond Fowkes; Redfuji6; Ricardo Sedan; Richard J. "Cthulhu's Librarian" Miller; Ricky Rimkevicus; Rob C; Rob Hansen; Rob Voss; Robert J. Nemeth; Robert Rhodes; Robert W. Cotter; Robin Powers; Roffles Lowell ; Roger Harvell, Jr; Ronald H. Miller; Ryan Idryo, Lorekeeper; Ryan Steffen; Samuel Frederick; Samuel Patrick McFadden and father,Michael.; Scarlett Letter; Scott Barnes; Scott Cunningham; Scott Edward Nash; Scott Kanger; Scott Meredith; Scott Turns; Sean Daley; Sean Guillemette; Sergey Pomerantsev; Seth E. Lindberg; Shane C Bradley; Shane Lacy Hensley; Simon Boy; Simone Rolim de Moura; Skeeter MF Green; Skulldoon; Stefan Flickinger; Stefan Pokorny (aka: Zaltar); Stephen Alexander BLAIR; Stephen Murrish; Steve 'elquesogrande' Drew; Steve Muchow; Steven Torres-Roman; Stewart Wilson ; Sven; T Broml; T.E. Hall; Terry Olson; Thaddeus Moore; The Disgruntled Poet; The Gibbs Family; The Naris Lords; The Peccant Paynim of Pestilence, Jim Skach; The Sandhorse; Thorin 'Son ov Thrain' Thompson; Timothy Ryan Deschene; Tobias Loc; Todd Stephens; Tomodeus Naught; Tony Hogard; Trevor Stamper; Troy Chrisman; Turjun the Panthan; Valerie Emerson; Vidal Bairos; Vincent Darlage, Ph.D.; Vincent E. Hoffman; Wade Harrison III; William DeGeest, Some guy who sometimes does things. Enjoys cottage cheese.; William Duckett; William E Craig Jr; William McGrath; YorkusRex; Zach Roberts; Zach Van Stanley; Zoë Himmah

Thank you to all the Legion of the Skull members who backed our initial Kickstarter!

ILLUSTRATION BY DOUG KOVACS

WHAT LIES IN ICE

A Gaunt and Bone Adventure

By CHRIS WILLRICH

SOUTHWARD the trireme chased the iceberg, for only in its wake could the ship escape the frozen sea. "Row!" the captain shouted, his spittle summing up his survey of the whiteness gnawing behind. "The ice will chew us up!"

The weary oarsmen found their strength, the sailmaster struggled to tap the mercurial north wind, and the navigator — that strange woman whom the captain hopelessly loved — narrowed her eyes at the ragged channel. For few would test Captain Dawnglass' temper, and his wrath had 'til this voyage kept them all alive.

He was far, far from the gentle Great River that washed blue through home's golden deserts. A black-bearded, bald-headed, dark-skinned man, he was distinct amongst a crew of mostly light-skinned northerners. They saw him as exotic, he, the most ordinary person in the world, son of dockside glassblowers. Silly as it was, he played on this notion, rumbling childhood songs under his breath that the crew took for charms against evil, but which were really lullabies.

It was a kind of falsehood. But he would tell any lie to get them through.

Alas, the same tricks wouldn't work on his passengers.

"But what of *them?*" said the nearer of the two, whose gesture took in none of *Sea-Glare*'s crew. Rather, the ferret-like, sandy-haired thief Imago Bone jabbed at the ribbon of the iceberg's moon-silvered wake and the ragged ramparts of its pinnacle — and at the uncanny crimson light oozing from crystalline depths. "*They* will come again soon. I'd draw no closer."

Bone's companion said, "We're indeed stuck between an iceberg and a cold place." She seemed a trifle fey, did Persimmon Gaunt — and Dawnglass, who'd known his share of women and still more of peril, treaded carefully around her. Gaunt had no supernatural talents that he knew, and claimed to be a simple farm-girl, toughened by a life on the road. Dawnglass didn't believe it. Beneath her auburn hair, the spiderweb-and-rose tattoo upon her pale face suggested mysteries. Gaunt might not be a sorceress, but she had a gift for piercing veils, whether with a poet's quill or a rogue's dagger.

"But it wasn't entirely by accident," Gaunt continued, "was it? You were *hoping* to find the frozen citadel."

Dawnglass looked away. "I admit it. What treasure hunter wouldn't? The tower of Salack Thorn! I grew up on legends of his enchantments, as did you both."

They'd traveled together before, Dawnglass and this poet and thief. He liked them, after a fashion. When he'd re-encountered them on a remote northern coast a month ago, begging transportation after some unspeakable caper up in Penultima Thule, he'd taken it as a good omen for an arctic venture —

"Captain!" interrupted a woman's voice from atop the mainmast.

Although *Sea-Glare* possessed no crow's nest, this was of no consequence to the navigator Irilee. She was the ship's greatest advantage, a mariner who'd once been an elemental creature of the sea. Though she'd given up that life, she retained a preternatural grace when sailing. Irilee perched as though she and the vessel were one.

There was nothing smooth or easy about her cry of warning, however. "*The Hands of the Sea!*"

"Stow oars!" Dawnglass bellowed, and the call was taken up by desperate voices across the deck and below. "Torches!"

It began again.

In the moonlight hundreds of once-human hands, wrinkled and barnacled and stinking of ocean slime, rose from the waters and clawed blindly at the hull. They covered the painted eyes that glowered at *Sea-Glare*'s prow, scuttled toward the oar-ports, and crawled up the rudder.

And among the death-grey hands were the paws of white bears and the claws of orange crabs, and here and there the rosy blooms of sea anemones, and the pink tentacles of squid, and many another thing that once grasped and tore beneath the waves. The mass of manipulators rose as one scuffling, clutching horde. Their swarming was even more unnatural than it first appeared, for if they lost their grip they dangled for a while mid-air like puppets on unseen strings, before grasping *Sea-Glare* once more. A maddening chorus of scratching and clawing echoed throughout the ship, amid the wash of waters, the creaks of wood, and the shouts of men.

The Hands of the Sea dragged one rower screaming into the night, rending him to red fragments.

His screams ceased as a merciful arrow found his heart. Gaunt had retrieved her bow from one of the chests upon the deck. Imago Bone clutched a torch. Dawnglass hefted a double-edged *kaskara* sword, and in the firelight he hoped he resembled a bold knight of far southern Ma'at, his homeland. Truth was, he was terrified, but half of being captain was theater. "To the tiller!"

Even now Viken, the huge oarsman he'd ordered to guard Tariq, the slight but strong-armed helmsman, waved a torch in one hand and an axe in another, forcing back the Hands. Other sailors joined them, their torches and moonlit blades swirling like a calamity of fire and ice. The clutching mass seethed onto the deck like a dozen cut nets billowing with a hideous catch.

Dawnglass and Bone slashed, and Gaunt targeted any of *them* threatening to snatch another man. Irilee called down directions to Tariq, whose brown face and black mustache shone with moonlit sweat, but who never released his grip.

They were lucky so far, for the wind and the iceberg agreed on their course. It might not remain so. The frozen mass, most of its substance far below the surface, was compelled only by deep currents. Meanwhile the surface ice shifted with the wind — as did *Sea-Glare* if the oarsmen couldn't intervene. Every moment the rowers battled was another moment the ship could scuttle.

The attack ended as abruptly as had the previous two.

All at once the Hands of the Sea dropped again into the waters.

Dawnglass had time for only one deep breath before his ship careened into the sea ice. But he welcomed battles with honest things — men, ships, nature. "Oars! Push off!"

With care and oaths and prayers, the crew shoved away from the ice and back into the channel.

"We lost five!" called down Irilee.

"Does Aurelius live?"

"Yes, we still have a sailmaster!"

"Good." Dawnglass shut his eyes. "Gaunt and Bone," he said, "join me up front." After a pause he called out, "Irilee! Find a relief for Tariq. Bring him and Viken to the prow."

Sunrise had begun, revealing a grey-white expanse stretching endlessly beneath pearly skies and striped by clouds resembling pink scars. In that light his handpicked group assembled. Dawnglass said, "Whatever blasphemy lies in the ice, it will slay us before we reach open sea. I will not wait for death."

Ahead, the iceberg grew rosy with sunlight, the unhealthy crimson glow fading for now. But deep within its vastness could now be seen an immense, leaning shadow of ebon stone, stretching unsettling crenellations and flanges like gargoyles' wings. Weird lights seethed from slivered windows.

Only a fool would go there — or a man whose ship was doomed, and the woman he loved with it.

"We're raiding the tower of Salack Thorn?" Irilee said, as if reading all his thoughts.

"Aye," he said, "and plundering it too." But the pirate bravado in his voice was like a chest of fool's gold.

• • •

IRILEE of Thessalonike had once been what humans, in their feeble understanding, called a *mermaid*. Sometimes the memories haunted her, of taking the shape of a fish-tailed woman, or a glimmer of coins in shallow water, or the shadow of land upon the waves. A mermaid's substance was mutable, and coalesced around observers' desires. Her primal state was a vortex, liquid and luminescent.

Then one day an extraordinary thing had happened; she'd had a powerful desire of her own.

When she'd become human her sisters had tried to slay her alongside Dawnglass, whom they'd believed had captured her love. They'd been wrong. It wasn't Dawnglass she loved, though she liked him well enough. It was his ship. She wouldn't lose *Sea-Glare* and its freedom lightly.

The little skiff, rowed hard by Dawnglass and Viken and steered by Tariq, bore Gaunt, Bone, and Irilee to the iceberg's shimmering edges.

Irilee closed her eyes to better sense the play of water — solid and liquid — all around. "I'll seek a passage."

Opening her mind to the sea, she remembered swimming as a mermaid to Scarcoil Reef. There the coral formed a thousand-mile glyph in a language even older than lost Nobeca's. At its innermost crook, in the crater of a sunken volcano, the Witch of Angles dwelled. She had granted Irilee's wish to become human, but there had been a condition.

You can never again echo another's desire, the Witch had declared, her jagged shadow appearing here and there within the bubbling caldera. *Or you will revert. You must be truthful about your own will, or you will again become water, and within minutes you will die.*

"Is that what it means to be human?" she'd asked. "To be truthful?"

The Witch of Angles had laughed a long bitter laugh. *You join a people of lies. But you will have gifts. You will have a sense of water, and be protected from it and by it. And you may swim deeper and longer than any other human. And you may lie too, if you wish — but not about your own desire. That alone is forbidden.*

"That seems little enough."

You may be surprised.

Now there came a splash, from something too small to have tugged at her senses. Gaunt was pointing toward an ice-shelf, ragged and blue-white. "It came from over there."

Viken, the huge, red-bearded sea-raider with the silver bird of the gentle Swan Goddess glinting incongruously at his neck, reached for one of the five axes he carried in an absurdly weaponized backpack. "What? What came from there?"

"Calm yourself," said Tariq, his cultured voice and white headdress hinting at his origin in Mirabad, a place as civilized as Viken's homeland was not. "A fish, surely? And yet…"

"A hand," Dawnglass said grimly.

"There are but two oars," Bone objected, as he often did to manual labor.

"*No*, Bone," Gaunt said, taking his wrist and pointing. "A *hand*. Look."

"Oh."

For there was indeed, Irilee saw, a pale severed hand, hard to distinguish from the swirling undulations of the iceberg's fringe, crawling from the water onto the shimmering slope. Yellowed bone was visible at the wrist. Strange, seemingly-writhing black inscriptions covered the back and palm, and its ring finger was possessed of an emerald in the shape of an eye. The stone glowed as though a tiny sun lay smothered behind it.

"Where are the others?" Tariq wondered, gaze darting here and there.

"It's alone," Irilee said, "I am sure." She watched the hand point at the rising mass of ice. "I think it's directing us toward a tunnel."

"It's surely a trap," said Viken. He made to throw his axe.

"Wait! It may not be hostile. The Hands of the Sea come always at night."

Gaunt added, "Have any of us witnessed *this* particular hand before, with those markings, and that ring?" All answered in the negative. "This is a new element," Gaunt concluded.

The hand twitched its way out of sight.

"Should we follow, Gaunt?" Bone asked.

"I think so…" Gaunt answered with a distant look.

"I sense there may be a better path," Irilee ventured, "further along the edge."

"I trust Gaunt's intuitions," Bone said. "More than I trust undead hands, admittedly."

"Hm." Dawnglass peered at the glinting ice as though hoping to consult his reflection. "I dislike splitting up, but there's no place here to beach the skiff." Some would have to go, and some remain. "Gaunt and Bone, you're normally a duo. Will you follow?"

When they'd nodded, Tariq said, "I have an interest in magic, Captain, and that ring arouses my curiosity."

"Fair enough; I did speak of plunder. But Viken and Irilee stay with me. Good luck to us all. If you must abandon the mission, try to reach *Sea-Glare*. Sailmaster Aurelius will bring the ship close if you wave."

Dawnglass neglected to add that these cold waters could kill anyone in minutes, Irilee thought. Anyone but her, that is.

Once Tariq, Bone, and Gaunt had scrambled out of sight, the journey was strangely quiet. Water melting from the iceberg's peak blew across them in a chilling mist. Ice fragments bumped against the boat with muted *thunks*. Waters lashed at the grey-white cliffs, carving caves. The irregularities spawned strange colors in reflected sunlight.

"There," Irilee said. "Into that cave."

Viken looked dubiously at Dawnglass, but the captain studied Irilee, smiled, and nodded. As they maneuvered inside the iceberg, Irilee found herself blushing. She could read a great deal in Dawnglass' stares.

The cave led to a watery tunnel, and the tunnel into darkness, but she sensed a hollow space in there, directly beneath the tower …

The boat lurched. "Swan's Blood!" Viken swore.

A mass of white tentacles, each wider than Viken, grabbed the launch and dragged it from the water. Irilee saw they were covered with eyes: brown eyes, blue eyes, hazel eyes — but all human eyes.

The ice below them was red.

• • •

THE mysterious hand was nowhere to be seen. What the thief Bone *could* see was ice, blue-tinted and darkening as they proceeded down a slippery tunnel. He hesitated to light a torch, not wanting to injure himself with fire before Salack Thorn's machinations got their fair shot.

Behind him he heard Gaunt telling Tariq, "Legends say the other wizards of Nobeca couldn't remove the sorcerer from his sanctum, but they were able to magically confine him to the tower. And while the citadel could fly, they pinned it to one location. It's said Nobeca sank not long after, while the tower hovered above the waves. Cold laughter followed the survivors' ships."

Tariq shivered. "Do you truly want to help me persevere? Tell me instead that Salack Thorn served his guests fine bread and wine, and that his dancing girls were sublime."

The dimming sunlight had just been augmented by a wavering green illumination. This, Bone discerned, emanated from archaic glyphs writhing around the edges an off-kilter doorway of black metal. The mutable green light revealed embossed images of nightmarish flying creatures.

Gaunt said, "The hand must have gone through."

"Is there a cat door?" Bone asked, half-serious.

"No," she answered with a faint smile. "We'd best proceed. The day grows no younger."

"I fear *I* will grow no older," Tariq said, shivering.

"Longevity is overrated," Bone said, dancing his fingers lightly upon the stone, trusting experience and intuition to warn him of traps.

"Oh?" asked Gaunt. "Are you planning to abandon it, my love?"

"Not at all! I prefer longevity to the leading alternatives."

"Good, for I prefer my child to have a father."

"I promise you," Bone murmured distractedly, "I will be there for you both …"

"You are pregnant?" Tariq exclaimed. "Congratulations!"

"No," Gaunt said. "Or at any rate it's too soon to know."

"Well, perhaps that's for the best," Tariq mused. "Surely a pregnant woman does not belong here."

"Oh?" Gaunt replied, with a suitably glacial tone. "Where do you estimate one belongs?"

"Ah, does *anyone* belong here?" Bone put in. "No distractions, please, a master thief is working."

"Why are *you* here, Tariq," he heard Gaunt ask in low tones, "and not in some civilized country?"

"Alas! I am the youngest son of nobility, and when one's a youngest son, one learns circumspection. Others interpreted this as shiftiness, and my deceitful reputation grew. Even if I bowed and said with pure guilelessness, *trust me*, people always studied me sidelong and clutched their coin-purses. Decades of this treatment engendered a trickster's grin, since if you're going to be called a scoundrel, you might as well look the part."

"Logical," Bone grunted. He flung handfuls of corn starch, raided from *Sea-Glare*'s stores, onto the glowing glyphs.

"And I followed the liar's grin out to sea, where I had a knack for encountering the most ludicrous situations. I've met birds the size of mountains and diamond-bedded rivers and a city of flying people. Can you believe it?"

"Well …" Gaunt said.

"Exactly! I have survived six unbelievable voyages and when this seventh is done, I will give up on convincing people, return to Mirabad, and write it all down as fairy tales."

"I approve whole-heartedly," Bone said, employing a paint brush (also liberated from the ship) to gently brush away excess starch. "Especially the part about escaping alive. Now then …"

Yellow fingerprints had appeared on three of the glowing glyphs. Excellent — although it was unnerving just how high the severed hand must have jumped. "Any guesses on these symbols?"

"No one alive is good with Nobecan," Gaunt said, squinting. "But if my neck depended on it, I'd say they are 'sorcerer,' 'rulership,' and 'world.'"

"So, *sorcerer-rules-world?* Thank you…"

"Wait!" Tariq broke in. "In ancient Nobecan, object proceeded subject. So, more like 'The world is ruled by the sorcerer.'"

"Much obliged …" Bone's erratic faculty for sensing magic, the result of a long prior association with angels of death, had nothing to say, even though sorcery glowed in his face. Surely that was a good sign. He quickly touched *world-rulership-sorcerer* in turn. It was like immersing his hand in ice-water and he could see the advantages of having undead fingers.

Nevertheless, the door groaned open.

The narrowness of the tunnel left him unprepared for the vastness beyond. The door opened upon a narrow balcony lacking any balustrade. The platform extended left and right, twisting to trace a vast hexagon girdling a tremendous empty space. Ice-dimmed light emerged from thin windows, allowing Bone to appreciate the extent of the chamber but not behold its depths. He did note a precipitous wall-hugging stairway corkscrewing up from the gloom, passing the balcony, and twisting up, passing a sort of chandelier.

This last took the form of a monstrous, elephant-sized iron head. Owing to the tower's tilt, the dark visage leaned against the stairway. The off-center face seemed to toss down a disdainful glance. It evoked a cruel impression with its jowls, ornately coiled beard, sneering mouth, and narrowed, ruby-filled eyes.

"I have seen the Caliph's palace in Mirabad," Tariq ventured. "It is magnificent but nonetheless built for the comfort of human beings. There are columned gardens and sparkling fountains and domes that catch the light in swirling patterns of turquoise and porphyry and amber. There are no precipitous plunges or giant sinister heads."

"I have a plan," Bone said. "Let's go to Mirabad."

"Gentlemen, keep your heads," Gaunt said, "and I mean that sincerely. Up or down?"

"Down," said Bone.

"Up," said Tariq. "If we're to meet the controlling intellect of the Hands, it's likely to be there."

"Treasure rooms are usually down."

Gaunt chuckled. "You're outvoted, Bone."

Tariq drew a scimitar engraved with a verse from the Book of the Testifier. Gaunt readied a bow. Bone roped them all together.

Bone led them past the iron head's titanic mouth, skirting (with a pang of greed) its jeweled eyes. Soon he was surprised to reach an ebon ceiling; it had been hard to detect in the shadows. The stairway led up through a gap beside the chandelier's chain.

Bone peeked through.

At once he pulled his head down.

"What do you see?" Gaunt asked.

"I —" Bone began.

"*Salack Thorn!*"

The voice came not from Gaunt or Tariq, but from somewhere far, far below. It sounded like Viken, the rower, in the grip of some deranged fear or fury.

In response to the name, crimson light flared to life within the jewels of the great iron head, and with a deep hollow bellow the thing rose demoniacally upon its chain.

Damnation. His glimpse of the upper chamber hadn't been reassuring. Best deal with this thing, somehow. Bone unsheathed a dagger, cut his rope, and leaped onto the chain.

Down he slid, considering the links. They looked rusted and weathered in places. That was something. "Sword!"

"I don't see a sword!" Tariq shouted. "I see teeth! Very big teeth!"

"No," Gaunt said, readying a bow, "throw him *your* sword!"

"Oh, indeed!"

The flung scimitar nearly took off Bone's head.

"I want it back!" Tariq called, leaping up the stairway just as the monstrous metal sphere half-crushed, half-chomped the place where he'd been standing, spitting out masonry.

"No promises!" Bone hacked away at the chain, a difficult maneuver when his platform was turning this way and that. Gaunt shot arrows, and Tariq threw broken black stones, and both clanged harmlessly against the face. Stairs again exploded into rubble. Dust made Bone blink, sneeze, and cough, but he kept swinging, and the chain began to give.

"Move, Bone!" Gaunt called.

Bone made a running leap, casting the scimitar ahead of him, forcing Tariq to dodge. Well, fair was fair …

Bone did not quite reach the stairs, but caught the edge with both hands.

"Did you have to carry *quite* so many daggers?" Gaunt grunted, grabbing his arms. She'd lost the bow to the abyss in her haste.

"They're like Dawnglass' stash … of Eldshoren sweet cakes … so hard to take just one …"

"Maybe lay off those as well —"

"Gaunt!" Tariq shouted.

The head swung up, still hanging by one frayed edge of a link.

It engulfed her in one gulp, just as the chain snapped. At the last moment she let go Bone's hands, so they would not be cut off.

Like mockery he heard himself voicing a promise that was now a lie. *I will be there for you both.*

He could only mouth the word *Gaunt* as he fell.

• • •

VIKEN of Smokecoast, all six-and-a-quarter feet of him, was accounted by his people a weakling. Although he grew up with foamreaver raiding songs resounding in his ears, an arctic wind toughening his skin, the heft of heavy wood-axes straining his muscles, and an active volcano dominating his sight, he'd been called *no true Bladelander* by his fellows. The reason? Of all his cohort, he'd been born last.

That was it. The simple, stupid fact of it was that he was always the smallest boy in any sport, and frequently the sport was *let's beat up on the smallest boy.* He'd adopted a stoop, lurked in the shadows, and sought refuge as an acolyte of the Swan. It wasn't until a decade later, when the local bishop's ship capsized in a storm, leaving Brother Viken as the only survivor *Sea-Glare* chanced upon, that Viken dimly understood what had been done to him.

Now, as the biggest man on the pirate ship, and the only one from the Bladed Isles, he was simply *assumed* to be a bloodthirsty berserker. He was really only thirsty for grog, but *Sea-Glare*'s crew didn't need to know that.

Fear was still a part of him, though, Viken reflected as the albino tentacles, puckered with human eyes, noses, ears, and mouths, whipped gibbering at them.

"*Salack Thorn!*" He bellowed in challenge while hurling an axe, the one he called Eagle-Scream. It wasn't magical, but weapons, like friends, should have names. Eagle-Scream stuck deep into the flesh of a tentacle but failed to sever it. *Perhaps I should change tactics*, he thought.

Dawnglass and Irilee drew swords, he wielding his *kaskara* and she a straight, slender *spatha* from Amberhorn. Viken readied a new axe from the straps at his back, Battle-Hag this time. When the tentacles withdrew a space, Viken jabbed Battle-Hag toward a formation of ice overhanging a tunnel. "If we can cross," he said, "bring that ice down …"

"It's ready to fall," Irilee confirmed.

"What we need is a distraction," Viken said. "Bladelander style. The skiff's wrecked, but we can turn it into a funeral ship."

"I'll light torches," Dawnglass said, in that voice of false confidence Viken knew and admired. Soon the captain was cursing the fickleness of pyrite.

The tentacles returned, babbling. Sometimes there were snatches of modern speech, even in Viken's native tongue. *Go back,* said some of the mouths, and *free us,* said others, but a few of the captive lips hissed *join us* in a bitter sneer.

Dawnglass now clutched two blazing torches. "Irilee, perhaps —"

"I dislike fire," she said.

"Very well." Dawnglass gave Viken a torch and kept one for himself. Together they jabbed at the immense tentacles as they'd fought the Hands of the Sea. The manipulators hesitated. Viken saw their origin in fissures high above, amid ragged projections of black stone, some plunging down as far as the icy cavern floor, testifying to the beginnings of the tower.

"Move!" Dawnglass yelled as the tentacles withdrew enough to let them scramble across the ice.

Viken reached the broken launch and stabbed down with his torch. Dawnglass did likewise. Irilee placed her hands upon the skiff, and perhaps the once-mermaid somehow coaxed away the dampness, for soon the wood ignited. The tentacles above quivered in consternation.

The pirates attained the far tunnel, smashing away at the vast icicles hanging nearby, blocking the path behind.

"Well, no way but forward," Dawnglass said with mock cheer, as if they were carousing the esplanade in Archaeopolis.

The blue-white, curving pathway, filled with only a hint of ice-filtered light, twisted upward in a seemingly random fashion. It did not appear artificial, yet its walls were smooth. Eventually they reached a sliding panel set into the tower's ebon stone, covered with bas-reliefs of sea life. The chosen sea life seemed immense, with a primary diet of sailors. They set to work budging it.

"This tunnel …" Viken mused. "Not right … Stop a moment … Ah. It looks like something made by rushing water."

Dawnglass glanced at Irilee, who closed her eyes. "He may be right. I do sense liquid beyond this wall."

Dawnglass frowned. "We can't go back."

Viken replaced Battle-Hag in its harness and brought forth Heaven-Scraper, an axe that was half-way to being a war-hammer. It had a long metal tooth which could serve as an ice-axe. He began hacking away at head level.

"You have gone completely barking mad, haven't you?" Dawnglass said. "I'm not judging. I'm halfway there myself."

"I think Viken's making a sort of shelter," Irilee said, "in case this tunnel floods."

Viken grunted.

"Ah," Dawnglass said, and he and Irilee stabbed at the other wall.

When they'd fashioned spaces large enough to hold all three, Viken said, "You two take shelter. The bloodthirsty berserker is the obvious choice."

"Not true," Irilee said. "I have an affinity for water."

Viken didn't like it that she was right. He could tell Dawnglass didn't either. The captain asked her, "Can *you* move the panel?"

"I think it's mostly there. Gallantry's pointless, Captain. I am a member of your crew."

"I … right you are."

As the men took shelter, Irilee yanked, snarled, and wrenched.

What roared out looked something like ink, and something like hot tar, and filled the tunnel almost to the level of their ice-shelves. It roiled and whirled with a chaos that seemed animate, disgorging dark tendrils that snatched at Irilee as she struggled to reach Viken's outstretched hand. The tunnel filled with warmth, accompanied by a reek of brine, oil, and rot. Viken grabbed one hand, and Dawnglass the other.

But a sudden surge of pressure snatched Irilee away and dragged her, with a muffled scream, out of sight.

In another moment the black liquid was gone as if it had never been, leaving no trace but a fresh sheen where it had coated the ice.

The panel rumbled shut.

Dawnglass crouched in the tunnel like a man just awakened from a nightmare. "No," he said, sounding years older.

"I will go after her," Viken said. "I know how you feel about—"

"No. She's gone. And she was right. We must get the job done."

Viken knew there would be no pirate bravado now, no talk of loot. This was no time for illusions; truth was, death lay all around.

They wrenched open the panel.

No flood assaulted them, but they heard a titanic crash, as of something falling from on high.

• • •

BY way of her motion sickness and bruises, Gaunt had ascertained that the sphere was empty, which, if she weren't seeing a bright panoply of exploding stars behind her eyes, might have been reassuring.

The sphere came to rest at last.

"Well. It seems I'm merely to be confined, not eaten."

"*Why/why would/would I/I consume/consume you/you?*" a strangely two-toned voice echoed around her.

Twin vast, oval, ruby lights glowed above. They must correspond to the jewels in the eyes of the face outside.

"*I/I offer/offer only/only kindness/kindness*," the weirdly echoing voice went on.

The stars faded from Gaunt's vision, and at last she managed the trick of hearing the voices as one.

"*I bring love and strength. I bring all together. Nobeca shall rise …*"

"Er …"

"*Of course you are intimidated by my greatness …*"

Gaunt felt her mind buffeted by the intensity of the doubled voice. Agree with it, the sound seemed to say. It is only good sense.

"*I am the most gifted of all beings and the source of benevolence …*"

As the words multiplied it came to her that the content of the words mattered not half so much as the texture of the sound. For it was relentless as a river, and it forced a response in an ancient part of Gaunt's mind, going straight and true to a place in her that wanted to trust in a parent, a priest, a noble, a monarch.

"*Wondrous is the People's Beast, symbol and embodiment of my authority. Yet it pales in immensity before my own mind …*"

She couldn't shut her ears, but she closed her eyes and placed her hands on the icy metal below her. Coldness. Iron. Symbols of that which will not yield to will alone. "Who did you say you were again?"

"*I am Salack Thorn. Mine is the gift of eternal life.*"

"Eternal slavery, don't you mean?"

In that icy place, the voice turned notably colder. "*It is the nature of all inferior men to be enslaved. Indeed it is their truest joy.*"

"What about women?"

"*Their enslavement goes without saying, unless they please me.*"

"Ah. And who are the superior men?"

"*A good question.*" The mirrored voice of Salack Thorn seemed to relish the idea of revealing its thinking. "*When I first ascended, I claimed it was all those sharing the ethnicity of the men of Nobeca. Then I claimed it was those within Nobeca only. Then I claimed it was Nobecans who followed the approved gods. Then I claimed it was the faithful of certain bloodlines. Then I narrowed those bloodlines to my own.*"

"So," she said, seeking the source of the voice(s), "just plain, old-fashioned nepotism?"

"*Ha! I am not so weak, to be shackled by family sentiment. All, including my own offspring, were inferior to me. Every step along the way Nobecans told themselves I couldn't truly be what I was: their future slave master, the destined lord of all beings. 'Surely,' they lied to themselves, 'he will reward me. I am special. I am party to the game.' Most believed this to the last. If only my consort had not betrayed me …*"

She found a fissure in the metal — the enormous "teeth" of the mouth. A hint of colder air met her fingertips as she explored them. They moved very gently as the doubled voice spoke. Aha.

Gaunt said, "How foolish of her!"

"*Surely it was jealousy. I was irresistible to women, of course, and any I chose came eagerly to my tower, tallest in the golden city.*"

"Perhaps they were too intimidated to say no?"

"*Ridiculous. None is more desirable than I.*"

"No doubt. Only …"

"*Yes?*"

"How can *you* be the true Salack Thorn? You seem to be only a very swollen metal head."

"*This! This is merely a vessel. For I have mastered every method of prolonging consciousness. Imprinting it upon gems is child's play. Thus I am immanent within the rubies of this sphere.*"

"You are within *both* eyes?"

"*Indeed.*"

"How is that possible?"

"*These two crystallizations of my personality are nearly synchronized. They act as one.*"

"I marvel at you! But then how do you control this tower?"

"*You attempt to flatter me. But there is no harm in answering. Other crystallizations are scattered about my sanctum. The ultimate source of command is my original mind, vastly enhanced. Together all my facets function as a unit, commanding the flesh-beasts I have created. Such flesh is what remains of the Nobecan citizenry, augmented by other creatures I have captured over the years.*"

"That's … repulsive."

"*No, it is glorious. I alone was able to unite thousands into one body politic. And you shall join it. But first I require your cooperation to re-link these crystallizations to the whole. You will emerge from the sphere and contrive to rejoin my chain to the tower's stone.*"

"Surely I will cooperate," Gaunt stalled, preparing to bolt when the mouth opened.

"*You will,*" said the echoes, and Gaunt felt twin mentalities pierce her mind. A slapped card-deck of memories seemed to whirl around her, her village on Swanisle, her first caper with Bone, their journey across the tundra, the sails of *Sea-Glare*. The memories began to alter, until it seemed she had grown up with Salack's anthems on her lips, Salack's red-thorn-on-black worn upon her arm.

History was rewritable, truth was mutable. The only constant was Salack Thorn.

I will not surrender… she told herself, in the last few moments while she could remember another life.

"I will surrender! But only to the strongest Salack Thorn."

The compulsion stopped.

"*What/what?*" came the voices. They had lost a bit of their cohesion.

"Only to the strongest!" Gaunt said, her voice gaining strength. "The ruby on the left."

"*Which/which left/left? Yours/yours or/or ours/ours?*"

"Isn't it obvious? The strongest one."

"*That is I.*"

"*No, that is I.*"

The argument commenced. The effect of the voices in the sphere was like two avalanches colliding inside Gaunt's head. That made it all the more urgent to get out of Salack Thorn's.

"*Mine is the purest will!*"

"*Supremacy is mine!*"

Yes. The maw of the sphere was opening up as the dispute intensified. More air rushed in, chilling but welcome.

"Amazing," she said. "Fought over by two such *powerful* male minds."

"*Let us end this. I will snuff the light of your gem.*"

"*Pathetic worm, I will crush your ruby's essence.*"

The words dissolved into shrieking cacophony, and the light from the vast rubies flickered. The maw opened wider.

Gaunt slipped past the teeth.

She stood in an ice-cavern whose floor was disconcertingly red, and there was a hint of briny reek. The skiff from *Sea-Glare* was burning in the midst, but she stood alone.

The sphere seemed to be trembling, and as it did so, the cracks in the surface around it expanded and multiplied. Gaunt backed away, as the great face of Salack Thorn groaned out of sight amid a keening, crackling, rending of ice. The cavern shook. Viscous red blobs spat upward in the sphere's wake, and the space where the head had lain became a crimson pool.

"Farewell, Salack Thorn," she whispered.

From the shadows, tentacles seized her. From many mouths came the words *Salack Thorn, Salack Thorn, Salack Thorn*.

• • •

TARIQ the Sailor grabbed Bone's arm, preventing the thief's slide into the abyss.

"No!" Bone yelled. "No, save *her!*"

"I cannot! Trust me! Now climb!"

Tariq helped him to the stairs.

"We must find her," Bone breathed.

"Come to your senses, man. I cannot imagine your loss, but —"

"I have not *lost* anything. Gaunt is in danger. We must go."

"The staircase is wrecked."

"We have rope. And with a running jump …" Bone's voice trailed off as he pointed toward the stairway above.

The severed hand had returned.

From the top of the stairs one desiccated finger pointed straight up.

"So," Tariq said gently, "what would Gaunt ask of you now? Go forward? Or throw your life away?"

Bone wore a blank look as he slowly ascended beside Tariq.

"Have you ever loved?" Bone's voice seemed to waft from beyond an open tomb.

"Three times," Tariq answered. Then, because that bleak voice demanded honesty, he added, "But only once was my love truly returned. And I didn't recognize it for the gift it was."

"Thirty-seven," Bone murmured.

"I hardly think this is the time to compare …"

"But only twice was it truly returned, as you say. The first of those true lovers is long dead. I never told Gaunt about her, never found the right moment." He was silent a few steps, then: "I caught only a glimpse, but I've the impression there's a pressure plate immediately ahead as you ascend. Dodge left, I'd say. The skeleton on the throne betrayed no movement save for a glint of ruby eyes. I would be wary of any gems here. I'd wager mangling the skeleton, while avoiding gazing into the jewels, is a good provisional plan. This should suffice." Bone halted.

"What should suffice?"

"My share of the treasure is yours!" Bone called as he sprinted down the stairway.

He leapt.

Bone didn't quite make it, but caught a ragged, crumpled edge and rose. "But not Gaunt's!" he added, cupping his mouth with bloody hands.

He lassoed his way across the next gap and darted into darkness.

The unbodied hand waited with an air of exquisite patience. Tariq sighed. "No one will corroborate my tale, will they?" He stepped forward.

The hand darted spider-like into the upper realm.

Tariq drew his scimitar and charged up.

He followed the thief's suggestion and dodged left before rushing the golden throne. Tariq was no thief, but he hadn't survived the world's weird oceans without being able to evaluate matters on the run. He noted there were many windows in this chamber, look-ing out through exceptionally clear ice and allowing the sunlight in. And lo! Far off there lay a ragged edge to the frozen waters and the bright glimmer of open sea, dotted with ice islands. *Sea-Glare* might not make it before nightfall, but Tariq dared hope.

He swung at the ruby-eyed skeleton that occupied the throne.

The skull, which had a peculiar gap in the cranium, came clean off. It shattered into bits upon the stone, and the rest of the skeleton sagged.

"Well, that's not so —"

Skull fragments and white dust swirled as a dust devil into the air, and the two rubies soared blazing like wraithlike eyes.

Tariq dove for cover.

This chamber was more laboratory than throne room, with grim ebon tables bristling with flasks, and jars crowded with peculiar fish and fowl from the outer realms of the Earthe. There was a thing like a huge cat-headed silver wasp with human-like eyes, glinting in the remote sunlight. There were rainbow-shelled clams covered with iridescent moss shaped like arcane symbols. There was a many-flippered thing with a mouth like a moray eel, dotted with black barnacles in the shapes of perfect polygons. All these and more were suspended in liquids of various hues, all frozen solid. Likewise frozen were various potions in flasks. What the cold did not affect, however, were piles of precious gems, mostly rubies but many emeralds, lying scattered upon the tables.

Here at last was treasure! But first he had to deal with the strange vortex —

Fire blazed from the flying rubies and nearly immolated Tariq. He darted behind a new table and dared a moment to pocket gems. But as he touched them voices screeched within his mind.

Take me, please! I was a noble; I can tutor you in the ways of power —

Me! I was an explorer; I recall treasure unknown on all continents —

I was a courtesan; I can fill your dreams with unsurpassed delights —

A new blast of flame jolted him free of the trapped mentalities. Jars fell, and one was so seared that blue liquid spilled forth, freeing the silvery cat-wasp; it stretched, blinked, and flew.

Tariq fled to the next table, blazing gouts chasing him.

Suddenly something grabbed his neck: twin somethings, hands that felt almost mechanical in their many-jointed, cold pressure. A rib-cage rattled against his back. Tariq spun and saw the throne empty.

Panicking, his vision blurring, Tariq smashed backward into tables, bookshelves, icy windows. Sometimes the grip weakened but it never surrendered.

The cat-wasp circled Tariq a few times before buzzing downstairs, dripping traces of blue liquid. *Liquid!* Desperately remembering family texts on potions, Tariq ransacked tables, grabbing flask after frozen flask and throwing them at the burning eye-gems.

As their fire catalyzed the potions there were flashes of purple light, billows of blue smoke, flickers of green lighting. The gems spiraled like drunk fireflies. At last Tariq seized and flung a purple flask, which produced an unearthly moan, a blazing glyph resembling a fist, and an acrid smell.

The flying rubies clattered smoking to the floor, and the bone dust was nowhere to be seen. The grip slackened. Gasping, Tariq dashed the skeleton down the stairs.

A new movement caught his eye. He shivered, before he realized it was only the undead tattooed hand with the emerald ring, a thing that by now seemed almost a friend.

It crouched beside his foot, aiming one finger at the throne.

"You — want — me?" Tariq scratched his chin. The hand hadn't so far pointed him awry. *A man must rise to his destiny*, he reasoned. *Or sit, as it were.*

Tariq sat. It was not a comfortable throne. It was icy and admitted no consideration of human aches and pains. Nothing of interest occurred. He began to rise.

The hand leaped onto his face.

• • •

VIKEN remembered the Swan cathedral he'd once served, and the region beyond the ebon panel possessed a certain kinship, albeit magnified by ten and bathed in gore.

A thousand human beings might fit comfortably within this space of black stone, amid carvings celebrating a bearded man with ruby eyes, whose favorite doings included sorcery, torture, dismemberment, and orgies, not necessarily as discrete activities.

The dozens of rubies all glowed, and in their weird light stood a vast dais, filled to overflowing with a bloated, manor-sized, squid-like denizen of the deep. The floor around it had sunken somewhat, and therein sloshed a shallow, noxious pool of the black, tarry effluent. The smell made Viken want to smash in his own nose.

"Drown me in Ma'at's river," murmured Dawnglass.

"Swan forgive my sins," whispered Viken.

The thing was no longer a true squid, for all that its tentacles stretched this way and that, sometimes downward through fissures in the floor. For one thing, there were thrice too many tentacles, and for another they were covered in human eyes and ears and noses and mouths. The quivering, rubbery main mass of the body might once have been a natural being, but it too had been grafted with parts from other creatures. Maws of bears and fish and eels and men crowded its upper reaches, and the legs, paws, and flippers of hundreds of hapless victims helped the monstrosity scuttle this way and that as it writhed upon the dais. Thousands of strange red pustules covered the entity's plump body like angry sores.

"Does the thing have the pox?" muttered Viken.

"Shh," Dawnglass said, trying to light the torches. "It might not have noticed …"

For something had clearly occurred just before their arrival, perhaps connected with the crashing din they'd heard. There was a roughly circular hole in the gallery through which the inky stuff dripped. The Thing on the Dais quivered in palpable outrage.

It's like a mad minister, Viken thought. For it had an audience. The loathsome Hands of the Sea writhed in their multitudes like ecstatic parishioners upon pew-like stone benches.

The chamber filled with sound. All the mouths upon the dais spoke nearly at once in a menagerie of voices. So too did words emerge from the stone maws of the surrounding bas reliefs. The effect was stunning, and only with effort could Viken resolve the sound into words.

"… *I was the voice in every ear* …" the mass was saying, "… *stirring Nobecans to greatness. For mine was the Art to manipulate both spirit and flesh. In my genius I could remove an ear from any slave, captive, or criminal, enchant it, and exchange it for the ear of a citizen. In time, this surgery was the duty of every adult Nobecan. Thus when I spoke, all citizens would hear. Rise! I said. Build! Burn! Slay! And few could deny the power of my voice. Have you come to worship Salack Thorn?*"

Dawnglass didn't answer the horde-voice, but only murmured, like a man who'd seen his death warrant, "Those aren't the pustules of a pox …"

"I worship only the Holy Swan!" Viken bellowed, for stealth seemed as ungraspable as dry land.

"*What are your pathetic young gods compared to my people? I have shaped them into the great Beast of the age.*"

"I remember mummification scrolls, back in Ma'at …" Dawnglass said.

"The Swan is she who died," Viken shouted, "to quench the Sun of Conflagration and save all humanity!" Viken felt a strange exaltation, as though his old self, the monk, had stepped from the shadows to keep pirate-Viken company. "She has redeemed us, if only we will be as brave and selfless as she."

"They're human brains …" Dawnglass hissed.

"*Your gods, your vessel, your garb, your very languages are absurd. Laughable! I have seen much while absorbing the minds of your crewmates.*"

Dawnglass was beginning to giggle.

Perhaps Viken too was losing his sanity. Now it seemed that his many-bruised boyish self emerged from darkness to join monk-Viken and pirate-Viken.

Together they all stood against Salack Thorn.

"The torches won't light!" Dawnglass laughed as if at a rich joke. "Soaked in that foul muck —"

"Go!" Viken said, tugging Dawnglass toward an upward-coiling stairway. "Find the others. I'll block the way."

"*I will overwhelm these upstart nations with their ridiculous names. Eldshore, Ma'at, the Bladed Isles …*"

The Hands scuffled forth.

"Viken? You can't be serious. I'm not worth …"

Viken laughed. "You may not be. Nor I. The ship's worth it, though. It was there I found my true self. Go! Find a way to bring this tower down around Salack Thorn's ears!"

"*I have many ears, and many mouths. I could whisper to all. Yet though I could speak to all simultaneously, my greatest power was to reach each individual in a manner specific to their own weakness…*"

"Viken, that burned boat should have been for you."

"Go!"

Viken guarded Dawnglass' retreat. In his mind's eye, all the fractured parts of him stepped into the same spot, defending it against doomsday.

"*You — tired, stupid, weak flesh-thing — who are you to oppose Salack Thorn?*"

"Just a man with an axe, who sometimes follows the Swan."

"*And what is this Swan's strength?*"

"She has none, truly. Only weakness. A weakness that bade her die for the world."

Laughter reverberated through the chamber.

"*Then she offers nothing. I can give you the world.*"

"She gives me infinity."

"*You are deranged.*"

Viken laughed at him. "I, greatest weakling of the Bladed Isles, challenge you!"

He backed up the stairs, wielding Battle-Hag. The Hands of the Sea followed, and some crawled while others levitated like a cloud of insects. Sixteen victims later, Viken's axe stuck in a white-furred paw and dropped over the edge. Viken was almost engulfed as he switched to Shield-Eater, and he gained still more steps before he lost his grip and drew Stern-Gaze, and astonishingly he wasn't dead before he returned to Heaven-Scraper. He swung and jabbed until the Hands overran him.

When it became clear that obedient to Salack Thorn's fury the Hands would salvage no piece of him, Viken laughed a red laugh that filled the hall. It was a sort of victory after all.

• • •

AS the hot black liquid snatched her, Irilee thought of home. The splendid underwater city had been raised by magic from images in the minds of drowned sailors. There were thatched cottages in a permanent sunset glow, and there were adobe huts rising from sands bright as desert noonday, and villas with slanted red roofs that seemingly glowed beneath starlight. In the city's heart soared minarets and steeples, onion domes and pagodas, gargoyles and moai, these and many another glimpses of home or paradise that had flashed before dying seafarers' eyes. There were even towers that mariners had imagined belonging to lost Nobeca, great spindly things of many-hued stone.

Now as she was washed away from a true tower of Nobeca, Irilee thought of that dream-city, amid the nightmare of this place. If she drowned, would her images of home be glimpsed by her sisters? Would Thessalonike gain a reflection of itself? Or would they reject anything that came from her now?

Thinking of them gave her anger, and from anger came strength.

The liquid spilled down the passage and washed her through the ice-cavern and clear out to sea. Water whorled and ice fragments stabbed.

She was powerful in the water, but she could die here, if she didn't reach a stable platform. Yet something nagged at her. Something about red ice.

She took a risk, swimming down, down, trying to take the measure of the whole iceberg. Was its only abnormality the tower? Her eyes adjusted to the gloom. Where before she'd shut them, this time she kept them wide as she tapped her water-sense, attempting to peer through ice itself …

• • •

PERSIMMON Gaunt struggled as two tentacles snatched her off the ice. *Flee, flee* said some of the nearer mouths.

"I … would … be … glad to —" Her hand reached for a glint of metal.

Kill, kill came the sound of other voices.

"I … am … willing … to … *oblige!*" Just a little farther.

Flee Salack Thorn …

Kill Salack Thorn …

"First things first, ladies and gentlemen." She reached the axe of Viken's that had been sunk into one tentacle.

Over and over she swung, aiming for the eyes.

The grip loosened, and with a body honed by months of sneaking into *this* mansion and *that* tomb Gaunt managed to break free. She dove skittering across the ice, stumbling past the crimson pool.

Now then.

She was below the tower itself, and things were *strange* down here in the guts of the iceberg.

Intuition nagged at her.

The guts of the iceberg …

"I wonder," she said, raising the axe. *The ultimate source of command is my original mind*, Salack Thorn had said, *vastly enhanced.*

She chopped and chopped at the red pool until ice shattered beneath her feet, flinging her into something vast and sponge-like

lying beneath the ooze. Encouraged by the rumbling all around, she kept swinging until her arms ached and scarlet waters closed upon her.

• • •

IRILEE, shaking and shivering despite her resilience, at last entered a chamber just below the great gallery of the winding staircase, wet footprints trailing behind.

Here was pandemonium. This room's heart had been rent by some falling object, and below lay another chamber from which a noxious briny smell arose. Open cages creaked on chains, and amid them Bone fought beside Dawnglass against five creatures that seemed all wings and eyes and claws, as though sea-birds had been augmented with parts from sharks and bears and medusae.

Irilee snatched a monster from the air.

Her elemental nature protected her. Pain seared as jellyfish-like tendrils lashed, but in another moment the agony seemed washed away. She flung the creature to the floor and crushed it beneath her boots. She dispatched two others, as the men skewered one apiece.

The three stared at each other, panting.

There commenced a pounding on the far door. Cacophonous laughter erupted from below.

Dawnglass said, "Irilee …"

"Easy. You've had only a little toxin, but enough to be excruciating."

"You … are … not … joking …" Bone managed.

"Irilee," Dawnglass repeated. "Sorry …"

"You could not have followed," she said. "I can take care of myself."

"I followed Gaunt …" Bone said, looking down at the gap.

Irilee hoped she spoke truth. "She can also take care of herself."

"Just don't want a promise … to become a lie …"

"What of Tariq?" Dawnglass said.

Bone answered, "He went … all the way up —"

The iceberg shuddered. The tower groaned and leaned before the quaking stopped. Now its tilt was more severe.

"*You will fail!*" cried many voices from below, all alike. "*I am everywhere! Your friend above cannot take control of the tower, and your friend below cannot destroy my mind! I will seize you and you will slay them!*"

The men reeled as something assaulted their thoughts, though Irilee felt nothing. The door buckled with fresh pummeling.

"Gaunt's *alive* down there," Bone said through gritted teeth, fighting the compulsion off.

Down there. "Listen to me," Irilee said, grasping Dawnglass' hand, the gesture helping him resist as well. "I saw, filling the iceberg's submerged bulk, a gigantic living thing, bigger than a dozen towers. Red, vaguely ovoid, with endless wrinkles."

"A brain," Dawnglass said, voice edging into hysteria. "Another gods-damned brain."

Bone murmured, "'Hovering above the waves,' that's what she said …"

"What?" Irilee said.

"I have an insane idea."

"You have a plan?"

"No, I have an insane idea. Someone must reach Tariq." He frowned. "With those broken staircases it has to be me." He ripped a birdcage and chain free from the ceiling. "A *truly* mad thief might be able to do something with a forty-five degree tilt, a rope, a chain, and a birdcage. Now, I am begging you two, find Gaunt, and get her away from here."

Before they could answer, he was off.

"There is no possible way," Dawnglass said to the air he'd abandoned. "It is purest nightmare down there. To the crew I pretend courage, but now …"

Irilee looked through the gap. She saw the Beast, and beside it the new hole leading down into deeper darkness, just below her feet. "Captain, did Viken say anything when he died?"

"Nonsense about infinity." Dawnglass looked away. "Shouldn't have died for me. Not worth it."

"Is the world worth it?"

"Not sure." He looked at the splintering door and back again. "Maybe if you're in it."

"Captain …"

"Irilee. If this is truly the end…" He stepped close, touching her face, right beside the edge.

She closed her eyes, made a choice. "I feel the same, Captain."

In that moment her human form dissolved.

Before the eyes of the doubly shocked Dawnglass, Irilee became a vortex of liquid glowing blue as sunlit turquoise.

She fell away from Dawnglass; she fell past the Beast; she fell onto the red ice. Nearby, Persimmon Gaunt lay face-down in a crimson pool, as the ice and the chamber and the tower all convulsed.

The blue vortex flowed over Gaunt and washed her up, up onto the ice; and it poured healing water into her and swirled back out, taking the tainted fluid with it. Gaunt sputtered and coughed and said "Swan's ghost … what are *you?*"

"You must escape," Irilee spoke from within a shining waterspout.

At that moment a gash of viridescent light rent the air, and through it they beheld a wavering image.

There was Tariq upon a golden throne, gazing down as if beyond a rip in reality. He wore a ring with a blazing green stone.

"*You there,*" Tariq said, but not in Tariq's voice. It sounded feminine, and possessed an echoing quality not unlike Salack Thorn's. "*This body and this tower are now mine! I, Ticheill Cerulean, consort of Salack Thorn, from whom he stole the secrets of gem magic, have waited millennia for liberty! Aye, and vengeance! But my new body insists you could be useful. Thus I take this moment to say, leave the iceberg. I will rescue you. Quickly!*"

Then out of nowhere Imago Bone appeared within the image, struggling with Tariq, attempting to shove the ring-hand into an iron bird cage.

"*No! You cannot stop me! I am unaffected by the wards against Salack. Now that I command the throne, I will fly this tower far from here and begin a new Nobeca — beautiful and harmonious! Unlike Salack I will welcome all humans, if only they worship me.*"

"Does Tariq agree?" Bone snarled.

"*Irrelevant,*" said Tariq's mouth. "*He is mine — how dare you use that cage to interfere —*"

Then: "No," gritted Tariq's own voice. "Trust me."

"I do," Bone said. "You're an honest man. You can end this, all of it. This tower can move? Send it down. Fly it through the iceberg and everything inside it. Wreck it at the bottom of the sea. Wreck everything."

"Yes," said Tariq's voice.

"*No!*" said Tariq's mouth.

Blue flame expanded from the ring, engulfing Tariq, blasting Bone and birdcage aside.

The vision vanished.

Suddenly Dawnglass burst from the ice-tunnel, sword in one hand and one of Viken's axes in the other. Gore-covered, he looked absurdly gallant and deranged. Perhaps in humans the traits were akin. Irilee withdrew toward the sea, though she could not help but train her senses behind her.

"Irilee, where?" she heard Gaunt murmur.

But Dawnglass did not understand. "Come! If I couldn't save her, I'll save you. I have to save somebody in this whole damned business."

"Bone —" Gaunt began. Ice fragments fell like rain.

A babble of identical voices followed them as they fled. "*Salack Thorn is everything! Salack Thorn is wondrous!*"

"Salack Thorn is getting a tower through his brain," Gaunt said, before she and Dawnglass leaped into the sea.

The magic of the Witch of Angles granted Irilee enough time, as if the witch had seen all from the beginning. Irilee became a current that dragged Gaunt and Dawnglass to safety, and when the tower of Salack Thorn stabbed through the gigantic brain, releasing hot gore that turned the iceberg into a steaming ruin, she flowed through the high windows, their ice now melted through, and snatched a startled Bone from beside Tariq's charred skeleton.

Rest in the deep, she said in the Tongue of Waves and Weeping. *Rest, Tariq and Viken, pirates, heroes*. The emerald ring fell into darkness before a silver cat-wasp gobbled it up. The tower and the red mass it speared were followed by schools of eager fish. Salack Thorn's lies were done, and all he had remaining were truths: kinetic energy, gravity, and the food chain.

She pushed Bone against *Sea-Glare*, and sailmaster Aurelius fished him aboard. Bone and Gaunt embraced, the first saying, "We are now going to settle down in the most dull village of the most prosaic country we can find," and the second saying, "You are such a liar."

Soon Dawnglass mourned Viken and Tariq, adding, "Let all searovers remember, how the one was brave, the other true." But of the third casualty he could not speak. He gazed out wonderingly to where the iceberg's destruction had cleared a path to open water, spread out blue and blazing in the afternoon sun.

"I will see you everywhere," he whispered: her captain, at the prow of her beloved ship, together again as they should be.

Strange, she thought before the last drop that was her fully rejoined the ice-dabbed sea. *It was false when I said it.*

ABOUT THE AUTHOR

Sometimes CHRIS WILLRICH thinks that sword and sorcery hits us in that primitive part of our brains that, since childhood, has never quite trusted reality, and which suspects that any moment now tentacled horrors will blast through the cupboards, windows, and manhole covers of our settled world and snag the mail carrier and the neighbor's dog, and that congresses, kings, generals, and priests will be powerless to save us, and that the only things we can trust in that moment are a length of steel and the wild-eyed comrades at our side. Or maybe it's just that unstable lunatics fighting monsters can be really, really cool.

ILLUSTRATION BY RUSS NICHOLSON

THE GUILD OF SILENT MEN

A Story of Morlock Ambrosius

By JAMES ENGE

THE sun still shed red light on the Thousand Towers that gave the city its name, but the street Morlock Ambrosius walked down was already evening-dark. A shadow moved among the other shadows in an alley as he strode past; it leapt out to grab him by the arm. But his arm was no longer where it had been; Morlock stood back, his hands open but ready to fight.

"Good evening," the shadowy figure whispered.

Morlock disagreed, but saw no point in saying so. "Then?" he rasped.

"I am a member of the Guild of Silent Men," the shadow replied. "We have troubles, Thain."

Morlock had troubles. He was a Thain, as the gray cape across his crooked shoulders proclaimed: the lowest rank in the Graith of Guardians, a voluntary order of seers and warriors who guarded the border of the Wardlands. His birth father had been judged a traitor by the same order and driven into exile before Morlock was born. On adulthood he had joined the Graith, in part to wipe out the stain of his father's disgrace. So far it had not gone well.

His current assignment was to attend on one of the Vocates, the second highest rank of Guardian. For some Thains, this sort of work was amenable and led to better things. But Morlock's Vocate was Fante the Dreamer, the Graith's most gifted illusionist—perhaps the world's greatest. Fante considered Morlock too glum and literal-minded and was always playing illusion-pranks on him.

But Morlock was bored with his troubles, and it occurred to him that the problems of the Silent Men might at least prove a distraction.

"Then," he rasped again.

"You must come with me," the Silent Man whispered.

Morlock speared the Silent Man with a glare from his gray eyes and waited.

"If you will," the Silent Man said at last.

Morlock grumbled a bit. He realized that what he had really wanted was an argument, or even a fight. But he made a gesture of consent. The Silent Man turned and led him up the alley to the Guild Hall of the Silent Men.

• • •

THE Wardlands were not ruled by king or council. Anyone who claimed lordship or mastery over them was killed or sent into exile. People ruled themselves there and, by and large, did pretty well.

But no one can stand alone all the time. Families and family-alliances, professional guilds and clubs: these were more important in the Wardlands than in the unguarded lands (as the Wardlands called the universal world outside their own borders). They avenged murders and other crimes against their members, among other things.

Some men and women had no kin who would acknowledge them; they had no professional guild or club that would admit them. These joined the Guild of Silent Men or the League of Silent Women, finding strength and help among the other friendless and helpless.

The Guild Hall of the Silent Men was a square tower built of dark blue nightstone. Its door was silvery *maijarra* wood. The Silent Man gestured at it, saying, "Open it, if you can."

Morlock put his hand on the blackiron doorhandle. It would not turn; the door would not open. He released the handle and stood back.

The Silent Man stepped forward and put his right hand on the door. Morlock saw that he wore a ring of blackiron on his right index finger. The ring and the doorhandle both gleamed briefly; the lock within the door clanked audibly and the door swung open.

The shadowy face of the Silent Man seemed a little smug as he motioned Morlock to enter.

Within the door, standing in the vestibule, were six cloaked and hooded men. The Silent Man who followed Morlock in made the seventh.

"Before you say a word," Morlock said flatly, "show me your faces and tell me your names."

The hooded men looked at each other.

"Thain, you must understand," said the Silent Man standing behind him. "No one brags about being a Silent Man."

"Then," Morlock said, and turned to leave.

"Wait!" said one of the Silent Men, and pulled back his hood. "I am Teyn. I can speak for the group."

The Silent Man who had first accosted Morlock threw off his hood as well and said, "I am Seetch. I will also speak. Is this enough?"

"If these others go," Morlock replied.

The others hesitated, and then departed through various exits from the entryway.

"Your problem," Morlock prompted Teyn and Seetch, when they seemed reluctant to speak.

"There has been a killing in our Guild Hall," Teyn said.

"Two killings," Seetch corrected.

Morlock sensed a certain rivalry between the two. He decided to ignore it. "You don't need the Graith of Guardians. You need the Arbiters of the Peace," he said, naming another voluntary order that investigated crimes and adjudicated quarrels.

"They've been and gone," Seetch said. "What they say is useless to us."

"It may have been true," Teyn said gently.

"It wasn't true," Seetch replied. "Thain Morlock—"

Morlock glanced at him in surprise. It was his first clue that the Silent Men had sought him out personally, not as a member of the Graith.

"—we face a crisis that could destroy our guild. The Guild Master, Danion, was killed last night. Reuk, our—the man who was campaigning to replace him, was killed in the same room with the same weapon. The Arbiters of the Peace say that Reuk killed Danion and himself and that, since the Guild claims right of vengeance for both men, it is an internal Guild matter and they will not involve themselves."

"Settle it yourselves, then," Morlock replied.

Seetch almost replied angrily, then refrained, clearly with great difficulty.

"Thain Morlock," Teyn interceded. Morlock turned to him. "Danion and Reuk were the leaders of the two largest factions in our guild. Their different philosophies would not interest you—"

"Tell me anyway," Morlock interrupted.

While Teyn hesitated, Seetch said, "The issue is whether the Guild should admit married men. Some say this violates the principle of the Guild's existence: that we stand together because we stand alone. Others say it would make the Guild still stronger to defend all its members. Danion held one view and Reuk the other."

Morlock noted that Seetch had not identified himself or any living Silent Man with either of the conflicting positions. And he had noted that Teyn had stepped in for Seetch, and Seetch for Teyn, even though they were clearly rivals. In the presence of an outsider, they stood together whatever their differences were. Morlock respected that.

"Then," he said to them both.

They looked at each other, then at him. "We don't know what you mean," Teyn said.

"What is it that you want from me?"

"Oh, yes," Seetch said. "Of course. We cannot believe—some us can't believe that Reuk killed Danion."

"None of us can believe it," Teyn added generously.

"But if the matter is left as it stands… It has been a difficult time for us, and this conflict could destroy the Guild from within."

"Suppose that Reuk did kill Danion and himself?" Morlock asked.

Both Silent Men bowed their heads.

"Then," Seetch said at last, "we will do what we must. But we do not believe it; we believe we have been attacked by an enemy who wishes to destroy the Guild. If the Arbiters are not allied with that enemy, then they have been taken in by the enemy. We beg you to help us. Your father, old Ambrosius, he was our friend. We beg you in his name to act as our friend in this matter."

They could not have chosen a worse argument. For as long as Morlock could remember, he had hated his natural father, this man he had never met, in whose shadow of disgrace Morlock had lived his whole life. That they shared a name enraged and sickened him.

But he had learned to master this anger, to mask this hatred which would shock even his father's enemies. And it occurred to him that this was another chance to cleanse his family name of disgrace.

"All right," he said at last, as the red tide of his rage receded. "I'll do what I can."

• • •

THEY took him to Reuk's and Danion's rooms, and on the way he began to understand the problem. There were no windows in the Guild Hall that weren't blocked with blackiron bars. Guards patrolled the halls and the central stair night and day, a coldlight in one hand and a sword in another.

Danion's room was at the top of the tower. Reuk's was on the same stair, several stories below.

In Reuk's room there was a table right up against the open door.

"Is this how he left the place?" Morlock asked, astonished. No one could have walked in or out of the doorway with the table there.

"It's how we found it," Seetch said. "We moved the table to go in, but pulled it back afterwards. We wanted you to see it as it was."

Morlock stared into the room. The bed was on the far side of the chamber. The bedclothes were thrown onto the floor, as if someone had rolled out of bed in a panic. Scratches on the floor led from the bed to the door: they'd been left by the feet of the table. Morlock crouched down and looked at the underside of the table. He ran his fingers along the sides of the polished table legs. He thought he detected rough patches, about the size and shape of sweaty handprints.

"He rolled out of bed," Morlock said, still crouching, "and hid under the table. He dragged the table over to the door and crawled out between its legs."

"That's how it seems," Teyn agreed.

They went on to Danion's room. Morlock thought he saw traces of blood on the pale flatstone tiles of the stairs. It looked as if Reuk had crawled all the way up the stairs, scraping his naked body on the sharp edges of the tiles.

In Danion's room there were two great bloodstains, not wholly dry. One was in Danion's bed, the other on the stone floor beside it.

"Where are the bodies?" Morlock asked.

"In the basement awaiting preparation for burial," Seetch said.

"Then," Morlock said, and they led the way downward.

They didn't speak on the long walk down except once. They passed a guard with drawn blade and coldlight and Morlock said, "Did the guards see nothing of what happened in the nighttime?"

"No," said Teyn. "But one of them fell partway down the stairs during the night. The—whatever happened probably happened then, while the guards were distracted."

"Very likely," Morlock said.

There was an attendant in a white smock guarding the entrance to the corpse-room. He was sitting at a table with two chairs, playing chess with himself: he would make a move on one side of the board and then hurry around the table to sit scowling at the board as if he hadn't expected the move. He looked up when they approached, then looked away as soon as he recognized his fellow Silent Men.

In the room within the two corpses were laid out on trestles. One was the body of a white-haired man, still in his nightshirt with his eyes tightly closed. The wounds in his torso were many: in the chest, the side, even one or two in the back, Morlock noticed, lifting the body to look. There were bloody hand-prints on the ragged nightshirt and the wax-white body of the corpse: someone had moved the already-wounded body to stab it in the back.

The other body was naked, with bloody scrapes all along its front from the shoulders to the toes. There were three great wounds on its chest, evidently self-inflicted. The knife was still in one of the wounds, still gripped in the corpse's right hand. Its eyes were open, glaring at the ceiling; the body was bent like a bow, as if it had been curled up when it began to stiffen. Morlock took the corpse by the shoulders and lifted it from the trestle. He gazed for a few moments at a boot print on the back, then lowered it gently back down.

"This, then," Morlock said, pointing at the naked corpse, "is Reuk, the other Danion."

"Yes," whispered Seetch. He and Teyn both had tears in their eyes.

"Did Reuk die with his eyes open?" Morlock asked.

"We think so. We found him this way," Seetch explained.

"Bring me a coldlight and a strong lens," Morlock said. "I'll also need a small hammer, a saucer and a needle. Come to think of it, bring me something to draw with as well."

The two Silent Men stared at him without speaking. He turned to look at them and opened his hands in a gesture of expectation.

"Right away," Seetch said, and hurried off.

• • •

THERE was no lens in the Guild Hall strong enough for the work Morlock had in mind, so in the end he went to his lodgings and got one he had made himself. But, an hour or so later, he was standing over Reuk's corpse with his instruments on a small table to his left.

He tapped the coldlight with the hammer, cracking it. He poured some of the pale luminous fluid into the dish. He pierced Reuk's left eye with the needle and then, still using the needle, introduced some of the glowing fluid into the eyeball.

"What in carnage are you doing?" demanded Seetch as Morlock picked up the lens.

"If Reuk died with his eyes open, as seems likely," Morlock explained, "the last image he saw will be lingering in the back of his eye. With the light fluid and the lens, I may be able to see it. It may be nothing more interesting than the ceiling of Danion's room, but there is a chance it will be something useful to us. Be quiet now, please."

Morlock held the lens close to Reuk's now glowing left eye. With his left hand he reached out for the charcoal and paper they had brought him and began to sketch what he saw: the image of Reuk's last sight.

When he had gotten the essential details down he stood aside to finish the drawing. He motioned for Seetch and Teyn to look through the lens.

"What is it?" Seetch whispered to Teyn, after they had both taken a look.

"It's a spider," Morlock said. "A large one, bigger than a man's hand, with bright red bands on its legs. It's not the only one; you can see others crawling over his body in the background. Reuk's knife seems to be piercing the spider as it crawls across his chest."

"We found no spiders," Teyn said dubiously.

"Of course not," Morlock said impatiently. "There were no spiders."

"Then how could Reuk see them? What does it mean?"

Morlock answered the last question, as the more urgent one. "It means that Reuk and Danion were murdered by an enemy, as you guessed. Tell me, if it's not a Guild secret: are you two now the leaders of Reuk's and Danion's factions?"

Teyn glanced at Seetch, who nodded. "Yes," Teyn said. "Why?"

"Together, you can speak for the Guild." Morlock sat down at his work-table and wrote a note in charcoal on a piece of draw-ing paper. Then he rolled it up with his drawing of Reuk's last sight and handed it to Seetch. "Send this to Jordel, of the Graith of Guardians. Do either of you know him?"

"We know of him," Seetch said reluctantly.

"If he comes here, your people should allow him to enter. Tell him how I made the drawing and, if necessary, let him do the same operation on Reuk's right eye."

"And—" Teyn began, but Morlock was already standing and beginning to walk away.

"I'll send you word as soon as I can," he said over his crooked shoulders. "Soon you should be able to bury your dead leaders with honor."

• • •

THE next day Morlock was not scheduled to attend on his Vocate, but he wrote Fante a note asking if they could meet. Fante wrote back, suggesting an hour after sunset. Now Morlock was at Fante's door, a little early, with a coldlight in his hand. There was still a smear of red on the edge of the sky where the sun had gone, but there was no moon aloft and Fante's house, situated in a grove of broad-leafed yalu-trees, stood in a private patch of midnight.

Fante opened the door himself; he had no night-watcher or live-in servants.

"Young Ambrosius!" the Vocate greeted him, smiling with mocking politeness as he ushered him in. "I hear you've been moonlighting!"

"Then?" Morlock snapped.

"I suppose you mean, 'And if I have?' You must really learn to speak in complete sentences, young Ambrosius," Fante said over his shoulder, as he led the way into his study. "It's an invaluable skill, if you want people to know what you're talking about. Just shut the door there! That's a good fellow. We'll want complete privacy."

The study had a reading lamp on the desk and a fire in the fireplace, but Morlock held onto the coldlight he had brought. If he set it down, he reasoned, he might never find it again, given Fante's prankish nature. He closed the heavy door of Fante's study and turned to face the Vocate, waiting.

"To answer the question you didn't quite ask," Fante said, seating himself between the fireplace and the open window, "I think you might have found more reputable employers than those repellent Silent Men, as they so mysteriously call themselves. I mean, it's a mystery to me. Get one of them to start talking about the injustices he's faced in this cruel life and you'll see just how silent they can't be."

"You dislike the Silent Men?" Morlock asked quietly.

"Not as individuals," Fante replied with an indulgent tone. "It's not as if I know them socially. What an idea! No, it's their group I object to. A body of outcasts, with no loyalty except to each other—a realm within our realm. It may someday prove a danger to the Guard."

"And that is why you killed Reuk and Danion?" Morlock said breathlessly. It was the question he had come to ask, but he had not expected to get to it so swiftly. It was unlike Fante to be so open, very unlike. It set warning bells ringing in Morlock's mind. That and something else: there was something about this scene that was all wrong, but Morlock could not quite decide what it was.

Fante laughed again and said, "Nothing escapes you, does it, Morlock? Of course I killed them. Or, rather, I made Reuk kill Danion, and then himself. Have you guessed how I did it?"

"An illusion of spiders."

"Yes! Reuk was terrified of them. He used to work in my garden, you know, and I noticed how odd he was about insects generally, but especially spiders. Not a terror of yours, are they?"

"No, I like them."

"You would. No, really, I can see it. They're gifted makers, like all the Ambrosii, and are generally feared and loathed, as—well, you know. Anyway, I managed to enter the Guild Hall along with Reuk the other evening, though he didn't see me, and when he woke in the night he found that the whole tower had been taken over by spiders. He was quite heroic about it: I gave him a window to leap out of, but he preferred to crawl through various webs until he had found the great King Spider, whom he bravely slew to save the Guild. Except the King Spider, you understand, was…"

"Danion."

"Yes. The Guildmaster, whatever his name was. Then the King Spider burst open and many smaller spiders leapt out to crawl all over Reuk. It was quite amusing to see him stabbing at them. I wish I could have let it go on longer, but there was always a danger the guards would notice."

"Didn't a guard actually stumble over Reuk on the stairs?" Morlock asked.

"Yes!" cried Fante, delighted by the memory. "Yes! How right you are. I'd cast a wilderment over myself and Reuk so that we couldn't be seen, but then one of the guards went and stepped right on top of him as he wriggled up the stairs! Oh! Oh! Oh! It was priceless, just priceless. Down the guard rolled, bouncing like a ball as he went. Oh! Oh! Oh! He must have broken his neck at the bottom. How I wish I could have seen it! How did you know?"

"He left a bootprint on Reuk's back," Morlock said quietly.

"Of course, you examined the body. No doubt plucked the dying man's last sight from his dead eyeballs. Well, of course, if you like that sort of thing. But should a young Guardian be spending his evenings at such morbid pursuits? Really, I ask you, Thain Morlock, aren't you the tiniest bit disgusted with yourself? I know I am."

"How do you justify killing two of the Guarded?" Morlock demanded, struggling to keep his temper. His eyes scanned the scene carefully. Fante must have a card he was not showing; he was easy, confident, contemptuous.

"Them!" Fante sneered. "We're not charged with guarding any particular individual, but the Wardlands, the realm. The Guild of Silent Men was and is a threat. If I could save the realm by sacrificing two worthless outcasts, am I not obliged by my oath to do it?"

"No," Morlock said flatly.

"It doesn't matter that you say that," Fante said, almost regretfully, "but there are others in the Graith who would agree with you. I don't suppose you could be persuaded to keep this secret?"

"No," said Morlock. "I've already sent messages to—to several Vocates."

"But you haven't heard back from them," Fante guessed, peering at Morlock's face. "No, I see that you haven't. Perhaps they were among the sensible minority. In any case, you'll tell me their names presently. And they didn't answer your pleas for help. That's why you came here alone. It was very unwise of you, young Ambrosius. I'm more than a match for you, as we both know."

Fante stood up, slowly, almost negligently, and Morlock saw that there was a knife in his hand. But Morlock did not react to the threat. There was something about Fante's appearance—something which did not…

Suddenly Morlock realized: it was the shadows. They fell about Fante's body, cast by the firelight and the reading light on his desk. But he cast no shadow by the coldlight in Morlock's hand.

Morlock threw the light out the open window. It passed through Fante's figure as if he was not even there. And, of course, he was not. Fante's bland features twisted for a moment in astonishment and the firelight and the reading lamp went dark. They, too, had been illusions: Morlock's light had been the only real one in the room and now it was gone.

From wherever he had been actually standing, Fante leapt forward to stab with his knife at Morlock. But by then Morlock was not where he had been. The older man was gasping loudly as he swung the knife wildly about. Morlock sneaked up behind Fante and grabbed at him in the dark, but failed to get hold of him. Fante was ware of him, swung around and slashed with the knife, slicing Morlock skin-deep across the ribs. Morlock knocked the knife out of Fante's hand and grabbed his enemy by the neck.

Light bloomed in the room again, a false light projected by Fante onto the world. Morlock was holding a tiger by the throat. The tiger snarled and writhed; it seemed almost impossible to keep his grip. The tiger prepared to slash him with its glittering claws. Morlock clenched a littler harder.

The tiger became a snake. It was as thick as a man's throat. Morlock had it by the middle of its body and its head reared above him, hissing. Venom dripped from its glittering fangs as it dropped its hooded head down to strike. Morlock clenched a little harder.

He was gripping a fountain of water. It was stupid to keep his hands closed. There was no way he could imprison Fante this way, not if the Vocate could transform himself into a glittering pillar of running water. Morlock gritted his teeth and clenched a little harder.

The water became a torrent of fire. He felt the pain of it, the searing agony of fire as he had never felt it before. His Ambrosian blood protected him from the pain of fire; it took a flame hot enough to melt gold to do any damage to his flesh. But this fire was agony to him; he could see his flesh crisping and fluttering away in dark flakes under the glittering blast.

Morlock clenched still harder and shouted, "Stop it, Fante or I'll twist your head off! I'll kill you, you murdering bastard, and take my chances with the Graith!"

The fire was gone; the room was dark. Fante was gurgling something, trying to speak. Morlock decided to break his neck then and there and have done with it.

The door of the study opened and someone bearing a coldlight walked in. There were four figures there.

"You see!" cried the one holding the light. "I was right, wasn't I? I was right! You can admit it; I won't think any less of you."

"Yes, Jordel," said a second voice, a woman's. "You were brilliantly correct. After Naevros and I explained our plan to you, you instantly agreed with us." This was Noreê, Morlock realized: of all the Vocates in the Graith of Guardians, she was perhaps the greatest seer.

"Let him go, Morlock," said a third voice. This was Naevros himself. "We'll take it from here." Standing beside him was his attendant Thain, Aloê Oaij, staring at Morlock with wonder in her golden eyes and amusement on her dark, impossibly beautiful face.

"No!" said Morlock hoarsely.

"You will learn to obey your seniors in the Graith," said Noreê icily, "or you will leave our order." She was well-suited to speak icily: her hair was white as snow, her eyes as blue as a winter's sky, and ice-white scars branched over the left side of her face.

"Shut your pie-hole," Jordel said dismissively to Noreê. "Don't you get it? How does he know we're not another illusion projected by Fante? We need to show him we know something Fante doesn't. Listen, Morlock, I have something: that sketch you sent me. You drew it with your left hand, didn't you?"

"Yes," said Morlock with reluctant admiration. "Could you tell by the strokes of the drawing?"

"Of course! Also, Seetch told me."

Morlock snorted. "Can you control Fante if I let go of his neck?"

"We wear talismans against illusion," Noreê said impatiently. "He won't be able to delude us. Release him, Morlock."

Morlock let go of the sobbing Fante and stood back. "Talismans against illusion?" he said, rubbing his hands. (They still throbbed with the phantom pain of Fante's fire illusion.) "How does one make those?" he wondered. He was thinking that they might have saved a couple of lives last night.

"If you ever need to know, we'll tell you," said Naevros mildly.

Jordel took Fante by the arms and started to hustle him out of the room.

"Wait!" said Morlock. "What happens now? What do I tell the Silent Men?"

"Nothing!" snapped Noreê. "You will contact no one in that guild again. On our authority you will proceed over the Hrithaen Mountains and put yourself at the disposal of Vocate Callion in Anglecross Port."

"We'll bring Fante before the Graith and make him testify on the Witness Stone," Naevros explained. "Then the Graith will take appropriate action, to exile or kill him. We'll tell the Guild of Silent Men when it's done."

"Why?" Morlock demanded.

"If you need to know—"

"If I don't know, I won't obey!" Morlock shouted. He clenched his fists. He'd fight them all if he had to.

"We owe him this, Guardians!" Jordel said. "Look, Morlock, I heard some of what Fante told you about his motives, and he's been complaining for years that the Guild of Silent Men is potentially dangerous. Well, some of us agree with him. But if we take vengeance for the death of their members, sacrificing one of our own for the purpose, they'll owe us a debt of honor. That gives us something to hold over them, decreasing their danger."

"You're wrong about them," Morlock said slowly. "I'm sure of it."

"In that case, this just makes the Wardlands a little safer. Don't you agree?"

Morlock didn't. If the Guardians lied to the Guild, and the Guild knew it, they would trust the Guardians less. They would think more and more about protecting themselves, care less and less about the land. A land needed to trust its guardians, and for that the guardians needed to be trustworthy. Morlock didn't have the words to say this, but he knew it. He looked at the Guardians, who were waiting for him to speak.

"Let me tell them—" he began.

"You'll tell them nothing!" Noreê broke in. "If the Silent Men owe a debt of honor to the Graith, then the Wardlands are safer. If they owe a debt to an *Ambrosius*—" She shuddered at the thought.

"They came to me!" Morlock shouted. "An Ambrosius! They came to *me*, not you!"

"Of course they came to us, Morlock," Naevros said patiently. "They sent word yesterday afternoon to Noreê and myself. We put our heads together and suggested they consult you. We suspected that Fante was the guilty party, but we needed to force an admission from him somehow before we could take him to the Graith. We knew he'd admit the truth to you because he enjoyed tormenting you. It has something to do with your father, I think. Fante and old Ambrosius never really got along—"

A red tide of anger, not far removed from madness, began to rise in Morlock's mind at the mention of his father. Wherever he went, whatever he did, he was still only young Ambrosius, struggling in the shadow of old Ambrosius. He met Aloê's golden eyes and she shrugged her shoulders in a graceful gesture: *What do you want from me?*

He could not speak. There was nothing more to say. There was nothing anyone could say that would make any difference now. He strode past them out the door, down the corridor beyond, out into the moonless night.

• • •

THE word came the next day around noon: the Graith of Guardians had found that one of its members had murdered two of the Silent Men. The Graith had executed the criminal, Fante the Dreamer, and turned his body over to the Guild of Silent Men. The new Guildmasters (against all custom, there had been two elected) publicly acknowledged the Guild's debt of honor to the Graith.

Morlock spent the next day tying up his affairs in the city. By nightfall he was done. He slung a pack over his shoulders and started walking out of the city westward, toward the high peaks of the Hrithaens.

Morlock's wolflike loping pace had taken him near to the edge of town when he found that, on either side of him, shadowy figures were walking. Each of them wore a blackiron ring on his right index finger.

Morlock stopped, and the Silent Men stopped with him.

"We wanted to tell you something," the Silent Man nearest him whispered. Morlock could not tell if it was Seetch, or Teyn, or neither.

"Then," Morlock rasped. He was in no mood to talk about recent events.

"*We know the truth.* We know it all, Thain. And we are grateful."

Morlock bowed his head. He found that what the Silent Man had said mattered to him—more than his frustrated longing for Aloê, more than his hatred for the father he had never met, more than his anger at those who hated him for his father's sake, more than his loathing for those who had used him like a prybar to break into someone else's secrets. It mattered a great deal.

"Thank you," he said at last.

The Silent Man handed him a blackiron ring. "In your need, call on the Silent Men!" the shadowy figure said. "Our blood is yours."

"And mine is yours," replied Morlock. He put the ring on his finger and walked away toward the crooked high horizon.

ABOUT THE AUTHOR

JAMES ENGE lives in northwest Ohio with his wife and two crimefighting dog-detectives. He teaches Latin and classics at a medium-sized public univérsity. He has published six novels and a raft of stories, many of them about Morlock Ambrosius, including the World Fantasy Award nominee *Blood of Ambrose* (Pyr, 2009) and *The Wide World's End* (Pyr, 2015). You can reach him on Twitter (twitter.com/jamesenge) and Facebook (www.face-book.com/james.enge).

ILLUSTRATION BY IAN MILLER

BENEATH THE BAY OF BLACK WATERS

A Tale of Shan Spirit-Slayer and the Banner General Bao

By BILL WARD

THE warehouse was on fire. The remaining members of the Fish-Gutter Gang, upon realizing their destruction was at hand, had dashed oil lamps against the planks of their hideout and flung glowing coals onto the heaps of stolen silks and sailcloth that filled the entranceway to the ramshackle depot. Dozens of attacking city watchmen slowed their advance, cupping hands over their faces and squinting against the smoke as the few survivors of their surprise raid slipped further into the building.

"Li Fan, take six men and douse that fire. The rest of you, attend me." Shan Wu-Tsi, Commissioner Extraordinary to the Imperial Throne, wiped blood from his slender straight sword as he dispensed orders. For weeks he had been investigating the Fish-Gutters and their distribution of the drug Black Pearl in and around the tangled alleys and rotting wharves of Long-He's dockyards, and today's raid was his best chance to eliminate one link in the chain between a hopelessly addicted city and the mysterious producers of the drug. He shouted as he flourished his blade: "Remember, I want prisoners. Onward!"

The men cheered, flush with victory. Stepping over the corpse of a gangster, Shan charged after the fleeing smugglers, and the city watch followed.

The Commissioner plunged into the billowing smoke, his tall silhouette knifing into the wall of roiling gray. A man shorter and broader than the guardsmen of Long-He sped after Shan, close on his heels. General Bao Guan, Imperial Bannerman and Shan's enforcer and confidant, scowled fiercely beneath his Hsung-du style mustache and raised his bloodied halberd into a ready position as he ran. Staff-armed watchmen followed in uniforms of black and green, each emblazoned with the silhouette of the great lighthouse that was Long-He's proudest feature.

More felt than seen, a knife-armed killer lunged at Shan through the dense smoke, and the Commissioner dispatched him with a rapid slash across the neck without breaking stride.

Leaping over the barely discernible body that was suddenly in his path, Bao called out: "Thought you wanted prisoners?"

"Not that one," Shan said matter-of-factly over his shoulder.

They proceeded deeper into the dockside warehouse, racing past a treasure trove of stolen and contraband goods: bales of fabric and tubs of exotic spice, stacked cages in which strange animals howled and screeched, casks of plum wine, urns of imported incense, and all manner of crates and chests of foreign design. Shan and Bao moved past it all quickly but cautiously, mindful of the potential for ambush that existed in that crowded place.

The smoke grew thinner, and a breeze blew in their faces as they came to the back of the warehouse. There, within a square cut into the floor over the waters of the bay, a skiff lay moored to a loading platform. Wind blowing over the water lifted the gray smoke from

their eyes, and the remaining smugglers could be seen loading the boat with identical chests of a kind the pair had seen many times before.

Here was a royal fortune in death—chest upon chest of purest Black Pearl.

"Seize them!" Shan cried, leveling his *jian* blade.

Before the words had left Shan's throat, General Bao sprang into action. Dropping his long weapon, he hurled himself over the watery gap and into the overladen boat, landing as heavily as a siege-stone. While the guardsmen raced around the hole in the warehouse floor to get to the loading platform, Bao slammed into the knot of Fish-Gutters that was desperately trying to cast off—the remainder of their product abandoned on the wharf in their haste to escape.

Bao smacked a hard fist into the jaw of one of the men he had tackled, and the thug flopped onto the deck like a fresh-caught fish. From behind, a brawny fighter tried to seize Bao's arm and the general twisted and flung his elbow in a vicious backward jab that toppled the man with the force of a smith's hammer.

He spun to take in all his assailants, shifting into a low fighting stance and keeping his feet wide to maintain balance in the rocking vessel. Before the city watch could intervene, the remaining three thugs attacked Bao from all sides with the long-bladed knives that were the Fish-Gutters' signature weapon.

The peasant general had fought a hundred battles, and been adrift in the surging melee of ten thousand men. Three opponents, in his estimation, were not so very much different from one.

He ducked a cut to the face and shifted to avoid a low thrust to his belly, catching his second attacker's knife hand and pivoting along with the man's momentum to drive the blade into the leg of the smuggler behind him. Bao chopped the hand that held the gangster's arm back against the man's neck, and the Fish-Gutter dropped with a whistling screech from his crushed windpipe. Wheeling to catch his first attacker's return slash with his right hand, Bao brought his left up hard against the man's elbow and felt it pop out of place. The man shrieked and tore himself away, falling overboard.

Bao turned to finish the final smuggler, who lay against the wall of tightly packed narcotics chests. With one hand the man clutched his bleeding thigh—with the other he held a loaded crossbow aimed at Bao's chest.

Without hesitation the Fish-Gutter loosed the bolt.

An arc of silver streaked before Bao's vision, and the crossbow bolt—neatly severed in twain—clattered to the deck between his feet. Shan stood next to him, slender *jian* sword in his hands, a look of detached amusement on his face. "Honestly, General, it seems I am forever getting you out of these situations."

"That's only fair," Bao said, smoothing his mustache, "as you are forever getting me into them."

More watchmen joined the group, their faces and uniforms covered with soot from putting out the fire. Shan snapped orders to his sergeants. "Escort this trash to the gatehouse for interrogation, and finish loading the boat—we'll pilot this poison back to the municipal docks and then . . . ." Shan, his long, elegant limbs far stronger than they appeared, pulled the crossbow-armed gangster abruptly to his feet by the collar, "we'll dump it all into a pit of quicklime."

Shan studied his frightened opponent for a moment and nodded to himself before releasing the criminal. He reached down and opened one of the unsecured chests of contraband and removed a dried ball of the substance he had been sent halfway across the Celestial Empire to destroy. Black Pearl was sticky and sweet smelling, like the resinous incense of the Al'harab traders, and each ball contained a million facets in the form of tiny, perfectly spherical granules. It looked to Shan like nothing more than fish roe. He pinched off a wad as long as his thumb and twice as thick, and kneaded it between his fingers.

Faster than anyone could react, Shan lashed out and grabbed the smuggler by the jaw, forcing the drug into his mouth and down his throat. The man bit Shan's fingers as he did so, and the Commissioner pulled back with a snarl, kicking the Fish-Gutter's legs out from under him and knocking him to the deck where he lay in a heap, sputtering and moaning.

"An utter lack of self control is apparently one of the drug's pleasant effects," Shan said. "In an hour or so, you and I will no doubt have a great deal to discuss about your mysterious supplier of Black Pearl."

• • •

THAT evening, with the moon full and silver above them, Shan and Bao and a contingent of watchmen piloted their newly acquired skiff—now unburdened of its illegal cargo—out across the dark waters of Long-He Bay to rendezvous with the supplier of Black Pearl. The story they had gleaned from the Fish-Gutters about the drug's origins was a strange and sinister one, and it did not sit well with General Bao.

"Drug-addled ravings—we are foolish to follow this trail." Bao, sitting atop a stack of massive silver trade disks as big as platters, stared sourly over the reed-choked and debris-laden bay. Suppliers from the sea made sense—foreign traders from Al'harab or Kund or even faraway Ferrencia. Suppliers from up-river made sense—Dhamhrad nomads or even Hsung-du caravaneers from the far north. But the swamplands? And apparently these suppliers—the nature of whom Bao was not prepared to speculate upon based on the lunatic gibbering of the man Shan, in his ire, had subjected to a near-fatal dose of Black Pearl—were never seen by the gang, staying as they did *under the water* during all transactions. Based on so wild a story, Shan, Bao, and a score of city watch under Captain Li were now rowing out from the island city and toward the mainland, toward the edge of the great swamp that stretched for leagues on the opposite bank, on a fool's errand to drop—actually drop—a fortune in silver into the bay to see what came up. Bao grumbled under his breath at the scale of their folly.

"None of your muttering, now, General," Shan said, in a near-festive mood. He had interrogated the prisoners all afternoon, and was so convinced he was on the right trail he nearly bounced with enthusiasm. "You of all people should keep an open mind. Have you not seen the hopping dead, fought spirits of the high places, and stood face-to-face with a veritable herd of horse-headed demons? As the poet said, 'There are more things under Heaven and in the Earth, Hong Hsiao . . .'"

"We'll see," Bao said, unsheathing his heavy broad-bladed saber to inspect its already keen edge. The guard rowed the skiff in silence.

Shan produced a silver-chased hand mirror from within his elegant robes, and examined his image in the moonlight. "Confidence, my friend. Remember, we are the discerning eye and punishing hand of his Most Imperial Munificence. Heaven's mandate flows through us."

Bao, who had won more than his share of battles, had not rated such intangibles as "confidence" highly on his list of essentials—good intelligence, training and preparation, high morale, thorough provisioning, choice of terrain, and able officers all ranked a good deal higher. In his experience, confidence was the guiding star of men who led their divisions into an ambush, or in an uphill charge against a fortified position. The general sullenly thumbed his saber's edge and said nothing.

The little bay was mired with snarls of seagrass and the rotting forms of dead ships, for it had long been the place where captains scuttled their unserviceable hulls. More than once the men on the little skiff had to thrust out their staffs at a looming hulk to keep from fetching up against the mossy sides of some ancient junk. As they crept nearer the far shore—a black expanse of swamp willows and wild-rooted banyan trees, Shan spotted the landmark that marked the Fish-Gutter's trading spot and ordered his men to extinguish their lamps.

"The ribs of the whale," he whispered, while the watchmen looked on in awe.

Vast, curving slats of algae-slick teak loomed above them in the moonlight like the ribs of some fantastic and undiscovered creature of the sea. But these were the ruins of a once-mighty vessel, the flagship of a great fleet that had brought the light of the Celestial Empire's glory to the far corners of the world before Imperial decree reversed itself, and the Empire drew inward once more. What was left of the fleet had been broken up and pressed into cargo service, but the colossal vessel that sailed at its fore—that had indeed led its progress around the waist of the world—was itself too expensive and impractical to maintain. This was its grave.

"'In its shadow, by the light of the midnight moon, silver will you provide,'" Shan quoted the smuggler's directives, more to himself than anyone. He set about readying his tools for this evening's investigation. From a pouch at his belt he produced a trio of brightly glowing Dragon's Eggs—fist-sized orbs of rock crystal in which was suspended a luminescent alchemical gas, each a miniature of the massive globe that sat atop Long-He's lighthouse. These he sat at the ready, while Bao assisted in unwrapping a larger device that rested on deck. Superficially it resembled a sailor's fargazer, but only if such an instrument had been crafted by a mad, metalworking giant. Jutting out from the instrument's large and ornately filigreed central hub of bronze was a telescoping flange carved to resemble an open-mouthed dragon of serene disposition. Within the dragon's jaw a lens of blue glass gleamed.

"Parter of Deep Waters," Shan said with reverence. "How rare and beautiful a thing. And how very lucky we are to have had one in Long-He, as Old Master Gu-Tzu was said to have made only five." Shan, admiring the device with a near-avaricious intensity, gave the watchmen orders to angle the boat into position where the longest rib-shadow terminated on the water's moon-silvered surface.

The Commissioner stooped and brought the Parter of Deep Waters up to rest on his shoulders, where contoured arms kept it resting snuggly in place and allowed the operator full use of his hands. Adjusting a dial, Shan clicked the flange into position in front of his left eye and went to the side of the skiff. Bao could hear liquid sloshing inside the instrument itself.

"Sympathetic vibrations, General. Water cancels water and thus . . ." Shan bent over until the dragon-carved flange dipped into the black water of the bay, and he was looking directly into it. "By the Ten Worthies, what an extraordinary device! General, get ready to drop a disk on my signal."

Bao sighed, and fetched one of the silver trade disks—each weighing about half as much as a grown man—and brought it over to where Shan peered into the bay. "I would like to point out, Commissioner, that His Most August Imperial Highness tends to value his silver more than the lives of his servants."

"True," Shan said, fiddling with a setting on the Parter of Deep Waters to bring it into sharper focus, "but you and I, Bao Guan, have the worth of rarest jade as we have never once failed Heaven's Son. Now please stop counting losses like a farmer's wife and drop that disk. Try not to splash."

Bao, the corded muscles of his arms bulging, slowly lowered the silver trade disk into the water and let it go, where it instantly disappeared into the dark. Shan dropped a glowing Dragon's Egg in after it, and the water beneath the boat was suddenly illumined in the orange hue of sunset.

"Amazing." Shan, fiddling further with the Parter of Deep Waters, extended its viewing flange to maximum depth and tossed a second light orb into the bay at a point further toward shore. "I can see remarkably well beneath us, though it's much deeper than it appears. More wrecks down there as well. In fact our once-great flagship is resting on a veritable mountain of naval hulks. The silver has plunged out of sight—get ready for another."

"This is wasteful," Bao said, not moving to pick up another trade disk. "We should search the opposite shore."

"Stop that carping, General, just—" Shan, still staring into the device, stopped in mid-sentence and tensed. Bao, knowing his comrade's every nuance, rushed to his side.

"What is it?"

"Shhhh!" Shan, reaching a blind hand out to gesture silence as he kept his focus beneath the boat, continued in a whisper. "I see them, vaguely, swimming upward. That Fish-Gutter was right, they aren't—these are no men, Bao Guan. Wait . . ." Shan made several fine adjustments on the Parter of Deep Waters and leaned intently forward.

Bao and the watchmen looked on in nervous silence as Shan leaned the device further out over the bay, with only the sound of the still waters gently lapping the skiff's sides and the sea wind carrying the murmuring sounds of the city to their ears, to fill the space of their waiting.

Then, in an instant almost too quick to comprehend, Shan was ripped from the boat—along with the Parter of Deep Waters—to plunge into the bay with a tremendous splash. Something had grabbed the instrument's flange and dragged it, and Shan, down into the deep.

Bao sprang into action. "Li Fan, they will need to know what we've learned back at the gatehouse," he said, his commanding voice brisk and betraying no hint of the surge of readiness that left his limbs tingling with the need to act. Captain Li nodded, though his men eyed each other in shock and uncertainly—a confusion compounded by Bao's hefting another heavy disk of silver. The general clutched the trade disk to his chest with both hands. "Give us an hour before you return. If you are attacked, retreat to the city. You have command, Captain." With this last word Bao dropped over the side, massive plate of silver held tightly against his body, and sank without a trace into the bay of black waters.

• • •

THE light helped. Rushing downward into the cold and dark without its radiance would have been much worse, Bao was certain. A stroke of luck brought him within arm's reach of one of Shan's Dragon's Eggs—the neutral buoyancy gas within the sphere keeping it drifting just a few spans below the surface—and Bao snatched it up and brought it with him on his downward plunge.

There were shapes in the murky waters around him.

Bao had seen many strange things on his journeys, but these *guai*, these freaks and perversions of Heaven's Order, filled him with a revulsion and fear foreign to his nature. Vaguely man-shaped, each swam with powerful strokes of their webbed and flipper-like limbs. The creatures were pale as cave worms, with lumpy, irregular flesh reminiscent of a waterlogged corpse. Their large heads were ringed with feathery appendages that Bao had seen before on certain kinds of newt—gills.

But it was the hollowness of their dead black eyes as they rushed him that unnerved Bao most of all.

Bao lashed a kick at the first *guai* to reach him, but such was the creature's agility and the difficulty of exerting proper force underwater that it did little to discourage his attacker. He kicked again, chest burning with the pressure of holding his breath. He held back a scream as one of the creatures latched onto his back with needle-like claws and bit his left shoulder. On reflex Bao hooked his right fist – the fist holding the Dragon's Egg—around to punch at his assailant over his shoulder. The freak released its hold before Bao made contact, the daylight glow of the Egg apparently enough to scare it away.

Bao's descent did not stop, and the heavy disk carried him past his attackers in a bubbling rush. Nearly a score of the creatures had noticed him now, and they angled their gross bodies downward and swam powerfully after him.

He was descending into a region of utter blackness, bringing the light of the glow globe with him. Bao scanned the depths beneath him, looking for any sign of Shan or the Parter of Deep Waters. What he saw instead at the outer limits of the Egg's illumination was a massive, black-hulled hulk halfway imbedded in a profusion of smaller wrecks of similar design.

Who can say how long it had rotted down in the dark waters of the bay? Fully as big as a war junk, the ship lay nearly inverted, with its keel pointing upward like the vast dorsal fin of some leviathan of the deep. Its plank sides were black-furred with algae, further reinforcing its organic appearance. A great wound of shattered wood lay halfway up its port flank.

If Bao had any hope of air, or of finding Shan, he felt certain it would be within.

Drawing level with the hole, he released the silver disk to arrest his descent and it continued its downward plunge into the dark depths of the bay. Curiously, Bao felt as if he had been suddenly jerked upward. The general made for the ship with all of his strength, his strokes made less efficient by the sphere of light he held in his hand and the agony of his protesting lungs. He did not risk a backward glance, but knew the *guai* fish-freaks must be close on his heels.

He entered the hulk, light held forward as if to ward against the dark spirits of the place.

Fetching against a bulkhead, Bao was momentarily disoriented, the sudden obstruction coming as a shock after his long plunge through so vast and boundless a space. He scrambled, pushing strongly off from the wall to move upward and further into the ship.

Emerging into a cavernous area—surely a cargo hold—Bao swiveled to get his bearings. Rotting cloth and rope drifted in the quiet tides of the place, and the water was brownish and flecked like broth. Light glimmered abstractly somewhere above him, and Bao swam to it in the last throes of desperation, his lungs like cold, heavy pieces of metal pounding against his rib cage.

Almost there—a white limb slapped his face, and grotesque, dead eyes stared into his own. Bao screamed—

—and was hauled upward into sweet air.

As Bao lay gulping on slanted planks, Shan reached down to pluck the Dragon's Egg from his hand.

"You cannot know how glad I am you brought this, not least because my little fire was fouling the air of this place even further." Shan stamped out the small smoking fire he had somehow coaxed to life on an old sailor's tunic. Bao lay still, gulping air, but took in the chamber as best he could from where he lay on the angled deck.

It was a small, irregular space lined from floor to ceiling with chests of Black Pearl.

"How did you ever manage to get here, Bao Guan? I relied on Yi Deng's fifteenth meditation to decrease my need for air—but I've never known you to meditate." Shan, seemingly oblivious to the overall state of peril and oddness they found themselves in, was genuinely curious.

"I—" Bao coughed wetly, "I just held my breath."

"Hmm." Shan raised an eyebrow, and turned back to a few of the crates he had emptied of their poisonous cargo, the black heaps of the drug glistening evilly in the light of the orb.

"It was dead. That *guai* fish-freak floating in the water just there was dead, yes?" Bao asked as he regained his feet. Shan nodded.

"I killed it. It was left here to keep watch on what they must have assumed was a corpse. I assume they put me in storage to, ah, *ripen*. What are these creatures, do you think?" Shan chatted as he lashed four of the empty chests together with some tarred rope, and Bao noticed for the first time that the Commissioner's robes were slashed almost to ribbons in places. Finishing his task, Shan set about smearing the outside seams of the chests with Black Pearl, as a kind of caulk.

"You're asking me? Shan Wu-Tsi, Spirit-Slayer and Queller of Devils? We have now crossed wholly over into your domain, Commissioner." Bao, ever quick to recover, was stretching the tension out of his limbs and taking slow, deep breaths. The air, he realized, was not so fresh as his first desperate gulps suggested—it reeked like a fish market. And somewhere above the stink was the sickly-sweet yet sinister smell of Black Pearl.

Shan shrugged. "I suppose you're correct. And, since I'm the expert, you'll indulge my theory—"

"Perhaps it can wait; dozens of those things followed me here."

"Quite right, General. Conjecture can wait its turn." Shan dragged his conglomeration of chests into the center of the tilted bulkhead room and hefted the Dragon's Egg. "Have you ever wondered why hardly anyone uses these glow globes? Why we don't see them in palaces and the homes of better men and the like?"

Bao, who had been warily eyeing the water for signs of approaching *guai*, grunted noncommittally.

"It is because . . ." Shan, tugging out the steel hair spike that kept his scholar's topknot in place, touched the point against the crystal globe and held it steady atop a chest, "Dragon's Eggs are extremely, extremely dangerous."

Shan drew his sword and, with the pommel, hammered the spike into the Dragon's Egg with one crisp, clean strike. Smiling in relief, he let out a long, quavering breath. "It didn't crack."

"They're coming!" Bao, ignoring Shan, drew his saber and squared off against the looming white shapes in the water.

"Forget them, just be ready to grab onto one of these ropes and hold your breath. Let's hope this Egg is enough to get us through bulkhead *and* hull. Still, this is much better than my original plan." Shan pressed a wad of sticky Black Pearl against the crystalline orb, and mounted the chests at the highest part of the room. Scrambling to the top with all the dexterity of a monkey, he affixed the Egg to an acute angle in the chamber's ceiling—which had, in point of fact, once been the deck floor. Quickly he removed the spike, and dropped back down to his lashed-together crates. "Hold your breath!"

But Bao was busy hacking the *guai* that tried to emerge into the room. The narrow pool seethed with pale forms, and the deck was alive and flopping with severed web-fingered limbs.

"Bao Guan!" Shan shouted in his ear, dragging him away, "Hold your—"

He felt the cold shock of the mountain of water that poured down upon him before he registered the sound of the explosion. Sword lost, eyes dazzled by a flash followed by the slap of cold black water, Bao felt strong hands guide his own to take a grip upon a rope. He was tugged sharply upward, through a fire that burned underwater and a hail of splintered wood that ripped at his arms and face.

Upward and out of the ship. Out of the ship and once more into the dark.

• • •

THE journey to the surface seemed longer than the journey down, and more than once Bao felt as if he would sip of the fatal water around him and breathe no more. Clutching the ropes of Shan's makeshift float—the air-tight and empty bundle of Black Pearl crates he had lashed and caulked so carefully together—Bao said a prayer to Fan Yin for mercy, and one to the patron of soldiers, Tuan Yu, for strength. He then started to beseech his honorable (and not so honorable) ancestors, starting with his father. Just as he was getting to great-grandfather Bao Meng-Chou who, it was said, had beaten back a bandit raid armed with nothing more than a chaffing flail and the aid of a particularly unruly ox, the float burst upon the surface of the bay, and Bao once again knew the sweet relief of those saved from drowning.

The sounds of combat reached them over the water.

There was the smuggler's skiff, waiting with its lamps relit. Drawn up against it—lashed firm, Bao suspected—was another, smaller boat. Upon both decks men fought and bled.

Shan and Bao met each other's gaze across the raft and, without a word, pushed off in the direction of the battle.

Shan, the better and faster swimmer because of his long limbs and slender proportions, reached the enemy boat first. He clung to the side, waiting for Bao, knowing that a concerted attack would improve their chances. Bao arrived moments later, breathing hard, silently cursing the loss of his sword.

Together they heaved themselves onto the deck of the enemy's vessel.

Shan's *jian* flashed in the moonlight, water and blood dancing from it as it arced and darted and claimed life and limb. Bao swung his bone-breaking fists, hardened to the consistency of stone by the daily punching of iron plates, and barreled into the melee, dropping men left and right like sacks of meal.

"It is the General with Commissioner Shan!" came a shout from the watchmen's skiff, and a cry of victory went up among men who had moments before thought themselves defeated. Bao roared back in answer.

"These are no gangsters," Shan said, dancing close to the general. He parried a spear-thrust at chest level and slid under his attacker's weapon to deliver a thrust of his own into the man's chest. The spearman died before he hit the deck.

"Rising Tide Cult!" Bao shouted back as Shan wove away. The few remaining cultists shrilled a cry of excitement at the sound of their name, and redoubled the ferocity of their attacks. Each man and woman of them—for even women fought and died for their mad, apocalyptic beliefs—was stripped to the waist, their flesh disfigured with a dense array of wavy tattoos symbolizing water. They fought well with spear and trident, testament to the training each received in the cult's martial temples hidden amongst the dockyard sprawl of Long-He.

And, it was rumored, somewhere in the swamps of the mainland as well.

Bao disarmed a cultist and broke her spear over his knee, then dove into the thickest part of the fight whirling both halves of the weapon in a deadly storm of wood and steel. Shan—already anticipating his next interrogation—slashed repeatedly at a burly fanatic until the loss of blood sapped the fighter's strength, then Shan ducked within his guard to crack his sword pommel against the man's jaw.

"It is too late to stop the coming tide!" The big man shouted hoarsely as he stumbled to the deck. Shan was swiftly at his side, hitting him again and knocking him unconscious with a sharp pommel-blow to the top of the head.

The few remaining Rising Tide fanatics fought on, refusing surrender, but the combined efforts of the watchmen and Shan and Bao subdued them.

"This is all starting to make some sense to me, General," Shan said, staunching the wounds of the unconscious cultist he had bled to exhaustion. The gleam of intense focus in the Commissioner's eyes, and the long wet hair pooled around his face, lent him an air as ferocious and strange as that of any of the cultists.

Bao, unlashing the boats after Shan dragged the man onboard, grunted in acknowledgment. "Makes one of us."

"Rising Tide worships a mysterious demon-spirit, an underwater entity they call Cui-Mu," Shan said, his voice taking on the singsong quality of a court lecturer. "The Fish-Gutters have always been allies of the cult, even in their days as little more than a fraternity of fish market cleaners and cutters. Sometimes they even have members in common, and it is the Fish-Gutters that have exclusive access to Black Pearl . . . say, has anyone else noticed we are moving backwards?"

The skiff was drifting away from the boat they had just abandoned, away from the city and toward the dark shore of the swamplands. The watchmen frantically looked for the source of their movement, and slashed their staffs and oars down along the outer hull of the boat to dislodge the *guai* that Bao was certain must be latched onto them. Despite striking flesh many times, the skiff moved steadily onward.

"Keep at those fiends, men. Captain Li, give me your knife." Bao, stripping his sodden clothes for another dive, reached for the re-

maining Dragon's Egg where Shan had left it on the deck of the ship.

"Good idea," Shan said, scooping the Egg up first. He placed it against the wale, and again produced his hair-spike.

Bao, focused on the fight before him, did not follow what Shan was doing. "Throw it to starboard, and I'll jump in from the other side. Should daze them—they don't like the light."

"I would not dive in there if I were you, General," Shan said, striking a perfect hole in the sphere with spike and pommel.

"Wait!" Bao shouted as Shan dropped the Egg overboard.

The eruption slapped the boat a man's height into the air, and turned the water beneath it the color of copper. When they recovered, and the few men knocked overboard were brought back to the skiff, Shan gave orders to make for the municipal wharves of Long-He in all haste.

Around them in the bay floated the myriad corpses of the *guai*, killed as surely as a fish must be when a man claps stones together underwater.

• • •

BAO drained the remainder of the strong, black tea from the kettle brought to him by one of the captain's daughters and suppressed a yawn. Rather than rolling into bed upon their return from the chaos of the bay as Bao would have liked, Shan instead roused the entire city watch and attendant municipal services and began full-scale preparations.

Preparations for an invasion.

And so Bao had coordinated the massive evacuation of the bay-side of Long-He that morning, reviewed plans for controlled arson with the city's firemen, drilled small teams of watchmen in the art of the ambush, oversaw the construction of barricades and the transport of cannon from the handful of war junks in port, and even led a contingent from the local army garrison on a raid of the dockyards to destroy known Rising Tide bases. Now, with dusk fast approaching and with it—according to Shan and his cultist prisoner—a pending invasion of the *guai*, Bao wanted nothing more than to stretch out for the next ten hours and dream of his wives. Particularly his third one.

"Nodding off before the big fight, General?" Shan, whom Bao had not seen for much of the day, entered the guardhouse with a thick tube of bamboo under his arm. His earlier dishevelment had been corrected, and the ever-vain Shan once again appeared in immaculate scholar's robes and topknot. "Always the case with the best military men, in my experience," he continued, "completely unfazed by impending danger."

"You . . ." the word turned into a massive yawn as Bao rose from his chair. The General covered his mouth with one gauntleted hand and waited impatiently for the yawn to dissipate. "You look awfully refreshed to me!"

"General!" Shan said, teeth flashing, "who needs sleep when there is work to be done? I brought this for you." The Commissioner Extraordinary held out the tube, and Bao noted it possessed something very much like a crossbow trigger.

"And it is?" Bao asked, cautiously accepting it. It smelled vaguely of fireworks.

"Fire-tube. Quite simple, ah, please don't tilt it like that." Shan darted a hand out to correct the angle of the device and continued. "Black powder, naptha, some ship's tar . . . just light this wick," he indicated a spirit-soaked rag at the mouth of the tube, "aim, and compress the trigger. Then I recommend you drop the tube and move away from it with all haste."

Bao grumbled as he inspected the makeshift weapon.

"I have a man in every forward team with one of these, and I've also dispatched them their new orders for this evening. I want you—"

"What new orders?" Bao asked suspiciously, just as shouts from outside indicated the first of the flares had gone up. Shan and Bao went to the window to watch the direction of the warning rockets. The *guai* had started their invasion.

"Fall back to the lighthouse square, and bring as many of them as you can with you once the barricades are overrun. I'll be there with the shore garrison." Shan slapped his friend's armored shoulder and turned to depart.

"The lighthouse? I don't see the reason for it," Bao called after the Commissioner. He snatched his halberd from the corner of the guardhouse and followed Shan outside.

"You'll see, General, I can't go into it now," Shan, nearly a block away, shot back over his shoulder. "Trust me—it's all going to plan!"

"Going to plan, it's always going to plan," Bao mumbled under his breath as he jogged through the empty street in the opposite direction and toward the nearest ambush position, massive *tuandao* halberd in one hand, fire-tube in the other. "And what of when we run out of plans? What then?"

• • •

THEY were innumerable as the grains of sand on the shoreline. White, hunched bodies glistening in moonlight and firelight, drooping gills like the filthy gray locks of beggars. An hour past nightfall the fish-freaks bubbled up from the water all along the bayside wharves and shanties of Long-He and moved without hindrance into the city. They were of radically different sizes. Many, seemingly less developed, hobbled along at knee-height on limbs little better than claw-tipped fins. Others were giants and captains among the host, their carp-like heads fused back along stiff necks, their hands bearing tridents and shell-tipped glaives. The majority were the *guai* that Bao had encountered, fast swimmers but ungainly on land, needle-clawed and spike-toothed and cold as the blackest ocean depths.

When enough of them had come within sight of the forward position where Bao waited in ambush with a unit of the city watch, he gave the signal to burn the wharves.

Flares went up. All along the forward line torches fell into oil-filled trenches and flames licked rapidly past sterile and newly cleared stretches of firebreak, and carefully prepared sections of the sprawling bayside of Long-He burst into flames. *Guai* blackened and died, or else fled to the water's edge and plunged—smoking and screaming—into its cool embrace.

"Now!" Bao shouted, charging from the house he and his men had occupied. There were *guai* in the street in front of him, and he could see more fleeing the area of flames beyond the misshapen heads of those closing in on his position. Bao had hoped the risky move of torching a large section of the city would serve to divide and panic the attacking army. So far, it seemed only to have made them more determined.

A freak launched itself at Bao, and he dropped the fire-tube he had been carrying and swatted it away with his halberd. More came on as his men joined him in the street to push the tide of creatures back. Dusk turned to day as the fire-tube armed watchmen in Bao's unit unleashed their weapons' fury into the crowd of *guai* and turned a score of them into howling, blackening wicks at the heart of a column of flame.

For a moment the horde was blind and reeling from the light, and Bao and his men counterattacked.

Spinning his *tuandao* in great, vicious arcs, Bao cleaved his way into the pack of creatures and his men followed his lead with spear and staff. Faster to recover than its lesser brethren, a giant *guai* intercepted the general, bringing its shell-tipped trident up to block Bao's whirling halberd with a clang. The ungainly creature was faster than it appeared, and its counterthrust against Bao scored a glancing hit as the general dove out of the way. Bao, halberd discarded, somersaulted along the pavement and sprang to his feet to the right of the giant, lashing a low kick into one of its flipper-like legs. The giant buckled.

Bao drew his sword, a replacement for the one he had lost in the hulk below the bay, and in one fluid motion struck off the creature's head.

"To the barricades!" Bao shouted, unwilling to lose any more men in this opening skirmish now that the *guai* were showing signs of recovering from their blindness. Backing away he hacked at the white forms around him, filling the air with a mist of black blood. His men retreated in good order, and Bao retrieved a torch from one of them before the man moved further back toward their defensive line.

Bao, surrounded and alone, had backtracked until he reached his own discarded fire-tube.

Sheathing his sword, Bao swung the torch in a rapid arc that halted the advance of the freaks. He lit the wick on the tube, leveled it, and unleashed a gout of orange flame into the mass of *guai* in front of him.

He dropped the tube and turned and ran, not watching the effect of the weapon—the screams of the *guai* at his back proof enough of its potency.

• • •

THE city was on fire. They delayed the rising tide of *guai* at the barricade for what seemed close to an hour while Long-He burned around them. Cinders, borne on the night breeze, quickly kindled fires in other parts of the city beyond the bayside docks. Units of firemen worked as best they could behind the line of defenders to contain a citywide catastrophe, while men of the watch and the able bodied of the town militia manned the barricades—operating cannon, throwing paving stones and buckets of hot tar, thrusting and slashing with spear, staff, and knife. Though every man to die sold his life dearly, taking ten *guai* with him, still the fish-freaks came on with cold-blooded determination and seemingly limitless numbers.

Bao knew it was time to try Shan's plan, though he dreaded what it would mean. Stepping back from the carnage on his section of the makeshift barricade of furniture and ship's masts that was their primary line of defense, Bao glanced back in the direction of Long-He's great lighthouse, the highest point in the city and for leagues in every direction. The slender tower terminated in a bulbous crown within which an alchemical sphere of incredible proportions—a true Dragon's Egg if ever such a thing were to exist—beamed its white light seaward as far as the horizon. From behind, seeing the black tower limned in its own glow, it appeared to Bao like some enormous scepter of a king of legend radiating an aura of power and majesty.

"Fall back to the lighthouse!" he bellowed, and the cry went up and down the line and men fell back—with more haste in their step than Bao would have liked. Exhausted faces pale in the torchlight filtered past him as the general stalked up the line to see that his men kept in good order. Shan would be waiting with fresh reserves of regular troops, but Bao had his doubts that even they could turn the tables on this horde. "Torches!" Seizing a burning brand from a nearby guardsmen, Bao flung it into the oil soaked barricade and other watchmen did the same, just as the *guai* began to clamber over the wall. Flame leaped hungrily into life the length and breadth of the barricade.

Satisfied that the fish-freaks would be slowed for some time, Bao jogged after his men and toward the lighthouse square.

He noticed the scaffolding first, or what he took to be scaffolding. A profusion of bamboo struts and beams caged in the great structure of the lighthouse, and platforms and oblong shapes surrounding the top of the tower stood out black against the glow of the Dragon's Egg within. More such platforms could be seen at various heights along the structure, and Bao believed he saw the glint of metal or glass emanating from several. Turning into the square the general caught sight of the soldiers arrayed close against the lighthouse base in a defensive formation. In among the soldiers he saw objects that he could not identify—surely some last minute cleverness of Shan's.

He had thought them at first covered boxes or crates, large rectangular shapes draped in canvas or sailcloth. Four such objects were spread evenly among the front line of soldiers, and each stood something like three times the height of a man. As Bao neared their position he heard a gasp from the soldiers and turned to look behind him—the first of the *guai* had reached the open area of the lighthouse square.

"Up here, General!"

Bao craned his neck to see Shan, sword drawn, standing erect upon a platform close beside one of the covered objects. The general roared orders to his men to file in behind the regulars and moved swiftly to the bamboo ladder that would take him to Shan's platform.

"City on fire and my men all but spent. Whatever you have planned had bet—"

"Yes, yes. Not now," Shan waved a hand for silence. "Steady men! Hold your ground and wait for my order!"

"Better to attack now rather than let them fill the square with the weight of their numbers," Bao said, leaning out over the makeshift scaffolding to inspect the nearest shrouded object. Unexpectedly, his own reflection peered back at him from an uncovered corner of what could only be a large mirror.

Below them in the square, the horrors from beneath the bay of black waters surged in malformed ranks of pale flesh and spiny limbs. Though thousands lay burnt and mutilated throughout Long-He, and though the defenders had nearly burned the city down to stop them, still they came on in numbers sufficient to overwhelm an entire Banner division. Bao whispered a prayer to his ancestors and prepared to climb back down to the square to do what little good his exhausted limbs would allow him.

"You may want to close your eyes," Shan said before drawing his sword and shouting at the limit of voice: "Now!"

A spear of white light blinded Bao, nearly sending him reeling off the platform. A horrible keening filled the square below them as the fish-freaks shrieked in pain and confusion. When his eyes had adjusted Bao saw that night had become day.

Mirrors. Hundreds, nay thousands, of mirrors—surely every mirror of whatever kind in the entire town of Long-He—were affixed up and down the height of the scaffolding and arrayed on the plaza floor itself. All channeling the light of the lighthouse's powerful Dragon's Egg around and down and into the square: straight into the face of the onrushing horde.

"Attack! No quarter!" Shan shouted, and every soldier, guardsmen, and hastily trained militia man in the crowd below took up the cry as they rushed to slaughter the now helpless *guai*. Bao moved to do the same and Shan stopped him with a hand on his arm.

"Stay, Bao Guan. That's mere butcher's work now and you've earned a rest for this evening." Shan leaned out to watch the carnage below, and whistled his appreciation at the scale of things. "Hard to believe there are so many of those *guai*. What, with them exporting their own eggs to the Fish-Gutters at the rate of thirty chests a week."

Bao, exhausted and enthralled at the spectacle below, nodded. But after a moment's reflection he asked if he had heard the Commissioner correctly.

"Oh yes," Shan said, sighing. From his robes he produced a lump of Black Pearl and held it up in the intense light. "Unfertilized, treated, then left to dry in that underwater chamber we destroyed. Half the city has been smoking or eating the eggs of those things for years, and who can say what long-term effects it may still have? Perhaps it would be best to burn the whole place down."

For the first time since they had come to Long-He, fatigue had crept into Shan Wu-Tsi's voice.

Bao looked away to admire the complicated array of mirrors that had turned night into day. Everything from the largest ritual pieces of buffed bronze and the massive bands of brittle polished steel that once fronted the custom house, to the myriad wall-mirrors of the city's well-to-do merchant families and the double-sided hand vanities that were all the fashion of courtly ladies of the south, all of these and more could be seen in Shan's precise reflective arrangement. The whole of it dazzled like lake ice beneath a noon-time sun.

"Very clever, Commissioner. Once again you demonstrate why you are the Emperor's favorite. This must be every mirror in Long-He—and I imagine it was quite a feat to pry these from the hands of the wealthy dragon widows of the cantonments," Bao said, turning away from the ingenuous arrangement to look at Shan.

The Commissioner had produced his own silver-chased hand mirror—an object clearly exempt from the general draft—and was intent on wiping a smudge from his face with the inner fabric of one of his long sleeves. Shan looked askance at his friend and shrugged.

General Bao threw his head back and laughed, a victorious sound lost among the din of slaughter, and the roar of a city in flames.

ABOUT THE AUTHOR

In his feckless youth BILL WARD discovered that he lacked the requisite sadism of a truly first class Dungeon Master, so he decided to be a writer instead. Many years and several beards later, and Bill's short fiction can be found in gaming publications, magazines, anthologies, and the occasional federal court transcript. He is often overheard mumbling to himself about figments of his own imagination, but so far no one seems to have noticed when the figments mumble back.

ILLUSTRATION BY BRAD MCDEVITT

BEYOND THE BLOCK

By AERYN RUDEL

MY cell is not far from the headsman's square, and I can hear he is already at work. The rhythm of capital punishment follows a predictable pattern. I hear boos and catcalls as the condemned is led up the steps to the gibbet, then a hushed moment of silence, and, finally, the dull metallic thud of the axe striking the block followed by an explosion of cheers from the crowd. I have heard this exact sequence play out over and over, and tomorrow they will come for me, and I too will serve as fleeting entertainment for the mob.

My cell is one of the few with a window, and a thin beam of late afternoon sunlight streams in from above, illuminating a cube of gray stone, its walls damp with lichen and etched with the hastily scrawled names of the damned. I have not added my own name to the litany of victims. I would rather no one remember me, my failure, and my inability to protect those I love. The headsman's axe will put an end to my shame, and I will go willingly into the dark.

Heavy footsteps echo down the stone corridor outside my cell and break the long silence of my imprisonment. It is likely the guard coming to bring my last meal. The footsteps end outside my cell door, and I step back as the key rattles in the lock.

The door opens and a man enters my cell. He wears the leather breastplate and carries the short sword and club of an Iron Citadel guard, but his face is youthful, his eyes bright and intelligent. His expression lacks the slow-witted brutality I have come to expect from my captors.

"Do not be alarmed, Matthias," he says in a low whisper. "I have come from Lucinda."

The mention of my sister's name sends a warm flood of hope through my body. I am here because of a failed attempt to free her from her new husband, the Lord Magister Gregor Vyard, a man of great sorcerous power and profound evil. I stood little chance of rescuing Lucinda, and my attempt to break into the Lord Magister's tower ended abruptly. He hadn't let his guards kill me, though. He preferred his enemies to die publicly, a spectacle and a warning to any who might oppose him.

I press my back against the wall, fear overcoming any thoughts of rescue. Vyard is cruel, and it would not be beyond him to send this man to torment me with false hope.

He sees my fear and steps close. "This is not a trick." He rolls up the sleeve of his shirt, exposing his right forearm. There is a tattoo there, a black rose. It is the sigil of the King's Shadow, a group of spies and soldiers who oppose the Lord Magister and the power he has attained, the control he wields over the king's court. The tattoo could be faked of course, but I have nothing to lose, so I take a chance.

"Is she well?" I ask, unable to hide my desperation. "Has he hurt her?" I know without doubt that my failed attempt at rescue will have incurred Vyard's wrath, and my beautiful, gentle sister will have suffered.

The man's face sobers, and he nods. "The King's Shadow applauds your bravery, Matthias, but you are a blacksmith, not a soldier. You put your sister in danger, but your failure has a silver lining. You will gain access to Vyard's tower, something no one else has done."

"I don't understand," I say. "I am to be executed."

"You are, and I am not here to save your life. I am here to give you a chance to free your sister, to strike back at Vyard, in *death*."

Fear casts a cold shadow across my mind, and I shake my head. "I don't understand. How can I help Lucinda if I am dead?"

The King's Shadow agent produces a vial of dark liquid from beneath his breastplate. "Your sister was chosen by Vyard for her beauty *and* because she was one of the more promising students at the Sorcerer's Guild."

None of this is news to me. Lucinda developed the gift as a small child, and when she came of age, the guild accepted her as an apprentice. This was before the Lord Magister came to power, before his black magic devoured the heart and soul of the kingdom, and before he had become enamored with my beautiful Lucinda.

The man continues. "She has learned some of Vyard's secrets, and this one," he shakes the vial of black liquid, "may be the Lord Magister's undoing." He holds the potion out to me. "Take it, and drink it now."

"What will it do?" I ask, even as I reach for the potion.

"I will not lie to you," he says. "This is dark magic, and I do not envy the course before you, but if you love your sister, if you care for the freedom and prosperity of the people of this kingdom, you will drink this potion down."

He is not going to tell me more than he had, perhaps out of fear the truth would keep me from his purpose. I am going to die; there is no avoiding that. The vial I hold offers some scant hope, a flickering candle in the darkness of despair. I seize on it.

"Tell my sister I love her," I say, and remove the cork from the vial. I bring the glass to my lips; the liquid inside smells of earth and rotten meat. I close my eyes and drink it down, gagging at the taste, then double over as the potion burns a line of fire down my gullet. The pain is fleeting, but I am left feeling strangely heavy, as if my limbs are encased in lead.

The King's Shadow agent takes the empty vial from my hand and hides it again under his breastplate. "You are a brave man," he says. "Tomorrow, you will understand the potion's magic, and I promise, you will have your chance."

A terrible weariness overcomes me, and I slide down the wall to a sitting position on the floor. I want to speak, to learn more about my sister, but my tongue has become a lifeless bit of meat in my mouth, and I can only mumble incoherently.

"Save your strength for tomorrow, Matthias," the man says. "We will be watching." My head nods forward and I fall into a black sleep to the sounds of his footsteps fading down the hall.

• • •

I AM awakened by a sharp blow to my ribs, and a gruff voice. "Get up, you sorry sack of shit."

I roll over and see one of the Lord Magister's guards staring down at me, the crimson lightning bolt on his doublet leaving no doubt about his allegiance. His face is a squarish lump of malice and stupidity from which two dull brown eyes stare angrily down at me. His stench, old sweat and cheap ale, fills my cell. He draws his leg back for another kick, but I scuttle away, and rise to my feet, swaying slightly. I can feel the potion's influence still, though it is muted, a slight tingling in my extremities.

"Turn around," the guard says.

I comply and turn toward my window. Morning sunshine lances trough the gloom of my cell, and it warms my face for a moment before the cold iron of the guard's manacles are clamped around my wrists. I feel the end of his club press painfully into my back, and I turn around.

The guard smiles, showing me a mouthful of brown teeth. "Time for your walk," he says. "There's a big crowd gathered to see you off." The man's delight at my impending execution is evident. "You're a big one, and that thick neck of yours might take two or even three licks."

I say nothing. My size and strength, gained from many years working iron and steel at the anvil, has availed me little. Though it would be a joy to wrap my hands around this man's throat and squeeze the life from his body.

"Alright, move," the guard says, obviously disappointed he can't wring a reaction from me. He's used to fear and groveling. I won't give him that pleasure.

I walk from my cell, the end of the guard's club pushing me forward. Outside is a long dim corridor lined with cell doors. We walk to its end, to another heavy door. The guard steps forward and raps the door with his club, and it opens. There are two Iron Citadel guards in the small room beyond. A trapdoor in the center of the room leads to stairs and the next level of the citadel.

One guard pulls the trapdoor open, and I am forced forward and down the steps. The journey from the citadel to the executioner's square is short. I pay little attention to the dismal surroundings, trying instead to focus on what will happen once I reach the gibbet. I am afraid, but there is a strange excitement beneath the fear. It is borne of hope, small and vulnerable though it is, and I cling to it.

The morning sun is bright as we cross the square. The gibbet rises from a small sea of people ahead, a wooden platform fitted with instruments of death. The headsman, a huge man in a black hood, stands before the block. His axe, nearly as long as he is tall, is in one hand.

The crowd of people parts, revealing a clear path to a set of short wooden steps. The crowd is silent as I walk through, which surprises me. Then I see why. With Lucinda, near the gibbet, stands the Lord Magister, a gaunt scarecrow in black surrounded by his guards, the three-pronged sigil of his office glaring from his breast, blood red in the morning sun. My heart breaks to see my sister, and her eyes find mine, though she offers no expression or words of comfort. Vyard's right hand is locked round the back of her neck like the talons of some carrion bird. His thin lips are turned up in a gruesome smile. He looks like a man about to experience what he enjoys most, the pain and suffering of others.

My manacles are removed when I reach the steps, and one more nudge of the guard's club moves me up the stairs. I am large and strong, but I am not a fighter, and surrounded by guards and the headsman himself, any attempt at escape would be foolish and short-lived.

The headsman approaches me, a towering figure of muscle and grim purpose. "Come forward and kneel before the block," he says. His voice is deep and grating, though not unkind.

The block gleams with congealed blood as I kneel before it. The headsman has already been busy this morning. He looms over me, and his eyes, a surprising bright blue, gleam from the depths of his black hood. He takes one hand from the haft of his axe, places a meaty palm between my shoulder blades, and pushes me over, forcing my neck into the notch. The block is cold on my skin, and it smells of the butcher's stall, coppery and rank.

"Don't squirm," the headsman says, leaning down to whisper into my ear. "Stay still, and the axe will bite clean." It is a kindness, this warning. I have seen the axe crack the spine of a man who jerked forward to avoid the headsman's stroke. His pained screams still ring in my ears. I will be still.

The headsman lingers for a moment, and he places one hand to the left side of my head. His sleeve rides up, and there, on his forearm, I see a black rose. I am terrified, but the headsman's action was deliberate. I was told the King's Shadow would be watching, but I had no idea how closely.

"One strike," the headsman whispers. "I promise."

I stare at the small crowd gathered before the gibbet. They are quiet, their eyes locked on me and the block. I do not see the usual bloodlust so common to the crowds gathered for executions. On many faces I see sympathy, even pity. How many of the King's Shadow are within the crowd?

The headsman draws in a deep breath, and I hear the honed steel of the axe-head scrape away from the gibbet. The crowd draws in a collective gasp, and I can feel the axe hanging over me. There is a moment of silence, and then the axe whistles down. I feel sudden, terrible pressure on my neck, just below the base of my skull. There is no pain as my head comes away from my body, just the dizzying terror of the world turning end over end.

My head rolls a few feet and stops, then I hear the heavy tread of the headsman moving in my direction. I open my mouth to speak but can make no sound. The throat and lungs that empowered speech are part of the body sprawled lifeless behind the block.

The headsman's thick fingers twine through my hair, and he hoists me up for the crowd's appreciation. I have a clear view of the executioner's square. I see the crowd, I see Lucinda on her knees before a puddle of vomit, and I see Vyard striding forward. He holds open a black silk bag, and when he reaches the scaffold, the headsman drops me into it.

I plunge into darkness, and here I wait for death. I wait for sight and hearing to fade. I wait to behold the gates of heaven or writhe in the fires of damnation. I experience neither. I come to the strange and awful realization that my head lives apart from my body. This realization is quickly followed by another. The potion I drank last night, the one supplied to me by my sister, created with her own sorcerous skill and whatever dark magic she has gleaned from her husband, has now taken effect. But for what purpose? I am a disembodied head, powerless, and destined for what? To spend the next days, weeks, months, even years in an impotent hell before my flesh rots away? Why would my sister inflict such horror upon me?

Time passes within the darkness; I have no way of knowing how long. I should be terrified, I should be struck dumb with horror at what I have become, but instead a slow and steady calm steels over me. I must wait. I must trust that my sister and the King's Shadow have a purpose, and my current state is part of that purpose.

Light returns as I am pulled from the silk bag. The light is from a torch carried in the left hand of man who is not Vyard. It is the same loathsome guard who awakened me in my cell this morning. I see a bare stone wall before me, and upon it a row of tall iron spikes. The man lifts me above the wall, and I see the executioner's square below and the city sprawling beyond. The height of my vantage point and the view tells me where I am—the Lord Magister's tower. The King's Shadow agent was right. I am within the tower, but what good can I possibly do?

There is sudden sharp pressure—again, no pain—as the stump of my neck is forced down onto a spike. The guard grunts with the effort of forcing the iron barb through the meat and gristle. I keep my eyes closed. I do not want this man to learn what I have become, lest he alert the Lord Magister. His task complete, he leaves me.

Is this to be my fate, to spend years uncounted as a ghoulish ornament upon my killer's wall? Am I to be condemned to a hell of slow and certain madness, another victim of the Lord Magister's cruelty?

Before I can slip further into despair, I am aware of a strange sensation. A feeling outside the prison of my skull, like an old memory I can't completely recall. Then it crystalizes, and joy surges through me—I can feel my hands, my legs, my body!

At first it is little more than a ghostly tingling, like an itch I can't quite scratch. It is reminiscent of the effect I felt this morning after consuming the potion the night before. Then the sensation intensifies, and I feel my fingers moving against soft and yielding resistance. I can see the empty square below and the pile of corpses near the gibbet. I focus on my body, forcing my legs to move, my arms to push. The pile of headless corpses in the square below topples over, and among them is my own.

I tell my body to stand. It obeys my phantom urging, and I can feel solid ground beneath its feet. I carefully pilot my orphaned flesh to the gibbet, mount the stairs, and move to the block where my mortal life ended. I tell my hands to pick up the headsman's axe, and its dread weight feels like something I have long been without. It feels like power, and it feels like vengeance.

I turn my body toward the Magister's tower. Guiding it proves to be a difficult task once I can no longer see it from my spike atop the Lord Magister's tower. Then I close my eyes and understand the true power of the magic that is animating my corpse. I can still *see*, but now my vision is a hazy shadow, a colorless world of grays and blacks viewed as if my head were still resting on my shoulders.

This strange dream-like state is both off-putting and exhilarating. I can feel my limbs move at my request, the weight of the axe in my hands, and the strange sensation of movement without breath. My chest is still and silent, and if there were ever any doubt I am existing beyond the grasp of death, it has been laid to rest.

I guide my body toward the Magister's Tower, a black finger of iron and stone jutting from the far end of the executioner's square. There are two guards outside the main entrance, both Vyard's men. They wear black tabards over chainmail byrnies and simple na-

sal helmets sit atop their heads. They are armed with falchions sheathed at their hips and each carries a round wooden shield strapped to his left arm. Both shield and tabard bear the blood-red symbol of the Lord Magister.

They are talking as I draw near, and I hear them not with my ears but through the shadowy plane from which I control my headless body. These men have done me no wrong, but they stand in my way, and I feel no remorse as I lift the executioner's axe and advance.

The first guard sees me, and his eyes grow wide with horror. He backs away, but his compatriot is made of sterner stuff. The second guard draws his falchion, a heavy chopping sword, and moves toward me, blade held high, shield close to his body.

For a moment I hesitate. I am no warrior, and I have never wielded a weapon in anger. This hesitation allows my opponent to close the distance and chop his blade into my torso. I feel the steel enter my cold flesh, feel the ribs crack, but there is no pain, no loss of strength. As the guard tries to free his blade from my body, I bring the axe down with all the strength I possesses, striking him between his head and left shoulder. The guard's armor is well made, but the executioner's axe is ten pounds of honed iron, and it cleaves through his mail as if he was wearing nothing more than cheese cloth. The axe carves a line of red ruin down the guard's body, stopping with a hollow metallic thunk as it lodges in his breast bone. Blood splashes my cold flesh, and I rip the axe from his cloven body.

The second guard turns and runs, dropping his shield on the ground. The entrance to the Magister's tower is a large set of wooden gates locked or barred from the inside. The guard shouts to be let in, his voice rising in a high terrified shriek. The gates begin to open, the men inside not understanding their peril.

I charge forward and bring the axe whistling down on the back of the guard's head. The blade parts helmet and skull, splashing the gates with gore. The guard collapses to the ground, and I continue forward, slamming my body into the gates and forcing them open.

Inside is a sizable chamber with a spiral staircase leading up into the tower. As I step through, I hear the heavy twang of crossbows releasing their quarrels. Both bolts strike true, sinking to the fletching into my insensate flesh. The two guards here stare at me with open-mouthed terror, even as they desperately try to span their crossbows for another shot.

I fall among them with the axe, beginning to revel in the strength and power of undeath. I split one guard's skull as he attempts to draw his sheathed sword. The other has managed to reload his crossbow when I turn to him. He fires, and the bolt pierces my abdomen, perforating organs that are little more than sacks of meat without blood flow or purpose. I smash the crossbow from his hands with one swipe of the axe, then remove his right leg below the knee with the other. He tumbles to the ground, screeching, until I silence him with another blow.

I mount the steps, still guiding my body through a dim hazy world. The next floor is a study of some kind, with shelves laden with books. I continue on, climbing higher and higher. The rooms get smaller as I ascend, and I can feel a strange heat in the back of my skull as my body gets closer to my head.

I reach a level that is largely open to the night air and surrounded by a ring of balconies enclosed by a spiked fences. There is another guard here, the oafish man from the Iron Citadel, the one who placed my head on the spike.

He is alone and terrified. He has no doubt heard the screams of his fellow guardsmen below, and now, confronted with the ghoulish apparition of my corpse, he stumbles backward. His sword and club are in hand, but there is no fight in him. His eyes are twin moons of dread within his doughy face. The other guards were simply obstacles, but I *want* to kill this man.

I open my eyes, and I now can see in full and living color the grisly spectacle of my corpse, lumbering toward the guardsman, crossbow bolts jutting from my chest and abdomen. I urge my body to charge, leveling a tremendous blow at the guard. He proves quicker than I anticipate and jerks aside. The axe smashes into the stone floor, kicking up sparks. The guard lashes out with his short sword, striking my right knee. A lucky strike perhaps, but it severs tendons, and I feel the weight of my body falling forward as the leg gives way.

The guard is not quick enough to avoid my falling corpse, and I drive him to the floor with me. He howls and begs as I claw my way up his body. I have dropped the axe, and I will simply strangle the man.

When alive I would have been much stronger than this fat guard, but in death I am possessed of a fell might he cannot resist. My hands find his throat, and his howls are cut short as I squeeze. I climb to my feet, lifting him from the ground along with me.

He struggles, but I have closed off his windpipe, and he is weakening. I drag him to one of the balconies, where my head sits upon the spike he chose as my final resting place. I want him to see what will happen to him before I crush the life from his body.

I am smiling, and I cannot imagine a more ghoulish final vision for the guard than my grinning, disembodied head. His neck breaks with a dull snap, but I am not done. I continue to squeeze, until my fingers sink into his flesh, ripping through the muscle and tendons. I yank upward and twist, snapping the vertebrae and freeing the guard's head from his shoulders. I place my grim trophy on the spike next to my own head.

The thrill of this minor victory fades quickly. I must find Vyard and my sister. The Lord Magister must be aware of what is happening now, and he may be ready for me. In Vyard I will face much more than steel swords and crossbow bolts; I will face his magic, the same magic that animates me now.

From the spike, I examine the state of my body. I pluck the crossbow bolts from my torso, but there is little I can do for my damaged leg. I can walk, but I must drag the limb crudely behind me. It will slow me considerably.

I guide my body to the spike and lift my head free. I hold it by the hair with my left hand, like a man holding a lantern in a dark night, and retrieve the executioner's axe. It is not designed for one-handed use, but I find I have no wish to leave my head behind and pilot my body as I have done before. I wish to be whole when I slay Vyard.

There are more stairs leading up, and I know I am near the top of the tower. That leaves only one more room above, and there I will find the man who has cost me so much.

I start up the stairs. It is a short flight to a heavy wooden door banded with iron. I push against it to no avail. It is stout enough to resist even my undead strength. I still have the axe, and I smash it into the door, its iron head biting deep into the wood. I strike the door again, smashing the blade completely through this time.

I hear a short surprised scream on the other side. *Lucinda!* My blows become frenzied, and soon the door gives way to my fury. I charge into the room, a spacious bed chamber adorned with fine furnishings and other luxuries. Vyard stands before the bed, behind Lucinda, his arm around her throat. He holds a long dirk in his other hand, pressing the point of it into my sister's back.

If I could have spoken I would have howled with fury, instead I can only glare. I take a step forward, raising the axe.

"Stop," Vyard says. "Or she dies."

I comply. I cannot risk this monster taking more from me.

Vyard smiles. "I had not expected this," he says. "I did not discover the makings for the potion until this night, and you might have succeeded, Lucinda, had you hidden them a little better."

"Matthias, forget me," she says. "Slay this fiend! End his blight on our kingdom."

I take another step forward, galvanized by my sister's words, and in response Lucinda jerks her head down and sinks her teeth into Vyard's forearm. He screams in pain and drives his dagger into her back.

I have never felt such despair or rage, and as my sister falls to the ground I rush forward, bent on ending Vyard with a single blow of the axe. He recovers with a serpent's speed, and the foul words of some execrable incantation fall from his lips. He points his right hand and a forks of red lightning burst from his fingers to engulf me. Now I feel pain as Vyard's spell burns my dead flesh. I drop my head and the axe and stumble backward.

For a moment I am blind before the pain subsides, and when I can see again, my head is lifted from the ground, in Vyard's grasp. He pushes the point of the dagger into my right ear.

"Leave your body where it lies," he says. "If I destroy your brain, all of you perishes."

Hopelessness washes over me. I have failed. Failed Lucinda, failed the King's Shadow, and failed myself. Vyard carries my head across the room, away from my corpse. "I think I will burn your body and place your head back on that spike," he says, his voice gloating and venomous. "I wonder what will happen first. Will you go mad or rot away?"

I can see movement over Vyard's right shoulder, and I hear a very familiar sound, the metal rasp of the executioners axe scraping against the stone floor. Vyard whirls around, taking me with him, and I see Lucinda with the huge axe in her tiny hands. Vyard opens his mouth to scream or perhaps utter another spell, but the axe comes down, and Vyard's head comes way from his neck in a gout of scarlet.

The world spins wildly as my head falls to the floor, but I soon feel my sister's soft hands as she lifts me from the floor, holding me so I can see her face.

For a moment I think she has simply survived Vyard's dagger thrust, but the cold horror of the truth is there on her face. Lucinda's flesh has taken on a grayish hue, and her eyes, once brilliant green, are now purplish-black, though she is somehow no less beautiful.

She kisses my forehead, her lips cool and soft. "Fear not, Brother. I made two potions."

ABOUT THE AUTHOR

AERYN RUDEL is a freelance writer from Seattle, Washington. He is a notorious dinosaur nerd, a rare polearms expert, a baseball connoisseur, and he has mastered the art of fighting with sword-shaped objects (but not actual swords). He occasionally offers dubious advice on the subjects of writing and rejection (mostly rejection) on his blog at www.rejectomancy.com.

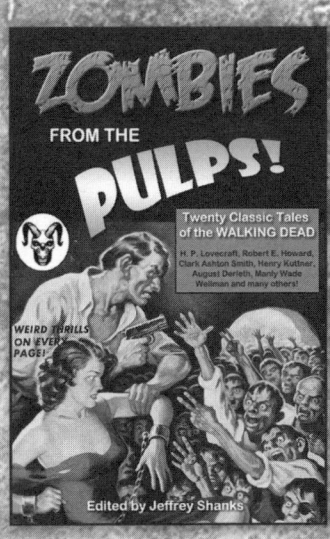

ILLUSTRATION BY WILLIAM MCAUSLAND

CRYPT OF STARS

From the Chronicles of Hanuvar Cabera

By HOWARD ANDREW JONES

INDAR couldn't stomach the screams. When his father told him he would be of service to a famous Dervani admiral, Indar hadn't expected he would have to endure so much screaming, or, for that matter, the dismissive contempt of the Dervani soldiery.

As the sound receded into a low masculine moan Indar stepped away from the long shadow of the outbuilding where the prisoner was being tortured and looked toward the ocean. The Dervani sentry had sent him here when he'd inquired at Admiral Mintra's quarters, but Indar was starting to think he should have insisted on remaining there, even if the admiral was overseeing the interrogation. Mintra had invited him to breakfast, after all, and there was clearly no breakfast to be had anywhere near the outbuilding.

The Dervani were determined, so the screams resumed. Indar withdrew further.

From the high hill where the ancient Volani garrison stood, Indar looked out upon three of the outer isles. The red cliffs rising from sapphire waters presented a certain stark beauty, set off here and there with clumps of green grass and low, dense bushes. Closer at hand, palm trees stood with curving leaves under the rising sun.

But, despite their hardy coastal foliage, the Isles of the Dead were no tropical paradise. Almost no fresh water flowed upon the majority of the isles in the maze-like chain, many of which were little more than sun-blasted rocks. The Volani soldiers formerly stationed to patrol the islands had always bemoaned duty at the garrison, and now the hundred odd survivors of the Dervani invasion had even greater cause for complaint, for the Empire had them digging up the very graves they had sworn to protect. Indar heard the steady chunk of their picks a few hundred feet behind him, along with the curses of overseers.

These, though, were lesser burials. The Dervani were intent upon recovering the vast wealth housed within the well-hidden tombs of Volani rulers and aristocrats. Tombs the Volani soldiers claimed secret even to them. That was probably the truth for all but a handful; unfortunately, it was not a truth the Dervan Empire wished to believe.

The screaming rose to a crescendo, and Indar winced in discomfort. Surely the torture could not last much longer. How could a man survive something that would cause that much pain? Yet he knew the Dervani would persist. They were barbarians, but as his father had said, their stubborn, relentless perseverance was key to their astonishing successes.

The scream abruptly died, and a short while later Indar heard the creak of the outbuilding door swing open. He turned to find the sentry stiffly at attention, for Admiral Mintra had stepped forth, blinking in the sunlight.

Though curious, Indar didn't ask whether the prisoner had died or passed out, or revealed anything of value. He but offered a formal bow and hand flourish.

Mintra answered this with a brief nod. The admiral was a lean, pale man, with hair receding behind a high forehead. Dark circles showed prominently under his eyes. His leather armored skirt and shining breastplate were scrupulously maintained and the admiral held his gaunt frame straight as a spear… yet his face had grown haggard in the week since Indar's arrival. The lack of actionable information wearied the admiral, and from little things Mintra had said, Indar was beginning to infer that the older man thought torture undignified. Indar found it profoundly distasteful.

The admiral's dark eyes settled on Indar. "Ah. Good morning. What are you doing here?"

"I have awaited you," Indar said. "For breakfast," he added.

The older man nodded once, and Indar wondered if the admiral had somehow forgotten.

Mintra closed the door behind him and they trudged the long distance across the square toward the Volani officer quarters, now occupied by the admiral. The dry sand crunched beneath their sandals as they walked.

"A nasty business," the admiral confided to Indar. "Are you certain none of your contacts know anything? We would naturally reward them for any information that produced results."

"What sort of rewards?"

The admiral looked at him sidelong. "Do you know something?"

Indar hadn't meant to imply knowledge he truly didn't possess. How could he so quickly forget the covetous Dervani interest in treasure? "I know the location of my own family's tombs, of course. But—"

Mintra finished this line of conversation with a decisive slice of his hand. "As I've said, they're inviolate. I have appreciated your counsel on Volani matters, Indar, but I think it's time to make better use of you. I want you to speak to the prisoners this evening before they eat. Offer any one of them their freedom if they reveal the location of a tomb."

"Me?" Indar could scarce believe the suggestion.

"They'll trust your word more than ours. You're a countryman, after all, and first-born to one of their greatest statesmen. Even if they don't like your politics, they must respect you."

Indar fought down a dark laugh. While he knew he was no traitor, other Volani had been less charitable, and he thought these captured soldiers – likely every one of them an adherent of Hanuvar Cabera and his family – would as soon kill him as look at him.

The admiral reached the door to his quarters, acknowledged the sentry's stiff salute with a nod, and placed his hand on the latch. "I'm prepared to offer concessions to any who step forward," the admiral told Indar. "If they see you, whose family prospers while they sit in chains, I think it might be considerable inducement."

The admiral opened the door and Indar followed him into the reception area, bustling with well-manicured slaves in bright tunics. One of them closed the door, shutting out the blazing sun and the distant crack of whips.

• • •

HANUVAR had observed the garrison from the height of the craggy cliff for the last three days. Careful scrutiny had provided him with the numbers, habits, and patterns of the Dervani. There were less than a hundred of them. Likely more had been used in the assault against the garrison—for over four hundred Volani troops had been permanently stationed on the isles—but the bulk of the force must already have sailed back to the empire.

The Dervani prided themselves on their soldierly precision, and Hanuvar was grateful to them for it. He now knew the quarter hour when the sentries changed, the hour when the prisoners were fed, even the time when the Dervani admiral took his breakfast.

He would have preferred to learn the names and habits of the enemy officers, but that would have required taking a prisoner, and the enemy would scurry like bugs if one of them were discovered missing. Their schedule would change. He couldn't have that.

Hanuvar climbed carefully down from the cliff and picked his way slowly along the rough shoreline hidden from above by a rocky overhang. It was early morning, and the sun was just cresting over the rust-colored cliffs, brightening the blood-red water to pink. Legend had it that the Lady Vazhan begged her lord each day to release those souls given over to his shadowy realm. Her greedy husband never relented, and thus she sorrowed, staining the water of the inner channels with tears of blood.

Hanuvar had seen the isles lashed with winds and rain on manifold visits escorting honored dead. When the water cascaded down the cliffs, the rock and soil turned it red. And so he knew that even if the lady of the underworld wept somewhere, it was the isles themselves that painted the waters their sinister color.

Only his errand coaxed him into open ground. He had to obtain the gatzi when they were at their most vulnerable. He moved swiftly between dusky purple shrubs that clung tenaciously to life on the rounded rocks. Yellow seabirds hung high overhead, almost motionless in the air currents.

As he climbed the slope, a shadow set in the cliff resolved itself into a deeper darkness—a jagged cave mouth. It was from here the gatzi flew forth each evening. Their meals of choice were the scuttlers that scavenged over the outer beaches and even some of the inner isles. Habitually the shelled creatures crawled up from the sea at night, and habitually the gatzi descended with their talons and razor jaws to devour them. Given the right stimulation, though, gatzi would attack nearly anything, and those unfortunate enough to stumble into a nest of the things seldom lived to tell of it.

The only folk Hanuvar knew who deliberately set out to find gatzi were suicides, sorcerers, or the occasional hunting party sent to destroy them. Hunters were inevitably well-armed with torches, pikes, and protective gear and even those brave souls never walked into a gatzi cave alone.

Hanuvar had no choice. He had fashioned thick gauntlets for his hands from canvas sacks that had once carried his supplies. Only two of those sacks remained, and these he bore over his shoulder, one sewn into the other. At his side hung a sword he'd brought from the distant isle of Narata. A fair blade, if not a fine one.

The stench of the cave hit him some twenty feet out. The gatzi den reeked of the dead things the ocean coughs up, fouler than the breath of a man dying from corruption. Hanuvar's mouth curled down in disgust as he trudged on over the rock, his sandals crunching pebbles with every step.

The odor grew stronger and, if possible, even more foul, and he paused to tie a torn cloth over his mouth and nose. It was neither as pretty as the painted masks the gatzi hunters wore, nor as thick.

Its elegance did not matter to him; he only hoped he would be shielded enough from the fumes that he would not succumb.

He paused upon the threshold of the cave, staring into the darkness until his eyes adjusted. The floor was sticky with a chalky lumpy substance he knew for gatzi droppings. Here and there it moved, for it was home to tiny worms, which thought the leavings the finest form of sustenance, and the larger insects that preyed upon them. They lived entire lives—eating, breeding, growing, dying, all in another creature's offal.

The cave was narrow, and high. He knew the gatzi would roost deep within, far from the hated sunlight.

Hanuvar advanced into the reeking cave, stepping cautiously over the soft, crinkly, occasionally writhing floor until the light was but a distant pinhole against the darkness behind him. He took to breathing through his mouth, and even then the vapor was so pungent his eyes watered.

He almost missed the gatzi. The front rank of them huddled on a shelf-like outcropping just below eye level; Hanuvar could not count their numbers, but he sensed the shelf stretching back into a vast space. Those gatzi nearest the rim resembled a rock formation, and it was the sharp regularity of their outlines which had drawn his attention; identical lumpy bundles of feathers, each head bearing an awful mouth tucked under a forewing. They were all roughly the length of his arm and spaced two handspans apart, arranged so precisely it looked like Dervani work.

Hanuvar had never thought to stand so close beside a single gatzi, let alone hundreds of them.

He slung the sack from his shoulder, his heart quickening, and reached up with one gloved hand to grasp the nearest of the things at the base of its neck. It was surprisingly bony, and light. The gatzi stirred only a little at first, but it hissed after Hanuvar dropped it in the sack. By the time he had slid a second through the opening, the objection from the container had grown louder.

Hanuvar snatched three in swift succession and dropped them in the bag. As he reached for a fourth its head snapped up and he found himself mere inches from the open, stinking maw with its double-rows of triangular-shaped teeth. He jumped back just as it snapped, and slid on the floor.

The monster that was the gatzi flock filled the chamber with echoing croaks, stirring the air with wings.

He turned and ran for the light, the bumping, writhing, cawing bag held at arm's length from his body. Behind him came a whispering thunder of wings, the hiss from a hundred throats rivaling that of the largest serpents.

He did not recall penetrating so deeply into the cavern. The light was so far away.

On he ran, uncaring, splattering cave muck with every stride. At any moment he expected to feel the talons rending his arm, the awful, diseased maws shredding the back of his neck like saw-toothed daggers. Something brushed the back of his shoulder, his hair—

And then he was in the light, blinded with its brilliance, kissed by the heat. He lost his footing on the rocks and swept out his arms as he fell. He dropped the bag. He landed with a thump, slamming his palms into the stone to take most of the impact, just managing to keep his head from striking stone.

He slitted his eyelids against the burning sun. A few black spots that were gatzi flapped out, circled dizzily, then fled back into the cavern. Hanuvar lay staring at a particularly fluffy cloud, then chuckled. What would the Dervani have thought of their hated enemy if they could have seen him then? He was nothing but a frightened, clumsy old man. In a better world his roaming days would be through. Now was the time of life to soak up the morning sun, to swap stories with old friends, to watch one's family grow and dare adventures of their own.

But that would never be.

Hanuvar climbed to his feet. His left knee was sore again, as it so often was these days. The gatzi within the bag rustled feebly. He tied their prison shut and lifted it. Later he would have to break one of his last light crystals to keep them quiet. Now, though, the sun visible through the cloth would leave them stupefied.

He started for his overhang. He used to be better at waiting, but now when he was not active his mind returned to his city, betrayed from within, and to his brothers. Once there had been four. Now there was only himself, and the ashes of his baby brother borne in a flask at his side. Melgar would be the last of them ever interred within the family crypt. Like his father before him, Hanuvar was certain when his own end came his body would know no hallowed ground.

• • •

IT didn't matter that the Dervani priest and two grizzled Dervani trions flanked him, that the prisoners knelt, that they were ringed by grim, helmed soldiers with spears. The Volani had simmered with anger the moment Indar entered their midst, an anger so pronounced he sensed they might attack him even under threat of death or injury. Had they greater savvy, they would have bowed their head to him and begged for forgiveness. They remained under the sway of the Cabera family, no matter the doom that allegiance had brought them.

The evening wind sapped the sun of its burning power, though its warmth was still heavy in the air. Indar sighed, and an image of Volanus rose unbidden to the forefront of his memory, with its cool evening breezes rustling leaves on the boulevards beneath the silver towers. He knew a sudden pang of loss.

Drilled on oration since his youth, it still took him a moment to gather his thoughts. He had practiced his speech for many hours, and now gave his audience the sympathetic frown he thought provided his best opening. "I've looked at you for days, wondering what I could do for you. You are victims. You were tricked; led down a path that your leaders could have seen, if they'd any kind of forethought. It isn't your fault. You were told to trust them. And now you are here."

"Traitor!" one of them shouted, and grumbles of assent rose from the throng.

The soldiers at Indar's side tensed, but he raised a hand. "I know that you're angry! You were soldiers, serving our country. And you did not ask for this! But I swear that I am not your enemy! Who really brought you to this point? Where is your council? Where is Hanuvar? They are the ones who told you Dervan could be bested. Had they listened to my father, you would not now sit here in chains."

Someone yelled something foul about his mother and one of the trions growled. The rest of the prisoners were silent.

"My family urged peaceful surrender!" he paced before them and offered a sad smile. "We knew the might of Dervan! Had the Seven possessed even a modicum of the vaunted wisdom they claimed, they would have seen what we saw. But because of them, you sit in bondage. Where lie the hallowed Seven? Most cowered in the temples!" Repeating the Dervani lie was necessary to convince his audience. While it was true Belevar had hidden in a temple and sobbed for mercy, the other six had died by their swords or on them, even ancient Mevlia.

He managed even greater conviction as he spoke on, for he knew, just as his father had long warned, that the Cabera family had guided Volanus to ruin. "And what of your great protector, Hanuvar? He didn't even turn up until the city was aflame! Dervani power flung him into the sea!"

He paused to look over the bleak, weary faces of the hundreds who watched. "The Cabera family brought you no lasting victories," he continued, pacing to the left. "They doomed our city with their deliberate provocations. But you need not be doomed. Life can be much better for you. If any one of you aids the empire, he could live as free as me. Dervan rewards its allies. Think of it. Wine. Women. And if nothing else, a life away from this baking sun picking at rocks! I ask you only to *consider* my offer this night. If any one of you knows the location of a tomb, he will be rewarded the moment he steps forward." Indar held up his hands. "Now this is a weighty thing, and I want no hasty decisions. Think on it for the night. Remember that the dead are dead. It is time now to think of the welfare of the living."

The faces were drawn and somber. He could not guess their thoughts, but he pressed on, hoping he'd led them to consider a changed perspective and witness a spark of hope. He wagered these qualities might weigh against stubborn Volani pride. "I will speak with you tomorrow after the morning meal. For now, I bid you a good night."

A few cursed at him as he turned away. He did not respond. Some would step forth in the morning, if protection were offered. He'd have to make sure they were immediately whisked away from the others.

"I think that was well said," the priest told him quietly as they walked away. "You have a wise way for such a young man."

"Thank you." Indar didn't feel that twenty-one years was especially young. He had already been married and divorced, and supervised the family holdings during the long months of his father's absences. He had argued in the hall of nobles so eloquently that even two of the Seven had praised his logic. But that was nothing to the Dervani, who seemed only to value men with gray at their temples.

The priest's scarlet robes swished against his thighs. His placid little face turned to Indar's. His voice was nasal, confident. "You may well inspire a change in attitude."

"One of them is bound to be smart enough, or miserable enough, to speak out."

"I prayed at length this afternoon," the priest continued matter-of-factly as they strode on across open, rocky ground for the living quarters. "And I spread the sacred bones. A momentous change is on the wind. I am not sure," he said, "what it entails for you."

The priest's smile was still affable, but his eyes were cold. What was he after?

"I am a friend to Dervan," Indar said. "I desire only peace between our peoples."

"Oh, of that I am certain."

Indar wasn't sure what to make of that. A Vazhan priest would never have dared such familiarity with a nobleman, but these barbarians tended to view all non-Dervani as beneath them. He feigned politeness. "What exactly did you learn from the bones?" he asked, although he knew that's exactly what the priest wished him to do.

"They spoke of fire, and a dead man. He is a man of some importance. I trust for your sake that the bones mean you will lead us to a dead man. I would hate to think that you would meet with any sort of… unfortunate circumstances."

"That's very considerate of you."

"Your father would certainly be disappointed. I know he has high hopes for you at the court." The odious little man cleared his throat. "Darkness comes. I have duties. You should report to the admiral. Good evening. May the Night Wise guard your steps."

"And may their blessings guide you." Indar pressed hands to forehead and bowed. He watched the priest leave, wondering if he hurried off to care for the mewling thing he kept in the wicker basket beside his window. Indar had no desire to find out.

• • •

ONCE the gatzi smelled the planks where Hanuvar smeared broken scuttlers they sped from the bag like arrows. The poor sentry didn't have a chance. He'd knelt to examine the carcasses piled upon his patrol route, which ensured he was not only closer to the scent but that he smelled more strongly of it. One moment he was a dark form hunched on the dock, the next he was a screaming and writhing mass collapsing under the devouring assault.

Hanuvar no longer knew the number of men he had slain, but he had seldom been responsible for so gruesome an end. He preferred quick deaths for his enemies, as he'd delivered to the other Dervani sentry whose cuirass, leather skirt, and helm he now wore. The helm was a bit tight, but Hanuvar had managed to squeeze it on. The night was dark, for only the brightest stars burned through the light cloud cover.

He heard the rest of the Dervani watch before he saw them, shouting from the wall above. Then came footsteps on the stone, shouts to aid a downed man, and the postern gate was thrown open. Four soldiers rushed onto the docks.

Hanuvar slipped into the garrison.

Shouts rang from various posts. He stayed to the shadows, walking swiftly for the old stone mess hall. All Volani captives were housed there, for the garrison had no prison, and the mess was the only room large enough to contain them under a minimal guard.

The Dervani had forged thick metal loops to either side of the hall doors, which were locked by placement of an iron bar. Hanuvar supported the bar gently so it wouldn't clang against the loops as he slid it free. Once it was clear he set it in the shadows and swiftly stepped inside, closing the door behind him.

"Olmar," he said softly.

The room's only light crept through high windows, recently mortared by the Dervani so that they were too narrow to accommodate a man's passage. By it he saw those within the dark chamber had not even the luxury of blankets. They slept curled on the bare floor, their arm or bunched up shirts for pillows. A few stirred at Hanuvar's call. They smelled of sweat and blood and fear and hopelessness. Some few among them, he knew, were women, the wives of officers who'd lived here with their husbands.

He pulled off the helm. "Olmar," he said again, and stepped deeper into the room.

"Hanuvar—" said a voice, and then the silent forms were sitting up. His name leapt from mouth to mouth, like fire on the steppe grass. Some cried that it could not be, others that he was a ghost. One laughed, madly, that he was there to rescue them, and even though Hanuvar was certain the Dervani would remain distracted, he worried the noise would bring them running

"Silence!" Hanuvar hissed.

And the Volani captives ceased their gabbling. They strained for better view of the figure before them, a silhouette against the gloom of the wall.

"Hanuvar?" One of the men rose tentatively and limped forward. Hanuvar knew the low-pitched voice, but not the limp. That was new.

"Commander Olmar." He had recognized him during the long days of watching, one of his brother Adruvar's best officers.

A figure halted a few paces off. "It *is* you—but you're dead..." there was a frightened quaver in the man's voice. "You plummeted into the sea."

Hanuvar spoke quickly. "I am no spirit. I am a man, and I have come to save you."

They began to chatter again, in joyous disbelief, but Hanuvar threw up his hands. "Quiet! We've little time. Listen to me, and you will soon sail free. Olmar. Come here."

Olmar walked forward, favoring his right leg, a thickly-built man with a wild mane of hair. "General?"

"They want our tombs—I want you to give them one. The family of my wife's." He could only hope, when he saw her at last in the afterlife, she and her forbearers would understand.

Olmar's voice rose in astonishment. "General?"

"I will tell you where to find it. And, if need be, a handful of other noble tombs. We must," he said tightly, "be prepared to make this sacrifice." Hanuvar turned his back to the others and whispered low to Olmar. The officer nodded, replying in the affirmative when Hanuvar asked him if he understood.

"There is much I would know," Hanuvar said, "but we will talk after." He turned to address the throng. Even though he could not see their eyes, he felt their attention fixed upon his every move.

"How many of you are fluent in Dervani? Show your hands."

Nine folk raised their hands, and when he asked how many spoke it with little to no accent, only three arms remained. "Make sure that you accompany Olmar tomorrow. Claim they have some special knowledge," he told the officer. It was vital that such men be close at hand from the first, should he have to improvise.

Olmar nodded sharply. "Yes, General."

Hanuvar could almost sense the sand grains falling in the hourglass. If some alert sentry were to wander by and seal the mess hall, everything he'd worked for would be lost. Yet he could not depart until he'd given them tangible hope. He considered them once more. "In the morning, Olmar will guide some of the Dervani to a wealthy tomb. Do your best to loot it dry, so the Volani will grow eager. Once they transport all of you there to begin work, you must await my word. Then we will strike."

Hanuvar smote the Dervani breast plate, then turned for the door. He left without a backward glance.

Outside the air was clean and cool. No one seemed to have observed his exit. He sealed his people in their prison as quickly as he dared, stepped clear of the building... and saw the postern gate was shut. A half dozen men clustered beside it. Four were clearly underlings. A fifth was cursing at them. Had they noticed a missing man yet? Had they already carried in the gatzi victim?

The efficient Dervani had moved even faster than he'd feared. He would have to rely on his backup exit strategy. Without hesitation he walked for a set of stone stairs that led to the upper level. A soldier was walking the crenelated wall above. "Is he going to make it?" the fellow called down.

"I don't know," Hanuvar answered in accentless Dervani. "It didn't look good."

As he climbed he saw the shutters opening on a small structure built against the wall by the stairs. Was someone looking out at him? He glanced back, knew a chill when light reflected off eyes too round to be human. No time to worry about that—he headed into the gloom away from the soldier.

The wall looked very different from this side, but he had measured carefully. On his left was the flat, dark expanse of the garrison compound, on his right the merlons of the outer wall. Beyond that lay a drop to the sloping shore, save for a narrow stretch… there. He checked both ways once more, stepped quickly to the battlement and hung down by his hands. The sea lapped against the wall below.

The soldier Hanuvar had spoken with heard a soft splash and strode over to investigate, calling out to the man he'd seen. But Hanuvar, kicking off armor and loosing his helm beneath the waves, didn't hear. It would have been ideal to swim with both the helm and the breastplate, but that was one miracle too many for him to work in a single night. They would have to remain on the seabed.

• • •

66 **I** FELT certain one of them would come forward," Indar said. "But I didn't expect it would be Olmar."

A half-eaten biscuit sat in a saucer on the admiral's desk, next to a few white danaline rinds and some empty shells. The remnants of breakfast. Indar had not been asked to join him this morning. He had begun to suspect that the admiral didn't like him, perhaps because of their age difference, or Indar's friendship with one of the emperor's nephews. Or it might be that the admiral had realized Indar's star was rising, while his own was surely waning. Else why would he have been given so miserable a post?

"You told me you had good news," the admiral said.

"He'll give us the location of a royal crypt. And," Indar could not help pausing for effect, "it's the tomb of the Idresta family."

The admiral's eyebrows rose precipitously. "The family of Hanuvar's wife?"

Indar smiled. "Yes, Admiral. Olmar had attended a family burial—one of Hanuvar's brothers by marriage. And Olmar's brother was one of the Vazhan priests – those sworn to oversee the sacred isles. He showed Olmar the locations of some of the other noble tombs as well."

The admiral frowned. Indar wondered if anything made him smile.

"He knew all that, and confessed nothing under torture?"

"I…" Indar couldn't dredge up any sort of clever answer.

The admiral sighed. "It makes one wonder as to the efficacy of our methods."

Indar had no doubt as to the effectiveness of Dervani torture. He was certain that he would have happily told them whatever they wished if he'd even been shown the instruments, much less endured their attentions. He flushed, feeling vulnerable and foolish, even a little fearful.

The admiral, he realized, was talking. "…wishes his own freedom for this information?"

"He asks for comforts for all his men."

The admiral's frown deepened and he sat back in his chair. "What specifically did he ask for?"

"Beds, blankets. More substantial meals. More breaks. No whips for men he swears will labor honestly."

"It is not so much," the admiral said finally. "He knew we could not grant all of them freedom, and so rather than asking solely for himself, he asked only for those under him to be treated like men. I wonder, Indar, if I would have done the same, in his place?"

Indar hesitated, unsure how to answer at first. "You would not have allowed yourself to be in such a situation, admiral. Your intelligence—"

"There will always be a victor and a vanquished, young man. Only the gods know which one will win out. My intelligence has nothing to do with it." The admiral fell silent. "I have requisitioned blankets for them already and they should be on the next ship." He fell briefly silent. "I will meet the rest of their demands as well, but they must first show me proof. Let us take two dozen of them to one of these burial sites and see if anything is there."

"Yes, Admiral."

"And if there is… then maybe you, at least, can depart these accursed islands."

Indar heard bitterness there, and sought to mollify the admiral's opinion. "I'm sure you will be able to return soon too."

The admiral's frown deepened. "I don't know if you heard last night, Indar, but we lost two men. Gatzi killed one near the docks. He seems to have stumbled on them while they were eating. A gruesome death. We think another might have been attacked by some on the battlement and fallen into the water, but we've found no sign of his body."

"I'm sorry to hear that," Indar said. He hoped that it wasn't a swarming year. If it was, there would be much worse in the days ahead.

"We shouldn't be here, pecking at the ground like chickens," the admiral continued sourly. "This place is for the dead, not the living."

"That may be so," Indar conceded with a forced smile, "but the emperor will surely be pleased with a new source of wealth for Dervan's coffers."

The admiral's tone changed abruptly, like the shutting of a door. "Go speak to Olmar and tell him I accept his offer, provided I receive proof this day. Have Olmar pick his twenty best men. Remind them the faster they work, the faster we can all depart these wretched islands."

"Yes, Admiral." Indar bowed and left, thankful that the sinister priest was nowhere in evidence. He'd begun to suspect the man was spying on him.

By mid-day a cadre of wretched prisoners were boarding one of the ships. The Admiral left more than half his contingent at the old garrison, assured he had men aplenty to shepherd the remaining Volani.

Indar watched the great red cliffs as they sailed south through the labyrinth of tiny islands. How many of his ancestors were interred within? What did they think when they looked down on him? Did they, too, think him traitor?

He had turned his back on the fools who drove Volanus to death, and his father had seen to it that the family would live on as valued servants to the Dervan Empire, but this was a different thing. He revered his ancestors and their accomplishments. Is that why he still felt so troubled?

Then again, his unease might be because whenever he turned he found the priest's eyes upon him. The fellow would smile, nod pleasantly, and look away — and then stare at him once more. What did he want? What was he watching for?

Worse was the wicker basket beside the priest. A cloying scent of unwashed flesh drifted from it. Occasionally it rocked a little and the priest hushed it tenderly.

Indar was glad he still had a knife at his belt. He might not be able to take down one of these soldiers, but if he had to, he was certain he could kill a priest.

• • •

THE Dervani had been thrilled with the riches in the tomb and, just as Hanuvar had supposed, quickly erected a temporary camp and relocated their prisoners there. It wasn't just that the Dervani were eager for the treasures; like anyone sane, they were desirous of completing their mission so they might put these desolate islands behind them.

He moved against the new camp in the deep night after the prisoners had been transferred. One by one he struck down the three sentries who watched the sleeping prisoners. Before too long the Volani most fluent in Dervani were in Dervan uniform and pretending to watch over their charges. Olmar and ten other Volani followed Hanuvar over the rocky ground, shovels and picks in hand. So far the plan had worked surprisingly well, and he wondered how long it would be before something went awry.

After an hour's walk they set to work on an unassuming block of stone around the cliffside from the camp. Hanuvar spoke only to guide their efforts.

They had but two lanterns, shutters directing ghostly beams upon the scarlet striated rocks. Olmar kept watch. The soldier did not speak of what the Dervan had done to him, but he often grimaced as he moved. He had insisted upon coming, so Hanuvar had given him a less strenuous task.

It took nearly an hour to clear the dried, baked soil from the stone slab, another quarter hour and the combined efforts of nine strong men to leverage it from the square of darkness it concealed.

They worked wordlessly, whether out of respect for the dead or for fear of the Dervani, Hanuvar did not know. Aside from his own instruction and the occasional grunt or low oath, the only noise was the clink of spade or pick and the rising wind, moaning through the canyons. Dark clouds drifted overhead, blanketing all but a narrow strip of sky through which a sliver of the golden moon shone down.

When at last they had dragged the protesting rock clear of the hole, Hanuvar called for Olmar, replaced him with a dour younger man, and descended the dark stairs with a lantern in hand. All but the sentry came with him.

It was cool down there in the old stone. A short walk of ten paces brought them to a round chamber with a black marble table built around an empty urn. Here of old were offerings made to the dead of his family.

A stark relief of Vazhan wept on the wall, leaning over the table, her colors long since faded. Hanuvar recalled her appearance from his last visit, noting then that someone should see to repainting her tears at least. His cousin had promised to do so.

"Olmar," Hanuvar said without looking from the relief, "do you know anything of my cousins' fates?"

"Not with certainty, General." Olmar's voice was grim.

"They are dead," Hanuvar said.

"That is what we have heard. But I know no details."

Hanuvar asked the question for which he dreaded the answer. "And my daughter?"

"They say she was taken. Her husband died in the street, fighting."

"Better she had died with him." He regarded the weeping relief, lost in memory, until finally Olmar cleared his throat.

"General?"

"There are weapons here," Hanuvar said. "We will need them in the coming hour. And hereafter."

He had never heard the voice of the gods as the priests did, but he had prayed to them that morning, wondering all the while why they should aid him now when they had allowed the Dervani to destroy Volanus. Might the Dervani gods be greater?

"General?" Olmar prompted.

He turned and faced them, the lantern deepening the lines and hollows in his face. "Forgive an old man lost in the past. This is the tomb of my family, down from the days of founding, and I bear with me the ashes of my brother, Melgar. He is the last of us who shall ever be interred within. And we are the last who shall ever pay homage here."

They waited for him to speak on, and he wished he knew all their names. There was not time.

"Since the founding, only those of our bloodline have passed this portal. Yet you may cross it with me, this day. There are so few of us left—we are all one, now." He turned to the relief and pressed in upon the eyes, hard. The ancient magics worked a final time, and an eerie whistle rose up from deep within the stone. The hairs along his arm and back of his neck stood quivering.

The relief sank slowly down. Before them loomed what at first seemed an underground lake, for the lantern beams plied over the space reflected off a liquid surface. And then those with him beheld what only the family of Cabera had ever seen; a stone walkway raised over an ocean of quicksilver, its waters forever lapping the shores of the miniature inner and outer seas spread to either side of the path. Hanuvar heard them talking in wonder as they walked on, pointing to the isles, the carved peaks and hills that rose from the ancient map. Someone noticed that diamonds were worked into the ceiling, arranged in the constellations, shining forever above the changeless sea. There too was a great emerald, near the shore. Eternal Volanus. Here in the tomb it still shone in all its beauty. And here in the tomb did it belong.

A metal door set with gold and silver waited at path's end, his family's crest of a swift ship with a soaring bird above carved into its surface. Hanuvar pulled upon the handle and the heavy portal swung easily outward.

Beyond, in niches, the bodies and urns of the centuries of Cabera dead lay in ranks of stone biers, stretching into the darkness. And here too, on the opposite wall, his lantern gleamed upon a martial display of swords and shields, mounted upon the wall almost to overflowing.

"They are treated with draden oil," Hanuvar said, "by the young men of our family each time someone is interred within. All but the oldest of these should be free of rust."

"You didn't say there would be armor, too," one man breathed.

"They're beautiful," said another, stepping forward to tentatively caress a hilt.

"Dress in the armor. Carry as many weapons as you can. And then we return to camp. We must capture and crew the galleys before the dawn."

"But where do we go?"

"That I tell you after our victory." They could not know, yet. What if the attack failed?

"Ready yourselves. I have a duty to perform." Only then did he lift the flask from his belt. It was a poor container compared to those upon the biers glittering with gold and jewels, carved with swordsmen and ships. "It is time to carry out the last wishes of my brother." So saying, he took one of the lanterns and left with it for the tomb's recesses, leaving the men amongst the shining weapons.

His sandals slapped over the cold, dark stone, his lantern's light flickered over the dusty bones, and his thoughts sped down through the years. Here was his grandfather's skull, and he recalled kissing that forehead a final time as they laid him there. Here were the bones of his aunt, and his baby sister.

Here was his father's niche, empty for want of a body slain by Dervani and left for carrion. Hanuvar caressed the carven letters of his name. What would his father say to him, now? Memories crowded for place like errant children vying for attention. How young *had* he been on that first campaign with father? He did not know; could scarce recall a time when an army camp had not been his home. He had wanted nothing more than to stand worthy in that man's eyes and to emulate all that he was. Later he realized that glory had been thrust upon his sire; that his father stood the line because there were none better, but given a softer world, Himli Cabera would gladly have been a gardener.

Hanuvar no longer wondered what he might have been, only what he might have said had he been granted more days with those he loved. This night, so close to the bed that should have been his father's last, he longed again to hear that calm commanding voice. What would father have done in his place? What counsel would he offer now?

He would urge him to waste no time.

Hanuvar stepped away.

Fabric yet clung to Adruvar's frame, the mighty hands withered and still across his powerful chest. There lay Hemlo, his crooked smile dust; death had reduced his handsome features to a grinning mockery and robbed him of individuality.

Only one of his brothers' biers lay empty. Here Hanuvar set Melgar's ashes. The youngest of the four, he'd been the brashest of the lot, a favorite of the ladies, quick of wit. A brilliant swordsman, brave to a fault… After he'd survived that chest wound, the slash that cost him his left arm and the illness that followed, Hanuvar had thought Melgar unkillable. But he'd sickened in the new colony, and on his deathbed asked only that Hanuvar bear him to the grave site of his family. Legends said that those close to death often saw the future, but Melgar must surely not have done so, or he would have foreseen that when Hanuvar's ship returned to Volanus the Dervani would be delivering the city's death blow.

Hanuvar knelt by his brothers one last time, his eyes straying to the stone bed that would surely have been his own, someday, had there been any one to carry him here after his death. He would die in some far off, lonely place, and his bones would spend eternity in a Dervani trophy case.

This moment, though, was for his brother. He bowed his head and began to pray.

• • •

INDAR awoke to horror, and knew a pressure against his chest. It was the quiet of the deep night, yet there was light in his tent, and by it he saw a black, skull-like face peering into his. He failed to scream only because he choked on an air bubble as he sucked in a breath.

The furred creature with scalloped wings chattered angrily at him and he felt its claws through the blankets as it shifted its catlike weight. It had a pungent, unpleasant scent as sharp as its talons. The priest looked down at him on one side, a soldier with a lantern on the other.

"You sleep deeply," the priest said.

"What is this?" Indar demanded more shrilly than he planned.

"You are coming with us."

"Why?" Indar's voice broke in fear.

"Because I have found you out, Indar."

The creature hopped off his chest and watched unblinking from the edge of cot.

Indar sat up quickly so it would not return. "What are you talking about?"

"You pretend it well. But my little servant has seen your friends."

"I have no idea what you're talking about." Indar was surprised to hear annoyance in his voice—he had assumed he would only project the fear that gripped him.

"We will see. Dress and come."

The priest exited the tent, thankfully taking the hideous creature with him. The soldier remained, scowling.

Indar threw on his clothing. Outside he found a dozen unhappy looking soldiers, as well as Admiral Mintra. Upon Indar's emergence they set out at a brisk walk, the priest leading, and Indar soon saw that they were leaving the camp. "Where are we going?"

"To meet your smuggler friends," the priest answered.

Indar fell in step beside him. A thin sliver of moon painted everything in yellows and blacks.

"I don't know what you're talking a—"

"You make things worse for yourself, Indar," Mintra said wearily.

"Palhecoc saw them at work on a tomb," the priest said. "And told me of it." He rubbed a finger under the chin of the stinking thing on his shoulder.

"It was not our men," Mintra said. "Our sentries and guards are in place and report all prisoners accounted for."

Indar struggled for inspiration. How was he going to convince the admiral that he hadn't been involved in whatever was under way?

"I swear by my grandfather's name that I know nothing of this," he said finally.

"Oh, don't play innocent," the priest sounded pleased. "You must have had a ship waiting nearby; you sent word to them once you finally knew the location of a tomb. Weren't the riches the emperor had already given your family enough for you?"

"That's ridiculous!" Indar could hear the conviction in his own voice—surely the priest did as well. "Admiral, I am a man of my word, you know it!"

"I know," said the man stiffly, "that you work against your own people."

"You're wrong," Indar snapped, wondering why he felt rage at the same time he knew numbing fear. "You will see I have nothing to do with any non-sanctioned operation and—" Indar's voice trailed off. He'd been contemplating a threat, and remembered he was surrounded by twelve men who'd kill him at a word.

It was a long, quiet walk, and his heart sped the entire way. The admiral commanded his soldiers quiet. The only conversation was that whispered back and forth between the eldritch creature and the priest himself. Indar was mostly thankful he did not understand them.

He guessed it was some forty-five minutes into the journey when the priest sent his winged horror flying ahead. He'd had the men shutter the lanterns before they rounded a corner in the cliff. Now a channel of water stretched along their right, a jagged cliff wall on their left with multiple caves and shadows.

There was no sign of any ships—which presumably one would see were there smugglers or thieves about—but he said nothing. Better if he remain completely silent, so as to give no cause for censure from the priest.

A dark shape winged out of the night and settled with a flap of wing on the ground before the priest. Indar gave an involuntary shudder. The thing bowed, then chattered at its master.

"It has slain one of them," the priest relayed after a moment. "A sentry, I think."

"Let us see," said Mintra.

The creature bounded ahead, flapping its wings determinedly until it had lift. It settled down beside a body, tore at its neck with the claws spurred along the back of its long fingers.

"You, look ahead," Mintra commanded, pointing two men forward. "Here is your man, Indar."

"That's not—" Indar stared. "That's one of the prisoners, Admiral. Olmar's friend with the missing fingers." The bulging, staring eyes rendered his visage horrific, but there was no mistaking the scraggly beard or the thick eyebrows.

Mintra stepped forward and peered down at the body. "He's right."

"There's an opening here, with stairs going down," the trion called to them.

"Someone's found and opened a tomb," the priest said to Mintra. The admiral frowned.

"As I said," Indar declared with stiff dignity, "I had no knowledge of any workings here."

The admiral paid him no heed. Indar wondered, as the admiral's gaze turned on him, if he would apologize. But the fellow faced his men. "This prisoner had a weapon. There may be more of them. Some of our workers must have gotten free. Stay alert."

"What would prisoners want with a tomb?" Indar asked, glad to be so obviously innocent of any involvement. "Wouldn't they just escape?"

"For riches, of course," the priest answered without looking at him. He scooped up his beast. "We will stop them."

Mintra called for lights once they arrived at the stairs. "They'll see us coming," he explained, "but we can't proceed without the light."

So saying, they descended the flight in twos, Mintra and the trion serving as his second-in-command, followed by the priest and Indar, and the rest of them. In moments they had reached the antechamber, and Indar scanned the walls. So too did the priest, and the two of them spoke almost as one as they recognized the Volani lettering. "The tomb of Cabera."

"This is Hanuvar's family," Indar said.

The priest chuckled. "Well, these slaves have done us a favor! The emperor himself will hear about this find!"

The men marveled at what seemed to be a lake beyond, and the vast map, taking in its beauty even before they noticed the riches set into the stone of the landmasses, a jewel sparkling at the site of every city. "Hands away," the priest said. "My pet is watching, and will tell me—this is all for the emperor."

Mintra took the whole thing in, looking troubled. Indar understood why. What could the soldiers possibly want with the tomb of their dead hero's family? Of all sacred ground, surely this was the last they would ever have wished to disturb.

The admiral led them across a stone walkway that bisected the map and was starting for the steps to the door when it opened before him. He backed away, grasped at his hilt.

At the head of the stairs, backlit by a blinding radiance, stood an aged man in armor. He was lean, powerful, with high broad shoulders. There was no mistaking that proud hooked nose, the silvery hair, the grey-green eyes. In the shining armor he looked for all the world like some war god descended to mortal realms.

Indar's blood chilled, and he stammered out what he knew, what many of the Dervani doubtless knew: "It's Hanuvar!" He did not say that he had returned from the dead, that he had risen from his own tomb. He knew it, just as every man there knew it. Even the veteran admiral froze.

The dead man leapt with a savage war cry. Too late did Mintra throw up his block — Hanuvar's sword cleft brain and bone and dropped him. The general ducked a half-hearted swing from the trion and plunged his red blade into the armpit gap of his cuirass. The Dervan officer screamed and fell backwards into a carved mountain range.

Behind Indar men cried out to their gods. Ahead, framed in the doorway, came more dead of the Cabera clan, each clad in shining armor.

The priest urged his pet forward but Hanuvar cut it down in midflight. The priest was still gaping stupidly as the sword cleaved off his own head.

"Spare me! Spare me!" Indar cried. "I'm Volani!" And he ducked low.

Hanuvar's ghost leapt over him, thrusting.

The Dervani soldiers screamed and ran.

"Chase them down! Hanuvar roared, and his dead men raced after, splashing through the cold, silver fluid.

Indar was hefted into the air by the scruff of his tunic and the blazing eyes of the vengeful wraith stared into his own.

"You've soiled yourself," Hanuvar said.

"Spare me—"

"Will you offer me riches?" The general's voice dripped with contempt. "What will you give me? My cousins' lives? My daughter? My city?" He pointed the sword at the younger man's throat.

"I followed my father!" he said.

And for some reason that gave the spirit pause, for the sword thrust did not come. Instead the ghost bore him backward, slammed him hard into the wall. Indar gasped in pain, felt something give behind him. A lever, he realized with a sickening lurch. Many aristocratic Volani tombs had them, and at their trigger the tombs would be sealed by falling rock. He cried out in fear at the sound of a great rumble from the doorway where Hanuvar had come, but the roof held steady. A dense cloud of dust wafted out from the entry to the crypt.

Hanuvar dropped him.

Indar, crouching in the quicksilver beside the path, trembled under the dead general's gaze.

"Live long, boy," the spirit said as it walked toward the distant clash of steel. "Squeeze every moment from it that you can, for you bought it dearly. If our gods yet live, they will not be kind to you in the hereafter…"

And then he was swallowed by the darkness.

Indar found that he was sobbing with both fear and dread. Even if he had desired to retreat deeper into the tomb he could not, for he was certain nothing lay beyond the doorway but crumbled stone. And he dared not follow the wraiths, so he sat in misery in the quicksilver beside the bodies of the Dervani, under a thousand diamond stars.

• • •

IN a little over an hour they had surprised and overpowered the rest of the Dervani. The surviving enemy soldiers loaded supplies aboard the galleys, and Hanuvar left them alive on the shore as the Volani rowed away from the isle.

It was only then that Hanuvar called Olmar to his side by the tiller and spoke to him of their destination. "We found a land, Olmar," he said quietly. "In the far southwest. Two weeks beyond the mountains of fire and the isles where the serpents run. Steer toward the top star in Sedrasta's horn." He presented him with a handful of gemstones. "Revictual at the isle of Narata. You know it?"

Olmar nodded slowly. Once, he had captained a ship in Adruvar's fleet. "I do… tiny and remote—"

"A friend rules there. See that no one learns your final destination. It must be secret. Our people must remain safe."

"This is all true?" Olmar asked. There was a tremor in his voice. "There is a new Volanus?"

"It's but a thousand folk in rude buildings," Hanuvar answered dully. "All that survived the trip." He'd planned it to be a new colony, his last great mission for the city. When he'd returned to Volanus he'd hoped to lure a few thousand more to join him there. It was best not to dwell on what might have happened if he'd arrived even a week earlier. "But it's better than this. Now. You will need to stop at this island—" Hanuvar pointed. "I left my skiff on its far side."

Something in his tone alerted Olmar. "You're not coming?"

"There is more that I must do."

"Hanuvar—"

"There are other survivors, aren't there?" Hanuvar asked him. "Scattered through the empire?"

"Surely—but not all of them will be close to ships. They will be slaves, trapped deep in Dervani lands. They may be too weak to travel. It's impossible. There is no hope for them. Come with us and live."

"Was there hope for you?" Hanuvar demanded.

Olmar stepped back in surprise.

Hanuvar had not meant to sound so vehement. His voice was softer as he turned away. "I will find a way, or I will make one."

The men and women scarcely knew what to say as they neared the beach and Hanuvar waded to shore; they called to him, blessed him, thanked him, watched him stride into the darkness. They did not expect to see him again.

Elsewhere, though, were others who felt sure he would be seen, for word spread quickly, borne first by official Dervani reports and then by rumors that grew in the telling. Hanuvar had risen from the tomb of his ancestors to wreak vengeance upon the empire of Dervan, a legion of undead warriors at his call, and he would not rest until his people were avenged and the emperor himself perished screaming on the altar to his dark gods.

ABOUT THE AUTHOR

HOWARD ANDREW JONES lurks in a tower beside the Sea of Monsters with a wicked and beautiful sorceress. When not spending time with her or their talented children he can be found hunched over his laptop, mumbling about flashing swords and doom-haunted towers. He has role-played regularly since junior high, long years ago, and game mastered so many adventures that he lost his mind and decided to become a writer. His publications include short stories, Pathfinder novels, and the historical fantasies of the Arabian sleuth and swordsman team of Dabir and Asim. You can find his musings on writing and gaming at www.howardandrewjones.com, and occasionally at www.blackgate.com.

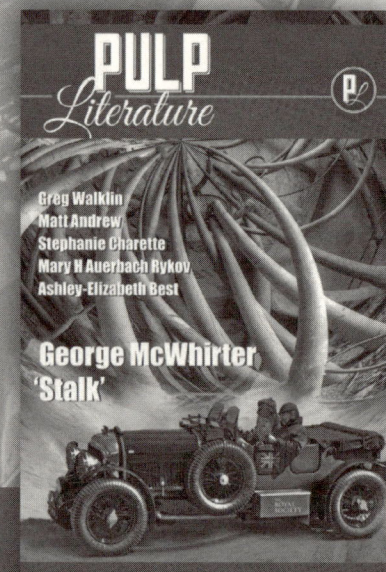

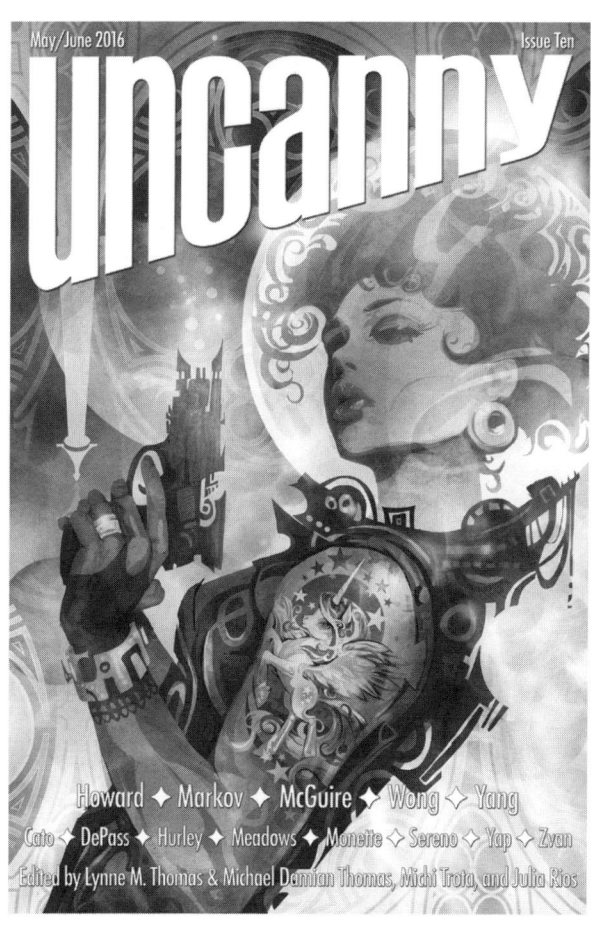
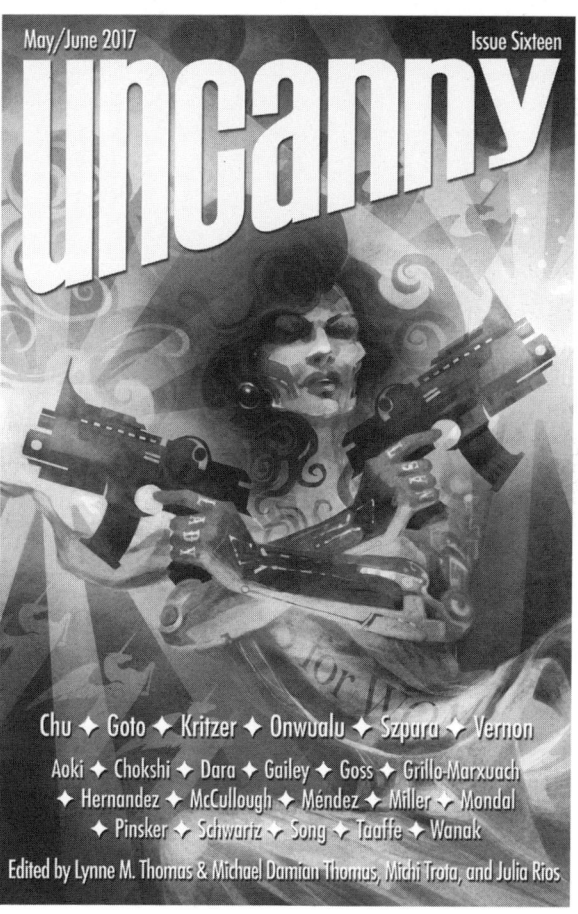

ILLUSTRATION BY STEFAN POAG

THERE WAS AN OLD FAT SPIDER

By C. L. WERNER

BLOODIED and torn, bones poking through ripped flesh, dried gore caked about ragged wounds. The hare had struggled fiercely to free itself from the trap, further damaging it upon the fang-like wooden barbs. The noise of its struggles had brought some predator to it – likely a fox from the size of the bites. When the fox had eaten its fill, the crows had come to peck away at what was left. The sorry remnant had been kicked and pulled until it was a good ten feet from where the trap had been set.

"Shadras take all stupid hares," Karl Rohlfs cursed as he looked down at his spoiled catch. The pelt was utterly ruined and between the fox and the crows there wasn't enough meat left on the hare to satiate a church mouse. What was more, the trap itself was ruined. Several of the wooden spurs were broken off and the curl of leather that held the whole thing together had been gnawed through, either by the fox or some scavenging weasel. It was bad enough to lose the hare but the destruction of the trap was an even bigger distress. If only the blasted animal had gone into the snare straight the catch would have broken its neck and killed it outright.

Karl shook his head and kicked the ruined tangle of flesh and wood. There'd be no meat in his bowl tonight, no coins to secure a corner of Brandower's stable to sleep in. It would mean a cold night shivering under the stars or sneaking into Hotchmueller's inn and hoping the taverneer didn't catch him before dawn.

That last thought brought a deeper scowl to Karl's face. No, however cold it got he wouldn't try sneaking into the inn. The humiliation of being caught and thrown out was too much to bear. Not because of Hotchmueller, but because of *her*. Even if Maria didn't see it she was certain to hear about it and that was something he just couldn't bear.

"You should have left Uerdingen a long time ago," Karl said to himself. It was true, there was nothing for him in the town. It was a place that had seen him brought low, worn down to the very bottom of society. There had been a time when he was a skilled craftsman, a woodworker who had even made pieces for the Baron. Now what was he? A vagabond, a dirty disheveled trapper and woodsman trying to eke out a miserable existence by snaring animals and burning charcoal. How very far he'd fallen.

Karl glanced one last time at the broken trap. He had four others, but all had been empty and now hung across his shoulder. Some of the shepherds grazed their flocks near Grimglen, so he had to be careful about setting his snares where they might damage an unwary lamb. Lacking the ability to make amends for such injury wouldn't stop the shepherds from taking repayment out of his hide. They'd beaten him through the streets of Uerdingen a couple times when one of their flock fell into his traps, usually with Ulrich Niebur goading them on. Not that Ulrich was above getting his hands

dirty, but the trader found greater enjoyment as a spectator than a participant.

The trapper put aside thoughts of Ulrich. There wasn't any good to come from focusing upon his animosity for the man. Ulrich had demonstrated most forcefully that Karl wasn't a match for him – in any arena. The merchant's triumphant laughter was a sound Karl'd heard far too often.

Leaving the dead hare, Karl set out across the green fields looking for a more advantageous spot to place his other traps. He saw a few sheep cropping the grass, heard a lark chirping away in the shelter of some bushes. Away to the left, the dark sprawl of the forest loomed. The woods were the Baron's land and everything in it belonged to the Baron. Stealing either wood or hares from the Baron would be courting a fate several degrees worse than a mere beating, so Karl was always careful to avoid taking such risks. So long as his traps were outside the forest his actions were tolerated by the Baron's beadle.

Karl shook his head. He wasn't the only commoner who exploited their lord's generosity. The reason the pickings were so slim in the fields was because of the townsfolk who hunted them. The real game was all safely beyond their reach in Grimglen. The trapper thought about his empty belly and emptier pockets, about getting thrown from the inn and the contempt in Maria's eyes when she heard about it. While he was thinking, Karl saw a lamb stray away from its flock, go wandering off into the shadow of the trees.

A plan came to the trapper. Looking around to see if anyone could see him, Karl tightened his grip on the traps he carried and set off into the woods. If the Baron's woodwarden found him, he could claim he was looking for the lost lamb. It would give him an excuse for being in the woods. After all, a poacher would come in cover of darkness, not stroll along in broad daylight.

The cool of the forest closed in over Karl as he ventured beneath the boughs. He saw the lamb ahead, its white wool vivid against the shadows. The animal was glancing around it in dismay, bleating quietly as it realized how far it had strayed. Karl stamped his foot against the earth, waving his arms at the animal. The lamb cried out in alarm and scampered off deeper into the woods.

Karl kept one eye on the lamb's retreating form while he nosed about the bases of trees and around bushes searching for animal tracks. It was the strange bleating of the lamb that made him turn away from his task. There was a quality of fright in the sound that sent a shiver through him. Drawing the skinning knife from his belt, Karl warily followed the noises.

The sounds led Karl to a small cluster of oaks. The trees had grown closely together, forming a dark hollow between them. Clearing a tangle of withered bushes from his path, the trapper opened a way into the hollow and the animal that had wandered inside. A tangle of wispy threads brushed across Karl's face, tickling against his beard. Irritated, he wiped the offending cobwebs away. The deeper he pressed into the hollow, the more numerous the webs became. He began holding his arm forwards, swatting away clumps of webbing from his path. There might be a thousand spiders creeping about the hollow to create such a nest. The trunks of the trees, the overhanging branches, everywhere was covered in a gray mantle of webs.

Karl spotted the lamb standing ahead of him, its wool fouled with stringy clumps of web and dead leaves. The animal stared blankly upwards, its dull eyes wide with fright. A terrified bleat rose from its throat. Raising his own gaze, Karl saw what so agitated the lamb. His own breath caught in his throat.

Overhead, nestled amid the thickest skein of webs, was a colossal black shape. A bulbous body easily the size of an ox, great segmented legs as long as a fishing smack, immense fangs that dripped with flecks of venom. The cobweb colony wasn't the work of thousands of spiders but a single giant, a monster of its verminous breed. Clusters of crimson eyes stared down at the trapper, contemplating him with their cold gaze.

Karl scrambled back, moaning in horror as the giant spider began to move. Slowly, ever so slowly, its spindly legs fanned out, groping along the threads of web. Even through his fear he noted the awkward lethargy of the creature, the hesitancy of each probing thrust of its limbs, the dry creak of its chitinous body as it moved. An impression of incredible age, of unfathomable hunger conveyed itself to him with every motion the monster made. Gradually the spider crept out from its cobweb lair.

The trapper retreated from the hollow, his eyes still riveted by the creeping monstrosity. That the spider was intent on seizing the lamb was obvious. Karl looked aside, seizing a broken branch and raising it to strike at the grotesque beast before it could seize its prey. As he watched, he saw the lamb shake itself from its numb terror. Easily it fled from the spider's reach, ripping through the feeble webs that blocked its escape. As the animal ran off, the spider arrested its advance, freezing in place, the segments of its mouth twitching in silent frustration.

So old. So hungry. So alone. Karl looked up at the spider, a strange sympathy suddenly growing inside him. There was something pitiable in the monster's state. Hidden away in the forest, wearing out what time was left to it, unable to catch even the most hapless prey.

Instinctively the lamb scampered towards Karl, seeking human protection from the spider. A moment before, the animal would have been safe. Now, however, a curious feeling of affinity for the gruesome spider moved him to action. Taking hold of the lamb, he removed a leather thong from his belt and lashed it around the lamb's legs. Stoutly secured, Karl set the helpless creature back into the hollow. The lamb bleated in terror as the spider started to move once more, as the long legs reached out towards it.

Karl didn't linger to watch the monster feed. Hastily he withdrew from the forest, fighting down a sense of revulsion at what he'd done. Giving the lamb to the spider, leaving it incapable of escaping the ancient beast. It was a despicable act that he couldn't reconcile in his mind. Whatever pity he'd felt for the old spider wasn't enough to blot out the image of the frightened lamb.

Once out into the fields Karl found himself amid the rest of the flock. The sheep were oblivious to the lamb's absence, unaware of its fate. Later the shepherds would worry over the missing animal. They'd go looking for it, but the trapper doubted they'd find the hollow and the monster that dwelt there. No, it was more likely they'd blame the animal's loss on Karl and his traps. Maybe they'd be so convinced he was responsible that they'd mob him again in town.

Through his dejection and fear, a small ember of hate blazed up. Karl looked back at Grimglen and towards the spider's lair. An idea took shape in the trapper's mind.

A vision of revenge.

• • •

THE atmosphere in Hotchmueller's tavern was somber. No boasting of harvests or sharp deals from the townsfolk, no bawdy ballads or boisterous songs. Those gathered about the tables stared into their flagons of beer and ale with dour expressions, worry etched across their faces. Occasionally one would turn his head to consider the man seated near the hearth. Almost a flicker of hope would manifest itself, but it was too feeble to offset the pall that had descended upon Uerdingen.

The man by the fire was arrayed in more finery than even the most prosperous of the townsfolk. His ruffled shirt was adorned with silver thread and gilded buttons, and a writhing dragon had been embroidered down the side of his leggings. Great jeweled buckles hung from the necks of his calfskin boots. Around his neck he wore a richly engraved pectoral, the royal eagle of King Heinrich IV clasping a sword in its talons.

The man himself was as impressive as his garb. Tall, handsome of face and broad of build, he was utterly unlike the rugged townsfolk. He was a man of refinement but who hadn't allowed his comforts to drag him down into decadence. One look into his piercing blue eyes was enough to inform any observer that here was a man who didn't shun hardship when it was required of him.

At present, Rudolf Goettinger was engaged upon such an enterprise. The comforts of the royal court had been set aside so that he might execute his duties to the King. For months, the little community of Uerdingen had been gripped by terror. Something was preying upon the town. When the depredations had been confined to livestock, there'd been little attention paid to it. Then people started disappearing. Vanished without a trace. Four shepherds and the Baron's woodwarden Bruno had all gone missing. That had provoked the Baron into action and through him an appeal had been made to the King.

Rudolf stared into the fire that crackled in the hearth, his mind turning over everything the townsfolk had told him. It wasn't easy to dig through the muddle of petty jealousies and barbed insinuations he'd been subjected to since his arrival. Adversity always tested people, brought out either their best or their worst. In Uerdingen, he'd found the worst. Gossip, prejudice, old grudges and new suspicions. Neighbor against neighbor, every man, woman, and child desperate to unmask the cause of their town's troubles.

"Can you help us?" The question was spoken in a soft, almost desperate voice. Rudolf looked up at the woman who stood near his chair. She was attractive even by the standards of the court, though the tanned complexion and calloused hands of a commoner would certainly be outre to the perfumed ladies of the palace ball rooms. Her blonde hair was just a bit too close to the color of straw, her figure just a bit too stout to pay proper homage to the latest silken stylings from Elven Ithylyr. All the same, there was a genuineness about Maria Hotchmueller that Rudolf found much more companionable than the vapid pretenses of the nobility.

"That remains to be seen," Rudolf confessed. He waved a finger to the small table beside him, waiting for Maria to set his goblet of wine down. The silver cup was the pride of her father, as was the wine that filled it. Reserved for important visitors and special occasions. Rudolf didn't have the audacity to tell the taverneer that any decent wine should be served in a glass vessel and that the wine he offered was a far distant relation to anything decent.

"You have to help us," Maria said. She looked aside at the solemn patrons clustered about the tables or gathered along the bar. "If someone else goes missing, I don't know what they'll do."

Rudolf noted the tinge of fear in her tone. He'd already heard the gossip about Maria's late mother, that the woman had been a witch. That an inquisitor from Bosenhelm had cleared the Hotchmueller family of any wrong-doing might be a matter of record, but facts were often the first casualty in a crisis. There'd been more than a few townsfolk who confided in Rudolf that perhaps the inquisitor made a mistake and that Maria had taken up her mother's dark art. As he looked around the room, he could see the furtive glances people threw at her when she wasn't looking.

"I am Beastcatcher Royal to His Majesty," Rudolf said. "I've hunted beasts great and small across the kingdom and beyond. Rare and fabulous, natural and unnatural, none have eluded me for long. It was my bow that brought down the Poelzimmer Peryton and my sword that ended the outrages of the Stanhoff Lioness. Believe me when I say to you... your neighbors aren't wrong when they believe there is some human agency at work here." He held up his hand to stifle any protest of innocence. "Even a clever beast is limited in its cunning. It will leave signs, evidence to betray its nature. It lacks the foresight to plan, to obfuscate its presence. I have searched where these men were last seen and found nary a trace of where they went. A beast might have the wit to hide its own tracks, but it wouldn't think to hide those of its prey."

Maria lowered her eyes, ashamed to broach the subject but compelled to do so all the same. "They say... it is witchcraft."

"Some do. Perhaps it is," Rudolf said. He was looking past Maria, watching the men at the bar. He saw the trader Ulrich Niebur trying to be inconspicuous while making frequent glances at Maria. It wasn't suspicion Rudolf saw in the man's gaze but a kind of offended pride – the look of a man who feels his primacy being intruded upon.

"Uerdingen isn't so far from Rheinstein," Rudolf continued, still watching Ulrich. "It was a few years ago when werewolves afflicted the community. All dead now, the whole pack. The inquisitors burned the ones we took alive. I'm minded however that there was an uncle who was unaccounted for. The family claimed he'd been wounded waylaying a traveler and that the rest of the werewolves cannibalized their injured kinsman. But there's a danger in reading too much truth into a confession ripped out through torture. It's possible the missing uncle settled around here. A beast with the brain to plot his crimes like a man."

Keeping watch on Ulrich, Rudolf was surprised when he saw an unkempt, tatterdemalion man approach the trader. Hotchmueller started to circle around the bar to remove the ragged man, but before he could, Ulrich waved Maria's father away. The man who'd joined him at the bar had shown him something, some object cupped in his grubby hand. Whatever it was, it commanded Ulrich's attention, even causing the trader to forget his jealous spying on Maria.

Rudolf nodded at Ulrich's companion. "Who is that?" he asked Maria.

"That?" Maria let a little laugh color her voice. "He's Karl Rohlfs." She went on to explain the trapper's lowly position in Uerdingen society with a mixture of both pity and criticism. The question utmost in Rudolf's mind, however, was the one Maria couldn't answer: what interest did Ulrich have in such a character?

After a brief conversation, Ulrich and Karl left the tavern together. It was clear from their respective attitudes that the merchant was calling the shots. At the same time, it was the trapper who was leading their way. Rudolf rose from his chair and made his apologies to Maria. Quickly he climbed the stairs to his room above. The finery of the court was suitable for impressing the townsfolk and getting them to divulge information to him, but it wasn't so suitable for his current purpose.

That curious arrangement between Karl and Ulrich intrigued Rudolf. Alert for anything unusual, watching for even the smallest incongruity that might put him on the track of Uerdingen's trouble, he intended to find out what the two men were up to. Hastily discarding his fancy raiment, Rudolf put on what he considered his working clothes – a set of black leather garments, a pair of hunter's boots, and a firm breastplate of ensorcelled steel. The deadly length of a broadsword hung from his belt while a dagger of cold-wrought iron slipped into a sheath inside his left sleeve. A knife of blessed silver hung from a scabbard beneath his shoulder, a weapon he'd been careful to keep close since Rheinstein's lycanthropes. Finally, a sylvan cloak woven from the shimmering wings of dusk-moths settled down around his shoulders. The enchantments bound into the cloak served to obscure the wearer from sight, only the shadow he cast serving as proof of his presence.

Kitted out for the hunt, Rudolf slipped out the tavern's side-door and hurried through the town's back alleys. Though his quarry had something of a lead upon him, Rudolf trusted his abilities as a tracker to pick up their trail. If his suspicions were correct and the men had something to do with the disappearances, then they'd be heading towards the fields where so many shepherds and animals had gone missing.

Rudolf's suspicions seemed to be bearing out when he found the distinct pairing of footprints outside town heading off in the direction of Grimglen. The expensive boots of Ulrich with their hob-nailed soles kept company with the ragged outlines of Karl's shabby shoes. It was a trail as clear as any the hunter had ever followed and he thought he should quickly gain on the men.

The first flicker of doubt crept into Rudolf's mind when the footprints steered away from Grimglen and the fields. He wondered if he'd jumped at a shadow, letting his thirst for action engender the strange association of merchant and mendicant with more importance than it warranted. Stubbornly he followed the trail, keeping after it until the tracks reached a small stream.

Here the hunter's flagging suspicions roared into even greater strength. There were no footprints on the other side of the stream. The two men had used the water to hide their tracks – likely at the insistence of the trapper. Rudolf didn't hesitate, but headed upstream, the direction that tended towards Grimglen rather than away from it. As he slogged through the flow he kept glancing at the banks, wary for any evidence of footprints, any hint as to where the men had taken to the shore.

Rudolf kept an easy grip on the hilt of his sword. Whatever Ulrich and Karl were about, it was clearly of secretive nature. It had been his experience that men with a secret didn't react kindly to being followed.

Or were they being followed? Rudolf scowled at the banks of the stream. He'd been moving up the channel for nearly half an hour without any sign of the men. Certainly he'd expected some sign of them by now. He frowned and looked back the way he'd come. There'd been a few rocky spots bordering the stream, places a wary man might have chosen to emerge from the water. The hard stone wouldn't betray any tracks. A merchant like Ulrich wouldn't have the woodcraft to think of such a ploy, but Karl would.

Turning around, Rudolf headed back. He would check the stony places and see if his quarry had left any clues. It might be too late to catch up to them now, even if he did regain their trail, but at least he would have a better idea of where they'd been going. That might count for much if the track tended towards Grimglen.

Rudolf would know then if he were closer to uncovering the monster that preyed on Uerdingen's people.

• • •

"HOW much farther is it? It seems I've marched halfway to King Heinrich's castle!" Ulrich tugged at the neck of his tunic, letting some air in to cool his sweating chest.

Karl nodded in servile sympathy to the merchant's complaint. "Not much farther now," he assured Ulrich.

"My boots are soaked," grumbled Ulrich.

"We had to be careful," Karl said. "Somebody might have followed us from town. We couldn't take that chance."

"I'm the one taking chances," Ulrich snorted. "I'll catch a cold with these wet feet." He reached into the pocket of his vest and drew out the object Karl had given him in the tavern. A silver mark, tarnished with age, the portrait stamped upon its surface worn down by time, but much thicker and heavier than the current coinage being issued. Melted down, the coin would be worth almost double its contemporaries – allowing a man was unscrupulous enough to defy royal decree and smelt a royal image into nothingness.

"You say there's an entire chest of these?" Ulrich asked Karl for the hundredth time.

"Why do you think I asked you to help me?" Karl's voice was just shy of being a whine. "There's too much for me to handle alone. I need your help to get it out and keep it safe."

A sly smile pulled at Ulrich's face. "The risk is considerable," he mused. "There's my reputation and standing to consider. I'm an important member of the community. It isn't so easy for me as it is for you."

Karl swung around. It was as well that the shadows cast by the trees hid his face from the merchant. For an instant he might have seen the expression of undisguised hate there. Angry words were choked off before they could be spoken, crumbling into a dry groan that Ulrich mistook for an expression of anxiety.

"No fear, my friend," Ulrich said. "I'll handle things. It won't be easy, but we'll do all right. Leave it to me. The excise-men won't find out about our windfall." The merchant grinned as Karl turned and led him deeper into the woods. The simpleton had swallowed every word about the hazards and risks Ulrich was exposing himself to. He'd agreed to letting Ulrich claim three shares of the treasure to Karl's one, and that was on the face value of the coins rather than what they'd really be worth when melted down.

"That's why we have to be careful," Karl enjoined Ulrich. "I think... I think that knight was sent here because of the treasure. I think he's looking for it. All this talk about helping the town is simply a distraction from his real purpose."

"You may have something there," Ulrich agreed. "It struck me as strange that the nobles would be so concerned about some missing sheep and peasants." He arched an eyebrow as he took the thought further. "The Baron might have been upset with Bruno disappearing. A good woodwarden is hard to replace."

Karl was quick to redirect the supposition. "Bruno could have heard about the knight being sent here and decided to leave before he could be discovered. I'm certain Bruno knew about the treasure."

"And that's what happened to the shepherds," Ulrich said. "They found out about Bruno and he got rid of them. Stole some of the sheep to make it look like a wolf's work." The merchant cast a puzzled look at Karl. "Which begs the question of why he didn't get rid of you." Ulrich chuckled at his own words. "Scared you off, didn't he? Why waste a bit of knife-work on somebody you can just frighten. You waited until you were certain Bruno was gone before trying to steal the treasure. And even then you needed help to get up the nerve."

Outrage boiled inside Karl as he listened to the trader's mockery. The jibes cut all the deeper because of how accurate they were. Karl had been a frightened, beaten little man. But all of that had changed. Ulrich would find out how much it had changed. Quite soon now, because Karl saw the hollow up ahead.

"Don't worry about the king's man," Ulrich said. "He'll lose interest soon enough. Nobles don't have much patience and I'm certain the novelty of slumming about in Uerdingen will soon wear thin." The merchant's voice dropped into a low snarl. "Then I'll have some words with that tart Maria about how she's been conducting herself. Sporting about with that poseur!"

"You'll leave her alone," Karl snapped, swinging around and glaring at Ulrich. "You don't care a damn about her! You never have! She's just a trophy to you, something for you to own. Something for you to show off and prove how much better you are than everyone!"

Ulrich flinched, drawing the dagger from his belt. Then a caustic laugh fell from his lips. The livid expression on Karl's face made him seem more absurd rather than less. "You're an idiot, Karl. You gave up everything for her and she couldn't care less. You sold everything you own to bribe the inquisitor and get him to absolve her mother of witchcraft."

"She doesn't know," Karl growled back. "I never told her. How could I tell her?"

"Maybe I told her," Ulrich sneered. "If I know what you did, why wouldn't she?" The merchant caught the glance Karl threw towards the nearby hollow. A greedy gasp rose from Ulrich's throat. "It's in there, isn't it?"

"Everything you've got coming to you," Karl told him.

This time there was such venom in the trapper's tone that it broke through even Ulrich's contempt for the man. Wariness shone in the merchant's eyes. Taking a step back he drew the dagger from his belt and pointed the blade towards Karl. "So that's it then, is it? I didn't think you had the stomach for it. Drop your knife on the ground." While he waited for the trapper to comply, Ulrich fingered the old silver coin. "Decided to keep everything for yourself, did you?"

"How would you have gotten rid of the knight?" Karl retorted. "Turn me over to him?"

"Not a bad idea," Ulrich said. He looked at the dark mouth of the hollow. An uneasy feeling tingled down his spine. "You go in first. Just remember I'll be right behind you with my dagger."

Looking defeated, Karl lead his captor into the hollow. As the two men stepped into the isolated space, Ulrich brushed away thick strands of web from his face. His attention was drawn to a strange clump that dangled from the branches overhead. As the clump swayed in what little breeze made its way into the hollow he found himself staring into the shriveled face of Bruno. The woodwarden's body was a withered mess of skin and bones bound within a cobweb basket.

Before Ulrich could fully digest the grisly husk, motion in the web-ridden branches above made him look upwards. His eyes went wide with horror as he watched an immense spider slowly emerge from a cave-like nest of cobwebs. Even as the merchant drew back in fear, a sharp cracking pain smashed against the back of his head. He collapsed to the ground, stunned by the blow Karl had struck him with a heavy stick.

The trapper leaned over Ulrich and tied his hands with a stout cord. "Not what you expected, is it?" It was Karl's turn to mock and the trader's turn to shudder. "I have a friend now. One who helps me deal with my enemies. All of them. While they're shocked by the sight of my friend I just give them a good crack to the skull with an old branch. Just to stun them. Spiders don't like dead food." Ulrich tried to beg Karl for mercy, but before he could say anything the trapper shoved a thick wad of cobweb into his mouth. "Can't have you screaming. The knight might be near enough to hear and come over to find out what's going on. And we don't want to disturb its supper." He pointed his finger up at the spider. The monster was continuing to emerge from its lair, forelegs twitching as they probed the air. Steadily it began to descend, eight sets of eyes glistening as they stared down at the doomed man.

Karl finished tying Ulrich's legs, then secured the bindings to a pair of pegs set into the ground. "Can't have you rolling away," the trapper stated. "Bruno did that when I left him here. Fortunately I found him before he could crawl very far and was able to bring him back. You should feel honored, Ulrich. I waited a long time before deciding to come for you. I had to make sure everything was perfect. I had to know my friend's habits. When it would be hungry. How long it would take it to kill its food."

The giant spider was creeping downward. Beads of green venom dripped from its fangs as it anticipated the prey waiting for it. The segmented plates of its mouth twitched eagerly. Ulrich flailed about in his bonds, struggling to twist away, but the peg limited his feeble rolls to a few feet in either direction. A muffled wail of terror rose from beneath the cobweb gag.

"Shall I tell you what it does?" Karl asked. He glanced up at the spider, judging the monster's distance before leaning down to jeer at his enemy. "It'll jab you with its fangs, fill you full of its venom. Everything inside you will be reduced to sludge. Flesh, sinew, muscle and organ. All of it turned to soup which it will then suck out of you until only skin and bones are left. You'll drain out, like pus from a wound. But don't think it'll be quick. Oh no, you'll be alive for quite some time while it's happening. When Bruno died, he was still moving when my friend started to drink his insides."

Karl frowned, a stray thought occurring to him. Looking again at the old spider as it crept downwards, the trapper reached into Ulrich's tunic and withdrew the silver coin. "You might like to know this is all there is," Karl told him. "There's no treasure except this. The first coin I earned as a woodworker. I've kept it despite everything and it has rewarded me well. It brought you here. It would be a shame to lose it now."

Ulrich's muffled shrieks grew more desperate as Karl backed away. The creak of the spider's segmented legs intensified as the beast drew still closer. Ulrich could see the thing looming above him, ready to jump down.

"Goodbye, Ulrich," Karl laughed from the mouth of the hollow. "Do be decent enough not to give my friend indigestion." A fierce light shone in the trapper's eyes as the mammoth spider fell upon its victim and the venomous fangs sank home.

"With you gone, Maria will notice me again," Karl said. "She'll appreciate my love for her. She'll see me as a man, not the fool you and the others tried to make me. Then everything will change. That is why you die, Ulrich. So that I can live."

• • •

VEILED by his sylvan cloak, Rudolf Goettinger followed Karl Rohlfs when the trapper left Uerdingen with Maria. A week had passed since Ulrich Niebur disappeared. The idea that Karl had anything to do with the merchant's absence was absurd to the townsfolk. None of them had noticed Ulrich leaving with him. The idea that a weakling like Karl could overcome a man like Ulrich was too ridiculous to entertain.

The attitude of the townsfolk made Rudolf keep his suspicions to himself. He didn't tell anyone about the tracks he found. He didn't bother expressing his theories. To do so would only put Karl on his guard. By keeping silent, the hunter hoped to lull his quarry into an illusion of security. Instead of denouncing him, Rudolf kept a careful watch on the trapper. He'd witnessed the distress Ulrich's disappearance had caused Maria. Whatever the merchant's own intentions towards her, it was clear the woman was devoted to him.

It was also clear that Karl was smitten with Maria. The trapper had been quite attentive to her, in as much as her father didn't chase him away from the tavern. Her indifference only intensified his efforts, finally escalating into a tense moment when the woman had herself exiled him from the tavern.

Why Maria was now in Karl's company, alone and headed away from Uerdingen, was explained to Rudolf by the conversation he overheard. The trapper claimed to know where Ulrich was, indeed, that the merchant had sent him to take Maria to him. Blinded by love for the trader, Maria had accepted Karl's claims without question. A decision that Rudolf was certain she'd regret. He didn't know how, but he knew the trapper was far more dangerous than he looked.

"He gave me a token to give you," Karl was saying as he led Maria to the stream. He reached into his shabby wool coat and withdrew an old silver coin. "This is why he had to leave. He found some treasure hidden away on the Baron's land." The trapper handed the coin to her, closing her fingers around it with a tender, almost despairing flourish. "That's why we have to be careful. We'll walk in the stream to hide our trail. In case anyone is following us."

"Why should anyone follow us?" Maria wondered.

Karl shrugged his shoulders. "They might know about the treasure." He smiled at the flicker of doubt he saw in Maria's eyes. "That's what Ulrich is afraid of," he added, mention of the merchant erasing that look of doubt. "He thinks that knight is here looking for the treasure."

"Rudolf is here hunting monsters," Maria told him. "He's looking for whatever has been taking our people." She shuddered and looked anxiously at the trees that lined the stream. "Perytons and werewolves..."

Karl managed a short laugh. "I've been in these woods for years and never saw anything more dangerous than a spider. Ulrich is probably right, that knight is looking for gold, not boogies." Again, the name of her beloved served to blot out any concerns that nagged at Maria's mind. With a little encouragement, Karl had her pressing onward, moving upstream until they reached a patch of rocky shore.

Rudolf followed after them, careful to avoid any betraying sound as he pursued his quarry. The concealment afforded by his magic cloak would count for nothing if some noise alerted the trapper.

As he knew it would, Rudolf found that the trail was veering back towards Grimglen and the scene where so many had gone missing. Maria realized this as well. Alarmed, she made protest to her guide. This time assurances about Ulrich waiting for her weren't enough to allay her growing fear. Karl tried a different tack.

"I'd never allow anything to happen to you," Karl assured her. The trapper reached out to her, trying to draw her close but Maria slipped from his grasp, stepping away and staring at him in confusion. "I've always tried to help you. I've always tried to keep you from getting hurt." A pleading note came into his voice. "When the inquisitor came for your mother, it was me who bribed him to leave her alone. I knew you'd suffer if she was exposed as a witch. But you didn't know that, did you? You didn't know I sold everything to make the inquisitor leave?"

Maria continued to back away. "I knew," she said in a soft tone. "I knew you helped. I'm grateful for that, but you have to understand that gratitude isn't love. Because you helped me doesn't mean you own me. As much as I am indebted to you for what you did, I can't be expected to feel something that isn't there."

The trapper sobbed, a low moan of anguish. "Ulrich said you knew. I didn't believe him. I didn't want to believe him. But it was the truth." Karl's face twisted into an enraged scowl. "You stupid girl. He didn't care about you. He never did. You were just something pretty to make those around him feel jealous. He wasn't worthy of you, but you were too stupid to care." A cold gleam shone in his eyes. "But I'll take you to him. I'll show you your dear Ulrich now."

Karl lunged for Maria, but before he could reach her he was himself caught in a powerful grip. Seemingly stepping out of thin air when he threw off his sylvan cloak, Rudolf seized the trapper. He pulled the skinning knife from Karl's belt and tossed it to the ground. The hilt of his sword smashed against the man's face, breaking his nose and dropping him to his knees.

"How about showing me where Ulrich is instead," Rudolf snarled. He lifted Karl by the scruff of his neck, shaking the little man. The hunter made a warning gesture to Maria when she came near. "Leave this to me," he told her.

"I want to know where Ulrich is," Maria declared, speaking at first to Rudolf and then directing her words at Karl. "What have you done with him?"

"Whatever he's done, you can do no good here," Rudolf said. "Ulrich, and the others as well, have been gone too long. There's murder at the end of this trail." He shook Karl again, glowering at the bloodied trapper. "Isn't that right, scum? You killed them all."

Karl nodded his head, weakly. He made a feeble wave of his hand towards the hollow. "They're over there," he said. Then a cunning smile flickered across his face. "It only needed a bit of knife work. None of them expected me to fight back." He gave a last, despairing look at Maria. "You know how they treated me."

"You murdered them," Maria spat, revulsion in her tone.

"Leave this to me," Rudolf repeated. "Go back to Uerdingen." He frowned when Maria shook her head. He could see she was adamant about remaining to the end. "Stay, then, but keep your distance until I've seen what happened to them." He turned back to Karl and shook the trapper violently. The cunning smile hadn't gone unnoticed. "Lead the way, scum. Just remember my sword will be at your back."

Rudolf wasn't fooled by the pretense of reluctance that Karl exhibited as he headed towards the hollow. The hunter suspected some kind of trap, a pitfall or some sort of mechanism that Karl had employed to overcome his victims. A knife in the back seemed too bold for the cringing man, but a concealed pit would be craven enough for him to try. As he followed his prisoner, he kept careful vigil, noting precisely where Karl stepped and how firmly he let his weight press upon the ground. He watched the man's hands, to catch his fingers brushing against a tree trunk or reaching for a branch. A few times he risked a glance over his shoulder to ensure that Maria was keeping far enough back that he could alert her of Karl's trickery.

The inside of the hollow was a murky, dusty place festooned with broad swathes of cobweb. Rudolf had an impression of grisly shapes wrapped in dirty gray webbing that dangled from the branches overhead. Then his attention was captured by the far more grisly sight that lay upon the floor of the hollow. A shocked gasp escaped him as he beheld a monstrosity beyond all expectation.

Lying crouched above the withered husk of Ulrich's body was the chitinous shell of a mammoth spider. Its long legs were splayed outwards, black as midnight and thick as steel. Its bulbous abdomen was arched backwards, resting partly upon the heavy webs behind it, a sinister crimson splotch standing distinct upon its black carapace. The comparatively small head was thrust forwards, sharp fangs protruding from thick mandibles. Four sets of eyes bulged from the top of its head, staring up at Rudolf with a dull, unblinking gaze.

For an instant Rudolf was overcome by shock and an instinctive horror of the spider's unnatural dimensions. That instant would have been enough for Karl to strike him. The trapper had grabbed up the stout cudgel he'd used before to such effect. But now he too was locked in a terrified paralysis. He'd come here expecting to find the spider; it was his great advantage over Rudolf. Instead he found a hideous surprise of his own.

The spider was dead. There was no shimmer of awful vitality in its eyes, no twitching motion in its limbs. The old monster was dead... and its killers were done with it.

Nearer to the spider than Rudolf, Karl could see the ugly split that ran down the center of its body. He could see the creeping movement that fluttered about the edge of that crack. He screamed in horror as the first fist-sized spiderling came crawling out of its mother's carcass. Unlike the old spider, the offspring was shiny and new, scurrying with abominable speed. It scuttled across its mother's head and with a tremendous spring launched itself at the horrified trapper.

Throwing his arms up to shield himself from the leaping monster, Karl screamed as the spiderling's fangs sank into his wrist. Flesh darkened as the creature pumped venom into his arm. The trapper clutched at the thing, trying to rip it away, but the arachnid's legs had tightened around his forearm with a vicious tenacity.

Any impulse Rudolf might have had to aid Karl evaporated when his gaze was drawn back to the shell of the mother spider. The eaten-out husk was vibrating wildly, a spasm of maddened excitement. Boiling up from the split in its body came a tide of crawling monstrosities. Scores of fist-sized spiderlings, their eyes gleaming with a ghastly vitality. The things surged towards Karl, leaping at him in hungry pounces. An instant and the trapper was borne to the ground, buried under a creeping mass of stabbing fangs and writhing legs.

Some of the spiderlings sprang at Rudolf. The hunter's sword clove one of the beasts apart in mid-air. A second became tangled in the folds of his sylvan cloak, helpless when he brought his boot stamping down on it. A third thudded against his arm, its fangs digging at his leather armor. Before it could free itself, Rudolf flattened it with the hilt of his sword.

More of the vermin came pouring out of the old spider's shell. With their kin devouring Karl's shrieking flesh, the other spiderlings came stalking after Rudolf. The hunter retreated before them, withdrawing from the hollow, slashing away at the monsters that sprang for him.

Suddenly an eerie green light filled Rudolf's vision. He saw the file of spiderlings explode under a sheet of emerald fire, their chitinous bodies bursting as the fluids within them boiled. The hunter

swung around to see Maria walking towards him, flickers of flame dancing about the tips of her fingers.

Without hesitation, Rudolf pointed into the hollow. "More of them in there," he exclaimed. "A whole swarm!"

Maria didn't say anything, just stretched her hand forwards. From her fingers, streams of witchfyre leapt at the clustered oaks and the dark recess between them. The massive trees and the cobwebs dangling from them swiftly took light. In a matter of heartbeats, a roaring conflagration was consuming the gruesome scene. Handfuls of spiderlings came skittering out of the flames, but Rudolf was ready for them. His broadsword was soon plastered in a pulped mash of the creatures.

A few minutes, and the oaks were charred and blackened. Foul-smelling smoke billowed up from the hollow. Except for the two people who stared at the old spider's lair there wasn't any sign of life. Maria turned towards Rudolf, her expression grave.

"Karl was in there?" she asked.

"Ulrich too," Rudolf told her, not without sympathy. "Karl did it. He lured Ulrich and the others here to feed them to the mother of those things." He kicked the husk of a spiderling, rolling it into the smoke.

Maria looked at the old coin Karl had given her. She could guess how Karl had lured them here. Furious, she threw the coin into the hollow. There was a challenging note in her voice when she turned towards Rudolf. "What will you do now?"

Rudolf shook his head. "I'm no inquisitor, but it is clear they weren't wrong about your mother. Or you. It isn't very safe to practice magic. Not without protection."

The witch studied Rudolf for a moment. "Protection?"

"Come back with me to the court," Rudolf told her. "Someone with your abilities is always useful." He smiled at Maria. "I think anyone who tries to meddle with you would come out the worst for it. Unless they knew the precautious to take. The inquisitors wouldn't be as feared as they are if every witch they found reduced several of them to ashes before they took her. Alone, even a clever witch would be brought down. But if she wasn't alone, things would be different. The inquisitors won't dare threaten someone in royal service. King Heinrich is pragmatic when it comes to matters of magic. Whoever serves him, they are protected by the crown."

"And what of you?" she asked. "Why would you shield me?"

The hunter waved at the smoke and boiled spiderlings. He suppressed a shudder. "It's easy to look the other way when a bit of witchcraft keeps you out of a spider's belly."

ABOUT THE AUTHOR

Exiled to the blazing wastes of Arizona for communing with ghastly Lovecraftian abominations, C L WERNER strives to infect others with the grotesque images that infest his mind. He is the author of almost thirty novels and novellas in settings ranging from Warhammer, Age of Sigmar, and Warhammer 40,000 to the Iron Kingdoms and Wild West Exodus. His short fiction has appeared in several anthologies, among them *Rage of the Behemoth, Sharkpunk, Kaiju Rising, A Grimoire of Eldritch Investigations, Edge of Sundown , Shakespeare vs Cthulhu, City of the Gods*, and *Marching Time*.

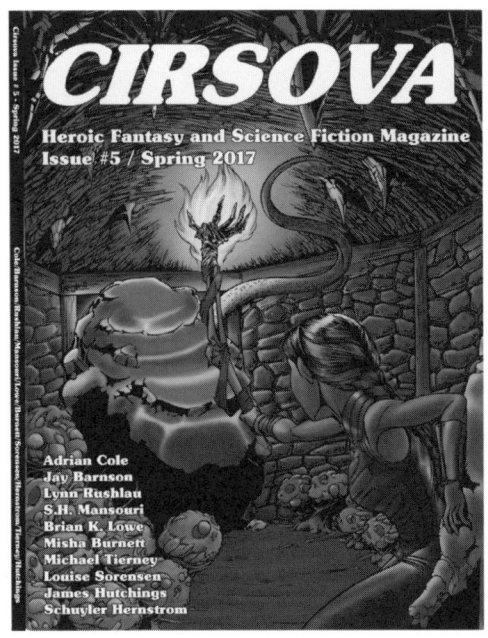

ILLUSTRATION BY JENNELL JAQUAYS

THE CRYSTAL SICKLE'S HARVEST

From the World of the Archivist

By JOHN C. HOCKING

THEY made their way through the long shadows among the trees, following a fence of metal shafts sharpened to wicked points. Benhus looked up and narrowed gray eyes at tree tops struck ruddy gold by the setting sun. He was young, less than twenty summers, and wore a cuirass of dark leather without a helm. His master, mentor, and employer of the past year drew up at a gap in the fence. Here, almost obscured by entangling brush, the metal shafts were twisted into an opening through which the two men bent and passed, entering the graveyard reserved for the city of Frekore's nobility.

"Sun's on its way down. Ever been in a graveyard at night before?" asked Thratos, the older man. He was tall and thin, almost gangling, with a narrow face framed by long, lank black hair beginning to show streaks of gray.

Benhus felt the urge to lie, to tell his master that he had been in many graveyards at night, but he had learned that Thratos enjoyed few things more than puncturing his most minor display of bravado, and didn't feel lying worth the risk.

"No," he said.

"Ah." Thratos cast a dark-eyed glance of amusement back at him. "An opportunity to extend your education."

Striding quickly after his teacher, long grass swishing about his shins, Benhus set his jaw and did not respond. When he had been assigned as apprentice to Thratos, the man sometimes called the King's Hand, Benhus was taken before King Flavius himself. His august majesty had praised him, sincerely but perfunctorily, for the skills he had shown in the Legion, and told him to look upon his new assignment as "an opportunity to extend your education." Benhus reflected that it was a rare day indeed that his mentor did not use that phrase in a manner that fell somewhere between wry and disdainful.

Headstones, grey and worn as old molars, scattered the overgrown meadow. A dark mausoleum, modest compared to those said to be found in the inner reaches of the cemetery, could be seen in a grove off to the south. Its shadowed outline, like a small dwelling forsaken among the trees, was oddly ominous to Benhus's eyes.

"So," continued Thratos at last, "I can assume that you've never hunted graverobbers before either?"

"Have you?" countered Benhus before he could stop himself.

"No," replied his mentor, his voice now lacking the edge it so often held when speaking to his apprentice. "No, I've never had to. And I wouldn't now if the King didn't have most of the army out chasing after Thracius Gavond and his renegade legion. A pox on him."

Benhus wanted to ask if Thratos was calling a pox down upon the rogue general Thracius Gavond or upon King Flavius, but kept the question to himself.

Instead, he asked, "Has the robbing of noble graves become so common that the King must send people like ourselves after the graverobbers?"

Thratos nodded curtly, stepping over an old grave capped by a pitted lid of grey stone. "Yes, I hear that it's happening often enough that some of the nobles sent an emissary to the King demanding his aid. I guess too many of them are spending their precious gold hiring guards to watch over the moldering bones of their grandparents and have grown weary of the expense."

"Times are even harder than I thought," mused Benhus, "that so many would turn to digging up the dead for a few baubles."

"You'd think their superstitions would scare off the peasants," said Thratos, "but I guess an easy profit is too tempting."

Benhus wanted to point out that neither he nor Thratos were anything close to nobility and might, but for their employment as tools, assassins, thieves and general catspaws of the King, be thought of as peasants themselves. He remained silent.

"Here," said his master suddenly. "What have we here?"

Ahead, a tall wall of fieldstone was a dark streak of shadow looming behind an irregular row of trees, and the meadow between the men and the wall was strewn with bodies. There was a partially opened grave, dark earth heaped beside a tilted headstone. Two men sprawled beside it, cut down, Benhus saw, by blades wielded accurately and with merciless intent on a quick kill.

There were more. About twenty steps from the violated grave a cluster of three bodies lay gathered back to back, as if to fight whoever fell upon them. Two still clutched weapons that had done them no good. All were dressed in motley armor, mostly leather, and appeared youthful and helpless in death, like children pretending to be soldiers caught by foes who weren't playing.

Thratos spotted a final body some distance from the rest. This one had apparently opted to strike off on his own and flee toward the wall. He lay on his belly with a ragged red wound in his back. The wound looked strange to Benhus. His master saw him squinting at it and spoke. "Killed by a bow. Probably a crossbow quarrel that the bowman reclaimed."

"But who slew him?" asked Benhus, only half aware he spoke aloud. "Who slew all these armed men then left their bodies lying where they fell?"

"Not the City Guard. They'd have cleaned up," said Thratos softly. The King's Hand rubbed his narrow jaw. "Who?"

"I think," Benhus began, "I think it might have been other, better graverobbers."

Thratos smiled thinly and raised an eyebrow. "And whence comes this sterling insight? How can you…"

"Look." Benhus pointed, sure he was right, yet still afraid he was wrong. "Isn't that wall broken?"

Across the meadow, beyond the trees, evening's failing light turned the wall into a dim barrier, vague with shadow except where Benhus was pointing. There was a brighter patch where there should have been none. Wordlessly, Thratos began to jog toward it, and Benhus followed.

The wall had a doorway torn though it. Fieldstone and mortar were strewn in a ragged fan-shape on the carefully tended lawn within. The wall, twice the height of a man and built to last, might have been breached by a powerful, yet precise, battering ram mounted on a siege engine, but there was no sign that such a device had ever been brought here.

Thratos touched the wall where it had been sundered, and his fingers came away coated with mortar dust. He cursed.

"This is new. Probably as recent as the bodies."

"How…" started Benhus, though he knew the answer.

"Sorcery, of course," answered his master. "This affair has changed its nature, my boy. Our graverobbers were discovered and killed by another group, a group with a sorcerer of at least modest power. And they used his skills to break into the Royal Cemeteries. This area is for those of the royal family, and none but they and their servitors are allowed inside."

"We go on." Hooded eyes gleaming, Benhus was not asking a question, though that was how his master took his words.

"Of course we go on. We'll find these trespassers, learn what we can of their motives and stop them." Thratos grinned humorlessly. "We'll move with care, in case we are overmatched, but I suspect we'll have the better of them."

Benhus followed his teacher through the opening in the wall and into the Royal Cemeteries as the sun clung to the dull scarlet horizon, night began to spread darkness among the trees, and the first stars kindled coldly above.

Thratos knelt in a dim grove, at the base of a grave marker tall enough to thrust out of the surrounding tree tops like a marble spear. Benhus crouched with him, and reached out to touch the moist grass, crushed down where his teacher pointed. He often mused that his master had little left to teach him, but knew his own knowledge of tracking to be weak and was careful to heed anything Thratos might say on the subject.

"This way," murmured his master, softly enough that he might not have been speaking to Benhus at all. "At least five or six of them."

They emerged from the grove onto a wide, well-tended lawn with few trees, and crossed a cobblestone path, flanked by a great stone vessel overflowing with white flowers, pale in the growing gloom. Ahead, the earth rose abruptly in a squared-off, unnatural hill. Benhus thought there were markings in the grass that showed those they followed to have turned left along the flank of the hill at its base, and was pleased when Thratos turned in that direction.

The low hill jutted from the flat sward of the cemetery steeply enough that one would have to bend and scrabble to climb it, but was only a little higher than a very tall man might reach. Its height was as even, and its rim was as regular, as a wall. It was covered with long grass, but clearly manmade. Ahead, Benhus saw the hill appeared to end at a sharp corner, beyond which he could make out dark flagstones.

Thratos approached the corner, lowering himself beside a carefully trimmed shrub. As he lifted a hand to indicate they should stop, Benhus heard voices, vague and indistinguishable. He tensed, swallowed, and touched the hilt of his sword.

The King's Hand stepped silently onto the flagstones and Benhus moved out and around him, flanking his master on the left. The flagstones, though dull from exposure to the elements, were black marble and of a quality that wouldn't have shamed a noble's bedchamber.

Coming around the corner revealed that this side of the hill was a wall of glossy black marble that matched the flags beneath their feet, except it was ornately etched in sinister patterns. At the wall's center, perhaps 15 paces from where they stood, was a frame of blocks that held a heavy inset door of black metal. The door looked to be thicker than a strong man's thigh. It had been pulled open just wide enough to allow a man entrance, and the darkness within was absolute.

Benhus saw that the hill was a mausoleum buried in the earth on all sides except this one, where its doorway faced a broad paved oval like a courtyard. He stared at the tomb's open door in mesmerized fascination, involuntarily anticipating some movement, any movement, there. It was a blackness greater than the night, and as old. He jolted with alarm when Thratos touched his shoulder.

"Wake up, fool," whispered his teacher. "Foes are near."

Benhus bit back a reply, and felt his face warm with shame.

Near the rim of the paved area, directly opposite the door set in the mausoleum's stark face, and right where the flagstones ended and the grass began, stood a six-sided cenotaph of the familiar black marble. At the top of that great dark dagger of stone a statue perched, and at its base a figure lay prone in shadow.

They moved swiftly and silently to where the man lay. He was clad in blue robes, and young, with a recently shaven scalp. He moaned softly and rolled his head from side to side as if with fever. His limbs twitched restlessly, and when he spoke it was in a desperate burst of words, like a sleeping man in the grip of nightmare.

"Don't do it. Don't go in. She can't do it by herself. Wait for me. Wait. Wait for me…"

Benhus bent to look at the man and saw his eyes were open, but the pupils were rolled back, showing only whites. Thratos seized his shoulder again.

"There, did you hear him? He came back. Never went far." The voice was near, but the pillar stood between the speaker and Benhus.

"Give thanks then," said a second voice. "As Strabo would have had me put a bolt though you if we'd lost him."

Boldly, without any apparent concern, Thratos stepped around the pillar, walked off the flagstones and onto the grass. Benhus, a thrill of mingled fear and excitement flaring in his breast, did not hesitate to follow.

Two armed men were not eight paces away, walking toward them and the mausoleum. All four stopped and stood facing one another. Benhus's gaze shot behind the two, saw that the earth lowered gently into a quiet hollow, beyond which dark trees rose. There were no others, only the two.

The one on the left, squat and wearing dingy, second-hand Legion armor, laid a hand lightly on his hilt but did not draw his short sword. The one on the right, taller and with unfashionably shaggy hair, held a small crossbow that he immediately hefted and pointed in the direction of Benhus and his master.

Benhus remained still but betrayed no sign of tension. He heard his blood hum in his ears, but fear seemed to drop away, not to vanish but rather to pull back so that it was a distant, less than pressing, concern. Thratos took another step forward, then put hands on his hips and gazed at the two men critically.

"What have we here?" asked the man with the bow. "What do you fellows think you're doing?"

"King's business," said Thratos curtly. "I'll ask questions and you shall answer them."

No one said anything for a long moment. The stout one did not remove his hand from his hilt. He glanced at Benhus, who watched the man's knees bend slightly as he set his feet. Above the little group, leaves rustled in a slow susurration, as an evening breeze moved through the trees like a long breath in the rigid silence.

"Point your sticker at this one," said the stout man, looking at Benhus. "I don't like his eyes. We'll ask the questions, dogs, and it may be better to have just one dog to answer them."

The bowman dutifully leveled his weapon at Benhus, then spoke up.

"Think I recognize the older one. Royal business indeed. That's the one they call The King's Finger."

Thratos's brow darkened, but Benhus was unable to restrain a snort of laughter. "What's so funny, you pawn of inbred royalty?" demanded the bowman.

"Hand," said Thratos, "the King's Hand."

"What amuses me is that you have a crossbow," answered Benhus easily. "I'm certain you're aware they are forbidden in Frekore. And I imagine that you've been slinking around the city with your little bow concealed in that foolish looking bag you've got on your belt."

The bowman's gaze dropped to his waist and the linen bag tucked into his sword belt.

In a single motion, fluid with speed that challenged the eye, Benhus drew his blade, lunged and slashed the bowman's throat. He immediately stepped back and to the side, crouching and wary should the man loose a quarrel. But the crossbowman did not trigger his bow. He dropped it, choked, and put both hands to his throat in a futile effort to stem the dark torrent there.

Benhus bent quickly forward and snatched the cloth bag from his foe's belt. He wiped his blade with it as the bowman hit the grass first with his knees, then with his face. The stroke had been swift and his steel was sharp. Benhus was pleased to see very little blood come away on the cloth. He dropped the bag and the breeze blew it over the bowman's corpse.

The stout graverobber's hand finally left his hilt as he spun and broke into a determined run.

Thratos dug a thumb behind his wide belt and produced what looked to be a small stick, a stubby length of weathered wood not much longer than a finger. He extended his arm, pointing the little wand, which sat in his fist as if whittled to fit there.

There was a sound like a powerful gust of wind funneled through the narrow opening of a door or window. At the rim of the hollow and just about to run in among the trees, the stout graverobber gave a strange wheezing cry, threw his arms up over his head and flung himself full length on the earth. He did not move again.

Benhus sheathed his weapon and looked at his teacher. Thratos grinned.

"Go on. Take a look. It's a new one."

Benhus started to walk to where the man had been struck down, began to pace faster, then abandoned pretense and loped to where the man lay. He knelt beside him, scanning the corpse, for the man was very obviously dead.

A circle about a handspan across marked the man's back, just left of his spine. The leather armor looked sunken and oddly withered there. Benhus squinted, unable to make out details in the gloom, when a beam of pure white light, brilliant as morning sun, spilled over his shoulder and fell upon the body, illuminating it completely. He snatched a brief glance over his shoulder and saw, as he expected, Thratos stood there holding aloft another of the little wands. This one cast a cone of bright white light.

Benhus touched tentatively at the sunken spot on the man's back. His fingers indented the strange wound with a dry crackle and he snatched his hand back as if scorched. The area he touched crumbled inward, fell into the man's body as if Benhus had thrust his fingers through a layer of long dead leaves, leaving a black little hole. He jerked to his feet swiftly enough to stagger. The light moved with him and he heard the low laughter of his teacher.

"This one parches utterly all in its path. First time I've used it."

Grimacing, turning his face from the light, Benhus snatched at his master's wrist, pointing the light at a leafy bush next to where the graverobber had fallen. The center of the bush bore a withered spot that ran right through the plant. Leaves were shrunken, dried to brittle husks.

"Its path goes beyond its target," rasped Benhus, choking back rage at both at his own discomfort and his master's clear enjoyment of it. "Use care when pointing the damn thing."

Thratos said nothing, but twisted his wrist from his student's grip and turned back toward the mausoleum.

Benhus followed sullenly. His master was supplied with weapons created by the King's own wizards. The little wand was a Nobleman's Comfort, a sorcerous toy the King was known to provide as gifts to family, friends, and favored members of the nobility. While some might be harmless enough to simply emit light, most of the ones Thratos had were justly feared as lethal. Each held a finite number of charges and each did something different. Benhus was fascinated by the things and Thratos knew it.

This one, Benhus reflected, was effective but not controllable enough, or dramatic enough, to satisfy. He had heard rumors that his master had recently received from the King a Nobleman's Comfort that instantly reduced an enemy to a skeleton brown and brittle with age. Now that was a superior effect, thought Benhus, and sure to be remembered by one's surviving foes.

"The bowman might have shot me," he said, catching up with Thratos. "Why didn't you take him first?"

"It was an opportunity to extend your education," replied his teacher drily. Benhus wondered if Thratos had entertained some hope that his student would take a crossbow bolt.

The robed man still lay senseless at the base of the cenotaph, and Benhus lifted his gaze to examine the statue at its summit. It was hard to make out details, but it was a hooded woman, in her left hand a wreath of flowers, in her right a curved dagger. Benhus squinted at the needle-pointed weapon. No, it was a sickle, like those used by harvesters.

"There's too much resistance. There are bonds on the inside, too. So it's twice as difficult to break." The prone man spoke more clearly now, and as if making a point in a vitally serious argument. Benhus heard his teacher chuckle again.

"See if you can get him to talk any sense," said Thratos. He watched the tomb's open door while his apprentice dropped to one knee beside the raving man. Benhus opened his mouth to speak but was cut off.

"Don't let Belsa try it alone! Don't close the door. It'll seal shut and I don't have the strength to open it again. How could I know it would be so strong?"

"The door?" said Benhus gently.

"There were bonds inside as well. How could I know? Took all I had to break them."

"Where's Belsa?" asked Benhus.

"She went in! With Strabo! They can't take her flesh without my help, they could…" The man blinked hard, then focused his eyes on Benhus's face. "Who- who are you?"

Benhus saw his master begin to draw his sword. He drew back a fist and punched the prone man full in the jaw with force enough to drive his head back into the flagstones with an ugly crunch.

"You've split his head," said Thratos.

"You were going to run him through," said Benhus.

"Well, we've learned enough from him, have we not?" When Benhus didn't answer his teacher pressed, "What have we learned?"

"This was a sorcerer who broke open the tomb. And it was warded with sorcery that was stronger than he was prepared to deal with. It sapped the strength of his body and mind."

"Hells, that's easy. Obvious." Thratos's tone was scornful. "Why are he and his cronies here?"

"To…to rob the tomb of course." Benhus fought to keep his voice steady.

"Gods and demons, weren't you listening? This is no simple group of graverobbers. This crew broke into the Royal Cemetery and have used sorcery to unseal a royal tomb. And they're not here for riches. What did he say they wanted?"

"He didn't…He didn't say…"

"Weren't you listening? They came to take her flesh!"

Benhus didn't trust himself to speak.

"Do you know whose tomb this is?" Thratos gestured back at the mausoleum. "This is the final resting place of the King's sister, Nervale. A skilled sorcerer could take the flesh of a royal and use it to afflict others of the same bloodline. These are not graverobbers, they are rebels against the crown who mean to strike at the King with magic. You know what this means?"

Benhus said, "They can't leave here. We have to stop them."

Thratos sighed with exaggerated relief. "Yes. And we have to go into the tomb. Now."

"Go in? Why?"

"They could be performing some rite to harm the King even now, simpleton. Here." Thratos fumbled in his belt, then drew out a small object, a Nobleman's Comfort. "This one's simple enough even for you. See the black spot? Press it hard, hard as you can, and point it at your enemy."

Benhus gaped at the little wand. It looked like a piece of jewelry, golden with black inlay. He reached for it, but his master drew it back.

"No," said Thratos. "You're not ready." He turned away and headed toward the mausoleum. "Come." Benhus followed numbly.

The tomb's heavy door was open, the interior as blackly forbidding as ever. There was an ornamental metal vine of sculpted roses running along the door's rim and overhanging it. As he drew near Benhus could see that it was matched by an identical one running along the doorframe, and that each dark metal rose or rosebud was split, with half on the door and half on the frame. When closed, each separated flower would meet and form a complete bloom. Peering warily inside, Benhus could see that this odd ornamentation was duplicated on the interior of the doorway as well. He hesitated.

"Go on," said Thratos. "I'll be right behind you."

"Get," started Behus, "get the light…" He wanted to ask his teacher for the Nobleman's Comfort that shed such clear white illumination, but knew Thratos wouldn't give it to him. Indeed, his master let him step completely into the black space inside the door before holding up the wand and lighting their way.

There was an open antechamber, wider than the doorway but empty. The floor was of plain flagstones, the walls of brick, all with a faint sheen of moisture. A wide corridor opened before them, leading directly away, and lowering into the earth.

The light from the Nobleman's Comfort seemed to dim, to fade and falter, forced back by the tomb's cloying darkness. They stood side by side, teacher and student, for a moment.

"Be careful," said Thratos. The advice was unnecessary, but Benhus was grateful simply to hear his master speak thus. "There may be more to reckon with here than grave-robbing rebels."

A few steps forward and the corridor could be seen to descend in stairs. The illumination from the wand was obviously dimmer now, unable to extend into the darkness ahead.

"What?" said Benhus. His stomach was clenched, but he drew his sword and was pleased to see that his hand was steady. "What else?"

"Nervale was younger than the King, and it was rumored that she did not die of a fever as was made known, but was put to death in secret for practicing necromancy."

They started down the wide flight of stairs, which dropped steeply into the earth. Thratos held the Nobleman's Comfort aloft, but the darkness ahead pushed back, keeping the light from penetrating more than a few steps ahead.

Benhus considered how he had never heard that the king had a sister named Nervale, much less than she might have been slain by her own family as a sorceress of the blackest arts. He noticed the dampness everywhere, the strange scent on the air, like an acrid, not unpleasant, spice, and that there was no sign of vermin whatsoever. No cobwebs.

Then he heard voices. They echoed hollowly down the hallway, not from close by, but it was impossible to determine how far off. Several voices, speaking at first, and then chanting together in unison.

"Gods!" ground out Thratos, "we've got to hurry!"

They moved down the stairs as quickly as they dared, suspended in their cramped sphere of light. The steps finally came to an end and they were once again in a wide corridor that led straight away. A few paces in and Benhus thought he could see light ahead. The chanting grew louder.

They hastened down the hallway, the light grew closer, and Benhus felt an odd moment of constriction, then the passage seemed to abruptly open up before them, filled with light and sound.

Benhus glimpsed a black gap in the floor ahead and lurched to a halt, automatically lashing back with an arm to arrest Thratos in mid-stride. The floor fell away in a sheer drop into utter darkness before their feet and, but for Benhus's reflexive action, both men might have stepped off into the void.

The gap was perhaps four paces across, and on the other side the corridor opened into a broad chamber with a ceiling high enough to be lost in shadow. In the chamber's center was a dais of three steps, and on the dais was a block of silver-veined black marble holding a plain stone sarcophagus. Three men held torches aloft while a woman in blue robes stood with her hands flat on the sarcophagus lid.

Benhus blinked, addled by the chasm at his feet, by the flaring torchlight and rising chanting thrust upon his senses as if revealed by the sudden opening of a door. The woman shouted an arcane word in a voice that rang like steel on steel, repeated it again and again while she leaned visibly into the coffin, pushing at the lid with both hands.

"Stop!" roared Thratos, and the word seemed to shatter in the air of the crypt, rebounding from the walls and boxing the ears with sound.

The sarcophagus lid slid halfway aside. The blue-robed woman choked on her chanted words as her head snapped around to stare at the intruders. The torch wielders gaped at the teacher and his student.

Thratos drew back, then leapt across the chasm, landing on the opposite side in a crouch and digging into his belt for a Nobleman's Comfort.

Benhus looked from the black chasm to his master and back again. He tensed his legs to jump, and the heavy stone lid of Nervale's coffin flew off, sailed impossibly through the air, and shattered against the tomb's back wall with a sound like lightning striking a granite outcrop.

The woman stumbled back from the sarcophagus, lifted her hands to her face and began to scream. Torchlight reeled in the chamber as the torch wielders recoiled. Thratos shouted words Benhus could not understand.

Something rose from the open coffin and lifted above the tumult. A figure in a ragged brown cloak, dusty and tattered as a collection of cast-off rags. Beneath its hood there was no sign of a

face, only a darkness featureless and blank. The narrow shoulders sloped down into a tapering twist of torn fabric, coarse and stained. There were no feet, no legs visible below it. The nightmare figure floated up, freed from the sarcophagus. As it rose, bone-thin arms, pale as snow, pale as death, lifted from its sides and extended as if in supplication. In its long-fingered right hand was a sickle of crystal, gleaming with a brittle light of its own, sharp and bitter in the dimness of the tomb. From the blank blackness within the ragged hood came a shrill titter of laughter, immediately followed by a terrible cackle of inhuman mirth, soulless and full of a venomous cruelty that made the hair on Benhus's neck stand up. A chill swept through his body like winter wind through a screen. The sickle lashed out, flashing. A scream, a throat-tearing fusion of agony and horror, lifted and entwined with the figure's unbroken laughter.

Benhus saw Thratos thrust a little golden wand at the laughing thing, now flourishing its crystal sickle gone scarlet. His master turned and leapt back across the black gap in the floor.

Then Benhus was running wildly, blindly back down the corridor. He almost tripped on the first steps, but caught himself, sheathed his sword, and leapt up them three at a time as another scream echoed nightmarishly along the stone passage. Gasping for breath, he topped the stairs and sprinted for the tomb's half closed door.

His heels skidded on the moist stone and his body rebounded from the heavy door frame, bruising his ribs. He clawed at the door, pulled himself through the opening and out into the clearing.

He shot a wide-eyed glance back into the tomb and saw Thratos trip and go sprawling not ten paces within, hitting with brutal force and releasing a tiny something that skittered across the floor toward Benhus. The golden Nobleman's Comfort.

Behind Thratos something dark seemed to float like a fog along the corridor, tittering with hellish delight. Benhus darted back into the antechamber, bent and snatched up the little wand, then ducked back out the doorway.

He was certain the slab-like metal door would be too hard to move, but it wasn't. Heavy, but with hinges oiled, it shifted with a deep groan as he leaned into it, pushing with both hands and the strength of his entire body, effort rising through his firmly planted feet, set legs and heaving shoulders.

"Benhus! For the love of the Gods!" Thratos voice rose to a timbre his apprentice had never heard before. "Stop!" The voice was almost at the door when Benhus pushed it shut. Thratos's voice, rising in a wordless cry, was clipped off.

There was a sighing sound, followed by a molten sizzle as each halved black metal rose on the door met its counterpart on the frame and sealed seamlessly together. Benhus took an unsteady step back from the portal. The rich scent of roses filled the air, sweet, incongruous, and somehow terrible.

Benhus listened intently but whatever sounds might currently be filling the space behind the door could not be heard. The courtyard before the mausoleum was silent. The moon had risen, casting an ashen glow. A breeze chased the rose-scent from the air. Benhus heard himself breathing.

There was someone behind him.

The blue robed sorcerer stood there unsteadily, blinking at him. The back of his head was matted with blood and his jaw was smeared with it where Benhus had struck him. As Benhus looked on, he frowned heavily and produced a wicked serrated dagger from within his robes. The blade was incised with black glyphs and its jagged edge gleamed a sticky green, like luminous malachite in the moonlight.

"What have you done?" he asked in a hoarse voice. He frowned and seemed to come to a greater awareness of where he was and what must have happened here. The sorcerer's face twisted with mingled disbelief and rage. "You sealed the door! Your comrade, my comrades…"

"Are dead now, or will be so shortly," said Benhus. "The King's sister was disinclined to provide graverobbers with samples of her flesh."

"Gods!" The man cast a glance over Benhus's shoulder, looking at the tomb's door. Perhaps, thought Benhus, he was less unhappy about the fact it was now sealed. "But you closed the door! Couldn't you have let them escape? What have you done?"

"I've protected the King from those who hoped to kill or control him by magic. I've slain a number of ill-prepared rebels." Benhus hesitated, smiling a little and hooking his thumbs into his belt. "And I've given myself a promotion."

"You monster!" All but weeping in rage, the young sorcerer lunged forward and slashed at Benhus with his envenomed blade. The merest scratch from that weapon would have produced a choking, frothing death, but Benhus was ready for it. He stepped back and triggered the Nobleman's Comfort.

There was no sound, just a passing chill like a gust of autumn breeze, and the air was filled with the scent of dry leaves and stale dust.

The poisoned dagger rang like a chime on the black flagstones. The sorcerer teetered on his feet, abruptly a thinner, almost insubstantial figure. He fell rigidly on his back, striking the marble pave with a disconsonant, muffled clatter.

Benhus stepped forward and looked down at his foe. Above the collar of his robes the sorcerer's head was reduced to a brown and sere skull. Worn, stained and cracked, it might have lain forgotten in the corner of a tomb for a hundred years.

Benhus studied the golden little weapon and smiled. Now that's just fine, he thought. This is just the one I wanted.

He tucked the wand behind his belt and began the long walk back out of the graveyard, into the waiting city. He would be home before morning.

ABOUT THE AUTHOR

Long before JOHN C. HOCKING wrote *Conan & the Emerald Lotus*, back in the mists of antiquity at the dawn of the RPG era, he gamemastered a Dungeons & Dragons saga so epic that the players cannot gather together almost forty years later without arguing about it. One of their primary foes inspired such terror that when he was finally fought and destroyed, the player who dealt the killing blow carried the eight sided die that slew him in his pocket for months, unsheathing it to flourish before the admiring eyes of his fellow players, and to roll in order to help make critical decisions in life, love and job search.

APPENDIX N:
INSPIRATIONAL READING

IN the 1979 publication of the *Advanced Dungeons & Dragons Dungeon Masters Guide*, the last entry before the glossary is Appendix N, in which Gary Gygax lists the fantasy and sci-fi novels that inspired his work on the game. This oft-ignored bibliography has received renewed attention in recent years. It is in fact one of the foundations on which fantasy role playing was built:

Anderson, Poul: *Three Hearts and Three Lions; The High Crusade; The Broken Sword*

Bellairs, John: *The Face in the Frost*

Brackett, Leigh

Brown, Fredric

Burroughs, Edward Rice: "Pellucidar" series; "Mars" series; "Venus" series

Carter, Lin: "World's End" series

de Camp, L. Sprague: *Lest Darkness Fall; Fallible Fiend; et al*

de Camp & Pratt: "Harold Shea" series; *Carnelian Cube*

Derleth, August

Dunsany, Lord

Farmer, P. J.: "The World of the Tiers" series; *et al*

Fox, Gardner: "Kothar" series; "Kyric" series; *et al*

Howard, Robert E.: "Conan" series

Lanier, Sterling: *Hiero's Journey*

Leiber, Fritz. "Fafhrd & Gray Mouser" series; *et al*

Lovecraft, H. P.

Merritt, A.: *Creep, Shadow, Creep; Moon Pool; Dwellers in the Mirage; et al*

Moorcock, Michael: *Stormbringer; Stealer of Souls;* "Hawkmoon" series (esp. the first three books)

Norton, Andre

Offutt, Andrew J., editor *Swords Against Darkness III*

Pratt, Fletcher: *Blue Star; et al*

Saberhagen, Fred: *Changeling Earth; et al*

St. Clair, Margaret: *The Shadow People; Sign of the Labrys*

Tolkien, J. R. R.: *The Hobbit;* "Ring Trilogy"

Vance, Jack: *The Eyes of the Overworld; The Dying Earth; et al*

Weinbaum, Stanley

Wellman, Manly Wade

Williamson, Jack

Zelazny, Roger: *Jack of Shadows;* "Amber" series; *et al*

APPENDIX: GAME STATISTICS
By TERRY OLSON

Publisher's Note: While this is a magazine of fantasy fiction, it is grounded in the aesthetic of the *Dungeon Crawl Classics Role Playing Game*, or DCC RPG. DCC RPG is heavily inspired by the stories of Appendix N, a collection of fantasy and science fiction works that inspired Gary Gygax to create *Dungeons & Dragons*. *Tales From the Magician's Skull* can be read on its surface as simply great stories, but players of role playing games (DCC RPG or otherwise) may also recognize that these stories are designed to pay homage to Appendix N and its role in providing inspiration to RPG games. Therefore we present this appendix of game statistics for the various creatures, spells, and items described herein. All of these stats are for the *Dungeon Crawl Classics Role Playing Game* system, although you may be able to easily adapt them to other systems as well. Gamers – enjoy!

Beneath the Bay of Black Waters

Dragon's Egg: A dragon's egg is a globe with a rock crystal shell, 4 to 6 inches in diameter, and a hollow interior. Filled with a glowing gas, the globe radiates a sunny day's light within a 60' radius, and gradually diminishes to candlelight 120' away. Nocturnal and un-dead creatures that suffer ill effects from daylight are similarly affected within 60' of a dragon's egg. It's not very heavy for its size, and floats just below the surface of seawater; in freshwater, it sinks very slowly.

The alchemical mixture contained within is very dangerous; if exposed to a tiny bit of moisture, even the little bit contained in normal air, the orb explodes. One may pierce a small hole in the shell, but he must pass a Luck check to avoid the shell cracking. In fact, a Luck check is necessary even for moderate impacts, though an egg automatically breaks when it lands from falls greater than 10'. If the shell does crack, the egg explodes at the beginning of the next combat round, doing 3d6 damage in a 20' radius (DC 12 Reflex save for half damage). If the shell does not crack, it explodes in 2d3 rounds unless the hole is plugged. An egg's explosion is greatly amplified if submerged (e.g., throwing a pierced egg into water). In this case, it does 6d6 damage in a 40' radius (DC 16 Reflex save for half damage). Of course, piercing the shell while submerged causes an instant explosion, and is practically suicidal.

Guai: Init +1; Atk claw +3 melee (1d6+1); AC 16; HD 3d8; MV 15' or swim 40'; Act 2d20 (on land) or 2d24 (in water); SP true amphibian (gills and lungs), latching bite (if both claws hit a victim, the guai bites for 2d4 dmg; gaui may stay latched for subsequent rounds, sacrificing actions but doing 2d4 dmg/rnd; DC 16 STR check to dislodge), photo-sensitive (suffers -2d penalty on all rolls in sunlight; DC 10 Will save each round or flee from light), infravision 100', immune to cold damage; SV Fort +1, Ref +3, Will +1; AL C.

Vaguely man-shaped, each swam with powerful strokes of their webbed and flipper-like limbs. The creatures were pale as cave worms, with lumpy, irregular flesh reminiscent of a waterlogged corpse. Their large heads were ringed with feathery appendages that Bao had seen before on certain kinds of newt—gills. But it was the hollowness of their dead black eyes as they rushed him that unnerved Bao most of all …fast swimmers but ungainly on land, needle-clawed and spike-toothed and cold as the blackest ocean depths.

Beyond the Block

Potion of Un-Death: Minimum *make potion* spell check: 36

Special ingredients: Dirt from a vampire's coffin and an intact zombie tongue

Effects: This potion is a dark liquid, and smells of carrion and corrupted earth. It causes the imbiber to become un-dead whenever he is killed. However, his brain must be intact; if the brain is destroyed, so is the imbiber. Upon un-death, his body turns a gray color. If his head is detached, the affected may telepathically control his body. The potion grants "phantom sight" for such circumstances, allowing one to hazily see his body's environment. PCs becoming un-dead retain their physical and class abilities, but they do not eat, drink, breathe, or feel pain. As un-dead, they are immune to *sleep*, *charm*, and *paralysis* spells, as well as other mental effects and cold damage. Additionally, the potion enhances the effective strength of the imbiber, who gains a +1d bonus to melee attacks, damage, and any other strength related actions.

I come to the strange and awful realization that my head lives apart from my body…My chest is still and silent, and if there were ever any doubt that I am existing beyond the grasp of death, it has been laid to rest.

Crypt of Stars

Gatzi: Init +4; Atk bite +4 melee (2d6+wound rot) and 2 talons +2 melee (1d4+1); AC 11; HD 2d8; MV 20' or fly 40'; Act 1d20 (bite) + 2d14 (talons); SP wound rot (DC 14 Fortitude save or wound is diseased; lost hp may not be healed until disease is cured), death frenzy (smell of death blood, including a PC bleeding out, bestows +1d to all attack rolls for Gatzi within a 20' radius), sun-stunned (suffers -2d penalty on all rolls in sunlight; DC 10 Will save each round or be stunned actionless), infravision 200'; SV Fort +1, Ref +2, Will +0; AL N.

Once the gatzi smelled the planks where Hanuvar smeared broken scuttlers they sped from the bag like arrows. The poor sentry didn't have a chance. He'd knelt to examine the carcasses piled upon his patrol route...One moment he was a dark form hunched on the dock, the next he was a screaming and writhing mass collapsing under the devouring assault.

Divine Familiar: If a deity is especially pleased with a cleric, it will consider granting the distinguished worshipper a divine familiar. In order to petition for this boon, the cleric must have performed a significant act for his religion (the completion of an epic quest, the felling of a divine rival, the destruction or recovery of an artifact, etc.); note that this requirement must be met just *to attempt to obtain a familiar*. In order for her request to be granted, the cleric must achieve a *divine aid* spell check of 22 or larger, with a +1 bonus to the check for every 1000 gp sacrificed during the week-long ritual. If successful, the priest is granted a guardian familiar, as detailed for wizards in the DCC core rulebook. As with wizards, if a familiar dies, the caster immediately keels over in intense pain, loses twice the familiar's hit points permanently, and suffers a -5 spell check penalty until the next full moon (or whatever condition the deity deems appropriate).

Palhecoc (Lvl 3 Dervani priest's divine familiar): Init +4; Atk claw +6 melee (1d6); AC 16; HD 2d4+4; hp 9; MV 30' or fly 30'; Act 1d20; SP clerical crit (1d12 crit table III), stealthy (+8 to hide in shadows and sneak silently), acute hearing (can hear whispers up to 300' away), infravision 300'; SV Fort +2, Ref +2, Will +3; AL L.

The Crystal Sickle's Harvest

Crystal-Sickle Wraith: Init +5; Atk magical sickle +8 melee (1d6+drain essence) and chilling cackle (special); AC 14; HD 10d8; MV fly 60'; Act 2d20; SP drain essence (sickle reduces PCs maximum hp by 2d3 points, no save), chilling cackle (DC 14 Will save or 1d4+1 Strength damage, all within 30' radius affected), chilling aura (all within 10' take 1d6 dmg/round cold damage, DC 18 Fort save to avoid), un-dead traits (immune to *sleep*, *charm*, and *paralysis* spells, as well as other mental effects and cold damage), immune to non-magical weapons; SV Fort +5, Ref +8, Will +7; AL C.

The nightmare figure floated up...bone-thin arms, pale as snow, pale as death, lifted from its sides and extended as if in supplication. In its long-fingered right hand was a sickle of crystal, gleaming with a brittle light of its own, sharp and bitter...From the blank blackness within the ragged hood came a shrill titter of laughter, immediately followed by a terrible cackle of inhuman mirth, soulless and full of a venomous cruelty.

Nobleman's Comfort: The Nobleman's Comfort is a tiny magic wand, about 4 to 6 inches in length. Unlike a "typical" wand, this may be operated by anyone. No arcane knowledge or command word is necessary; all one must do is press a tiny button, or so most believe. Actually, a PC using the device must make a spell check, though the minimum check for success is much smaller than required to cast a spell of equivalent power. Non-spell casters make the check with a d10, though thieves may use their *cast spell from scroll* die. Failure deactivates the device for 2d4 hours. A natural one on the check results in minor corruption. The nobleman's comfort's ease of use and concealability make it highly desired. Any given wand has 1d6 + Luck modifier charges when found. Some examples are given below:

• **Withering Parcher** (Min Spell Check 4): This looks like an aged wooden elongated finger. It makes a whooshing sound when activated, and emits a ray of energy that withers and desiccates objects in its path. Living beings take 2d10 damage (DC 14 Fort save for half). If the ray inflicts 11 or more points of damage, it passes through its target to strike whatever is next in its path, up to a maximum range of 50 feet.

• **Illuminator** (Min Spell Check 2): This tiny porcelain cylinder emits a cone of sunlight, with diameter half its length up to 100' (10' diameter at 20' away, 50' diameter at 100' away). It radiates light for 1d3 hours with each activation.

• **Decomposer** (Min Spell Check 7): This looks more like jewelry than a wand, as it is golden with black inlay. When activated, a scent of dry leaves and stale dust precedes the almost instantaneous decay of the target. A living target becomes a hundred year-old skeleton within a few seconds. The target must pass a DC 10 Fort save or die, with no "recovering the body" check allowed. The device's maximum range is 10'.

The Guild of Silent Men

Coldlight: A coldlight is a glass cylinder, about a foot long, filled with luminous fluid that provides light similar to torchlight. This frozen liquid radiates as it slowly melts, until it becomes sufficiently warm and goes dark. Once taken off ice, a coldlight will radiate from 2 to 8 hours, depending on ambient temperature and whether it is held with insulation. A bare human hand holding one on a summer day will warm it within 2 hours; a thickly gloved hand holding one on a cold night will warm it in 8 hours. If the glass cylinder is cracked, the exposed liquid still radiates, but dims about 10 times faster. Nevertheless, clever uses of coldlight liquid abound. The judge may decide whether the liquid comes from a creature (e.g., the blood of a white dragon), is the product of alchemy, a gift from the gods, or the product of a basic wizard's spell.

He tapped the coldlight with the hammer, cracking it. He poured some of the pale luminous fluid into the dish. He pierced Reuk's left eye with the needle and then, still using the needle, introduced some of the glowing fluid into the eyeball.

Talisman Against Illusion: This talisman is a thin azurite disk attached to a fine platinum chain. The chain is worn on top of one's head (like a head band) with the azurite placed in the center of the forehead, serving as a lens for the "third eye." When so placed, the talisman becomes magically invisible (an illusion in itself) and may only be removed by the bearer. For non-spellcasters, it imparts a +2d bonus to all saves vs. illusory effects (e.g., PC saves with a d30 instead of a d20). If worn by a spellcaster, the bearer saves vs. illusory effects by rolling a d100 (percentile dice).

Illusory Self	Level: 3
Range: self	Duration: varies
Casting Time: 1 action	Save: Will vs. spell check

General: With this spell, the caster creates the illusion that his body has another form. Unlike the *phantasm* spell, this illusion has aural and tactile elements in addition to its visual deception. However, it can neither change the caster's scent nor create illusory odors. Nonetheless, wizards use *illusory self* for disguise, subterfuge, and even combat (though casting the spell while in combat incurs a -1d spell check penalty).

While maintaining the illusion, the caster may move at half speed and take physical actions with a -1d penalty (such as melee attacks). He may not cast spells or use magical devices requiring spell checks. If the caster takes any type of damage (weapon, ability, subdual, etc.), he must make a Will save vs. 10 + damage taken or the spell expires. Thus, if the caster takes 6 points of damage, he must pass a DC 16 Will save.

The caster may choose a form only from things he has seen and experienced; if he has never encountered a dragon, he may not choose a dragon's form. His illusory self may perform melee-range, physical attacks. Such damage is limited by the caster's melee weapon at lower spell checks, but with larger spell checks the illusion provides additional damage.

Those experiencing the caster's illusory self are granted a Will save vs. spell check to realize the illusion. Allow a cumulative +1d bonus to the save for every inconsistency that is noticed, stopping at a d100. Such inconsistencies may include seeing the illusory form change, noting an inconsistent smell, saying atypical things, etc.

Manifestation: See below.

Corruption: Roll 1d8: (1) One of the caster's limbs appears to be a non-sensical inanimate object (such as a forearm appearing as a scabbard); (2) caster appears to have a small animal protruding halfway out of his chest; (3) the caster's face changes appearance uncontrollably, once per minute (few people trust or recognize her); (3-5) minor; (6-7) major; (8) greater.

Misfire: Roll 1d4: (1) For 1d6 hours, the caster sees her hands as made of stone; she must pass a DC 15 Will save each time she wishes to use them; (2) the caster sees his body constantly changing, and is paralyzed with fear for 2d3 rounds; (3) For 2d3 rounds, all within 30' see the caster as their worst enemy; allies must pass a DC 12 Will save to avoid attacking the caster; (4) the caster's body appears to uncontrollably change size, shape, form, etc., for the next 1d6 hours, drawing unpleasant reactions to him in nearly all circumstances

1	Lost, failure, and worse! Roll 1d6 modified by Luck: (0 or less) corruption + patron taint + misfire; (1-3) corruption; (4) patron taint (or corruption if no patron); (5+) misfire.
2 - 11	Lost. Failure.
12 - 15	Failure, but spell is not lost.
16 - 17	The caster appears as an inanimate object (table, bench, etc.), similar in size to himself, for 1d3 rounds. He does not do melee damage in this form.
18 - 21	The caster appears as a mundane animal (such as a tiger or snake), similar in size to herself, for 2d3 rounds. Her melee damage is limited by held weapons.
22 - 23	The caster appears as a humanoid for 3d3 rounds, of any race or gender, similar in size to himself. His melee damage is limited by held weapons.
24 - 26	The caster appears as an inanimate object, of any size from 1/2 to 2 times his own. The effect lasts for 1d3 + caster level turns. He may change his illusion (to other inanimate objects) a number of times equal to caster level, but must pass a DC 11 Will save with each change or the spell expires. He does melee damage equal to weapon + 1d6. However, such attacks grant saving throws with bonuses for inconsistencies (a limb falling from a tree is self-consistent; a table attacking someone is not). The illusion grants a +1 to AC.
27 - 31	The caster appears as an animal or humanoid, of any size from 1/2 to 2 times his own. The effect lasts for 2d3 + caster level turns. He may change his illusion (to another animal or humanoid) a number of times equal to caster level, but must pass a DC 11 Will save with each change or the spell expires. He does melee damage equal to weapon + 1d6. The illusion grants a +2 to AC.
32 - 33	The caster appears as a ferocious monster, of any size from 1/3 to 3 times her own. The effect lasts for 3d3 + caster level turns. She may change her illusion (to another monster) a number of times equal to caster level, but must pass a DC 11 Will save with each change or the spell expires. She does melee damage equal to weapon + 1d6 + caster level. The illusion grants a +3 to AC.
34 - 35	The caster appears as any inanimate object, animal, humanoid, monster, or elemental form he desires, of any size from 1/5 to 5 times his own. He may change his illusion once per round with ease. He does melee damage equal to weapon + 2d6 + caster level. The effect lasts for 1d6 + caster level hours. The illusion grants a +4 to AC.
36+	The caster appears as any inanimate object, animal, humanoid, monster, or elemental form she desires, of any size from 1/10 to 10 times her own. She may change her illusion once per round with ease. She does melee damage equal to weapon + 3d6 + caster level. The effect lasts for 3d6 + caster level hours. The illusion grants a +5 to AC.

There Was an Old Fat Spider

Old Fat Spider: Init +2; Atk bite +5 melee (1d8+2 plus poison) or webstream +3 missile fire (webbing, range 100') or charm (special); AC 15; HD 6d10; MV 20' or climb 20'; Act 1d20; SP poison (DC 14 Fort save or 2d4 dmg/round until death; for successful save, 1d4 temporary STA damage), webbing (spider gains +1d bonus to hit target, which is penalized -1d to all rolls, half movement, requires 1 round's actions to remove), charm (DC 15 Will save, spider may paralyze victim with fear for 1d3 rounds, or evoke friendly sympathy from the victim for 1d3 days), death throe (spiderling swarm erupts from body, attacking all within 10' of spider's corpse); SV Fort +4, Ref +2, Will +7; AL N.

It'll jab you with its fangs, fill you full of its venom. Everything inside you will be reduced to sludge. Flesh, sinew, muscle and organ. All of it turned to soup which it will then suck out of you until only skin and bones are left. You'll drain out, like pus from a wound. But don't think it'll be quick. Oh no, you'll be alive for quite some time while it's happening.

Spiderling Swarm: Init +3; Atk swarming bite +2 melee (2d3 plus venom); AC 13; HD 3d8; MV 30' or climb 30'; Act 1d16 special; SP swarming bite all targets in 20'x20'x20' volume, half damage from non-area attacks, venom (DC 12 Fortitude save or helpless for 1 round); SV Fort +1, Ref +3, Will -1; AL N.

The eaten-out husk was vibrating wildly, a spasm of maddened excitement. Boiling up from the split in its body came a tide of crawling monstrosities. Scores of fist-sized spiderlings, their eyes gleaming with a ghastly vitality.

Sylvan Cloak: This cloak is a rare prize, and its fabrication is a closely guarded secret among the fae of Elfland. The garment, being constructed from exactly 103 wings of dusk moths, is exceptionally light, though its arcane nature makes it quite durable. When donning the cloak, the wearer is magically invisible, but she still casts a shadow. Although it prevents most detection by sight, it does not mask sounds, odors, etc.

Elemental Witchfyre	Level: 1
Range: 60' unless specified	Duration: varies
Casting Time: 1 action	Save: Reflex vs. spell check

General: Witchfyre is a fusion of raw phlogiston and glowing elemental energy. Casting it is unpredictable, as it can have both offensive and defensive results. Nonetheless, it has some of the largest damage potential of any first level spell, but unlike similar spells (e.g. *flaming hands* and *magic missile*), targets receive a Reflex save vs. the spell check. If multiple streams of energy are directed toward a single target, that target receives only one save. If the save is successful, there is no effect from the incoming streams. The spell can be especially potent against un-dead, doing significantly more damage.

Witchfyre causes either heat, cold, or shock damage. When the caster learns the spell, she must specify which one of the elemental forms she'll perfect. She may cast the other two elemental forms with a -1d spell check penalty. Note that creatures with immunities to a particular type of damage (such as un-dead's immunity to cold damage) are not damaged by that type of witchfyre.

Manifestation: Roll 1d4: (1) streams of emerald fire; (2) eerie green globs of viscous liquid; (3) tiny spiraling viridian comets; (4) shards of glowing yellow-green light.

Corruption: Roll 1d4: (1) eyes have a faint green glow; (2) fingertips are permanently lit with witchfyre; (3) entire body glows green light, equivalent to candlelight and imposing a -2d penalty to hide checks; (4) the caster is averse and phobic toward the element that caused the corruption, and takes double damage from that element.

Misfire: Roll 1d4: (1) the caster causes a flash of witchfyre in front of her eyes, blinding her for 1d3 hours; (2) the caster covers himself in witchfyre, taking 1d4 + caster level damage; (3) the caster and all allies within 20' must pass a Luck check or be struck by a stray witchfyre stream for 1d3 damage (no save); (4) the caster inadvertently summons minor witchfyre elementals that attack the caster until killed; the number summoned is equal to the caster's level. **Minor Witchfyre Elementals:** Init +1; Atk witchfyre stream +2 missile fire (1d4); AC 12; HD 1d8; MV fly 30'; Act 1d20; SP immune to witchfyre; SV Fort +0, Ref +1, Will +2; AL N.

1	Lost, failure, and worse! Roll 1d6 modified by Luck: (0 or less) corruption + patron taint + misfire; (1-2) corruption; (3) patron taint (or corruption if no patron); (4+) misfire.
2 - 11	Lost. Failure.
12 - 13	The caster shoots a thin stream of witchfyre toward a single target. A faint glow emits from the victim. For the next round, he grants anyone attacking him a +1d bonus to hit, while he takes a -1d penalty on all actions. An un-dead target takes additional 1d3 damage.
14-17	The caster fires 1d3+1 streams at a single or multiple targets, each stream doing 1d4 + caster level damage. Un-dead take 1d6 + caster level damage.
18-19	The caster himself radiates witchfyre from within, and his body is covered in glowing flames. Anyone within 30' physically or magically attacking the caster receives a retaliatory stream doing 2d3 damage. Un-dead take 2d4 damage. The effect lasts 1d3 rounds.

20 - 23	The caster shoots a stream of witchfyre toward every enemy within a 30' radius. A strong glow emits from each victim. For the next 1d3 + caster level rounds, each target grants anyone attacking them a +1d bonus to hit, while he takes a -1d penalty on all actions. Furthermore, each target takes 1d6 damage. Un-dead take 1d8 damage.
24-27	Extending fingers outwards, the caster projects 3d3 streams of witchfyre, which may be directed at a single target, or divided among multiple targets as the caster desires. Each stream does 1d8 + caster level damage. Un-dead take 1d12 + caster level damage per stream.
28-29	The caster herself radiates witchfyre from within, and her body is covered in glowing flames. Anyone within 120' physically or magically attacking the caster receives a retaliatory stream doing 2d8 + caster level damage. Un-dead take 2d12 + caster level damage. The effect lasts 2d3 rounds.
30-31	Spreading his arms to the sides, the caster unleashes a semicircular "sheet" of witchfyre with a 60' radius. All within take 4d12 + caster level damage. Un-dead take 4d16 + caster level damage. The caster may choose a number of targets less than or equal to his caster level that the sheet does not affect.
32+	Drawing from the elemental planes themselves, the caster flings a concentrated sphere of witchfyre at a single target within 120'. The target takes 6d12 + caster level damage. An un-dead target takes 6d16 + caster level damage.

What Lies In Ice

Hands of the Sea (swarm): Init +3; Atk rend +3 melee (1d6); AC 10; HD 4d8; MV 25' or swim 15' or fly 15'; Act 1d20 special; SP rend all targets within 30'x30'x30' volume, half damage from non-area attacks, fire-averse (fire-based attacks do double damage; hands avoid fire-wielding combatants if possible), un-dead traits (immune to *sleep*, *charm*, and *paralysis* spells, as well as other mental effects and cold damage); SV Fort -2, Ref +6, Will +6; AL C.

Imperishable Hand with Gemmed Phylactery: Init +3; Atk rend +2 melee (1d4) or face-palm +4 (1+soul crush); AC 14; HD 2d8; MV 30' or swim 20' or jump 10'; Act 1d20; SP soul crush (DC 10 Will save or victim's soul/being is irrevocably lost, and gemmed ring's soul transfers to body), intelligent (gemmed ring retains life force of wizard, and intelligence drives hand), psychic senses (can see, hear, smell, etc., without the need for organs), regeneration (1hp/round, gem must be crushed to destroy hand), un-dead traits (immune to *sleep*, *charm*, and *paralysis* spells, as well as other mental effects and cold damage); SV Fort +10, Ref +5, Will +8; AL C.

Colossal Brain-Poxed Squid: Init +7; Atk tentacle +7 melee (2d6+constrict) or scalding ink +5 missile fire (60' range, blinding) or stunning babble (special); AC 15; HD 12d12; MV 40' or swim 60'; Act 2d24 special; SP multi-tasker (squid may focus 2 attacks on up to 15 different opponents per round), constrict (the round following a hit, tentacle constricts for 1d6/round; DC 20 STR to escape), blinding (DC 13 Ref save when inked, or blinded for 2d6 hours), stunning babble (babbling mouths on tentacles stun listener to helplessness for 1 round, DC 12 Will save), un-dead traits (immune to *sleep*, *charm*, and *paralysis* spells, as well as other mental effects and cold damage), many-brained immunity (cannot be turned), all-around sight (eyes on tentacles allow simultaneous sight in all directions); SV Fort +12, Ref +6, Will +16; AL C.

The thing was no longer a true squid, for all that its tentacles stretched this way and that, sometimes downward through fissures in the floor. For one thing, there were thrice too many tentacles, and for another they were covered in human eyes and ears and noses and mouths. The quivering, rubbery main mass of the body might once have been a natural being, but it too had been grafted with parts from other creatures. Maws of bears and fish and eels and men crowded its upper reaches, and the legs, paws, and flippers of hundreds of hapless victims helped the monstrosity scuttle this way and that as it writhed upon the dais. Thousands of strange red pustules covered the entity's plump body like angry sores.

Monstrous Iron Head: Init -2; Atk crushing chomp +5 melee (1d12) or crystalline assimilation (special); AC 22; HD 20d10; MV 20' (along attached chain); Act 1d20; SP engulfing crit (on a crit, head engulfs victim in addition to critical damage; DC 20 STR check to escape), crystalline assimilation (DC 13 Will save or engulfed victim's soul is absorbed into crystalline network, leaving body lifeless; head must be connected to network, e.g. via chain, to make this attack), half damage from mundane slashing or piercing weapons; SV Fort +10, Ref -4, Will +8; AL C.

Mutomorphic Flyer: Init +3; Atk muto-attack (see Muto-Attack Table below); AC 13; HD 2d8; MV fly 30'; Act 1d20; SP spell resistant (saves with d30 vs. any spell, even if spell normally doesn't allow a save), muto-memory (remembers and can duplicate attacks from previous creatures it encounters); SV Fort +1, Ref +2, Will +3; AL N.

… creatures that seemed all wings and eyes and claws, as though seabirds had been augmented with parts from sharks and bears and medusae.

Muto-Attack Table: The mutomorphic flyer is a winged fleshy globe composed of eyes, teeth, appendages, etc., that changes form constantly; each attack is unpredictable. Roll a d12 for each attack to see what suddenly-morphed body part tries to inflict damage.

Roll d12	Attack and Damage
1	Eagle foot: talon +3 melee (1d4)
2	Shark head: bite +5 melee (1d8+2)
3	Jellyfish tendrils: stinger +2 melee (1d3, DC 12 Fort save or paralysis for 1d3 rounds)
4	Bear paw: claw +4 melee (1d4+2)
5	Seagull head: peck +1 melee (1 dmg)
6	Snake head: bite +3 melee (1d4, DC 14 Fort save or take additional 2d4 from poison)
7	Manticore tail: spike +3 missile fire (1d6, 60' range)
8	Most recent melee attack: +3 melee (dmg as whatever weapon last hit creature)
9	Mystery appendage, unrecognizable to PCs: +3 melee (2d6)
10	Gorgon Face: Single victim must make DC 11 Will save or turn to stone. Range 60'.
11	Roll again, that attack happens twice!
12	Muto-Split! Instead of attacking, flyer divides itself into two separate flyers (same hp)

GYREKIN CLASS / RACE

Description: You are a creature birthed between the planes of elemental water and prime material. Your natural form is that of a shining liquid vortex (see below), though you can transform into a form similar to a human's to walk on land and breathe the air. However, there is always some not-so-human feature, such as gills, webbed fingers, second pair of eyelids, a dorsal fin, etc., that betrays your true origins. While the less adventurous of your kind stay in the water, teasing mariners with visions of fish-tailed women, unattainable gold in the shallows, land on the horizon that never gets any closer, and other such illusions, you prefer the company of the land-based races. Consequently, you divide your time between land and water, changing from your humanoid to vortex form as needed. Water is your element; you can manipulate it, summon creatures from it, and outperform any other class within it. Indeed, you can even cast spells completely submerged! On land, however, you have a limited time to perform your best. Eventually you must return to water, or perish.

Hit points: A gyrekin gains 1d6 hit points at each level.

Weapon training: Gyrekin only train with piercing weapons, since bludgeoning and slashing attacks are less effective in the water. These weapons include blowgun, crossbow, dagger, javelin, short bow, short sword, spear and long spear (as polearm).

Alignment: Most gyrekin have neutral tendencies, and try to not choose sides in the eternal struggle of Law vs. Chaos.

Vulnerability to Fire: Gyrekin are extremely averse to fire. They suffer double damage from all fire attacks, and receive a -1d penalty to any saving throw, skill check, etc., that involves a fire effect. Gyrekin do not willingly come within 5' of a burning flame. Thus, they do not hold torches, candles, huddle close to a campfire, etc.

Magic: Gyrekin have mastered the manipulation of water, being able to achieve fantastic spell-like effects. They make a spell check as a wizard does, but add their Stamina modifier to the check instead of Intelligence. Sages debate what whether the gyrekin actually perform magic, or something entirely different. Regardless, they can suffer the effects of corruption, just like wizards. Gyrekin have a limited selection of spells they may learn. When one does learn a spell, she transforms it into a manifestation that uses water, and does water elemental damage, if applicable. Gyrekin cannot learn or transform any spell that contains a fire effect. The following spells may be learned; the judge is encouraged to use these as a guide to determining whether a gyrekin can learn a spell not found in the DCC rulebook.
- Level 1: animal summoning (marine animals only), charm person, color spray, force manipulation (uses water instead of "force"), magic missile (water manifestation), ropework (rope is made of twisted water), sleep.
- Level 2: arcane affinity (illusionist, summoner, or aquamancer), ESP, forget, locate object, mirror image, monster summoning (marine monsters only), Nythuul's porcupine coat, phantasm.
- Level 3: consult spirit, dispel magic, eldritch hound (but "shark" instead of hound), haste, slow, water breathing (effects for "caster" may be applied to someone else)
- Level 4: control ice, polymorph (only marine forms), wizard sense.

Caster level: Caster level is a measurement of a gyrekin's ability to channel his water magic. A Gyrekin's caster level is equal to his level as a Gyrekin. A 3rd-level gyrekin has a caster level of 3.

Water-Resting: In order to perform his best, a gyrekin must periodically water-rest, which is spending at least 8 hours resting submerged in a natural body of water (no bathtubs!). In fact, water-resting is the only way a gyrekin can naturally heal hp and ability damage. Resting on dry land offers no healing benefits. Consequently, most gyrekin have marine-based occupations, and are rarely found more than a day away from a natural body of water.

Land Weakness: A gyrekin can function for a limited time outside of the water. She may be away from the water for a number of days equal to her level. If she does not water-rest by that time, she loses 1 point of Stamina per day and suffers a -1d penalty on all actions until she does water-rest. If her Stamina reaches zero in this manner, she evaporates and dies irrevocably.

Infravision: A gyrekin can see in the dark up to 60'.

Vortex Form: The natural form of gyrekin is a luminescent, liquid vortex the size of a human adult. The gyrekin can assume this form whenever underwater, but leaves clothing, weapons, armor, and carried items behind; when a vortex-formed gyrekin transforms back to humanoid form, they do so in the nude.

This form has some advantages. As a vortex, the gyrekin's AC is 10 + gyrekin level + Agility bonus, and base movement is 60'. Although they cannot wield weapons as vortices, gyrekin can perform buffeting melee attacks that do 1d3 + gyrekin level + Strength modifier damage. They may also surround one item in their currents, effectively carrying it, with a maximum weight of 100 lbs per gyrekin level. Despite these limitations, gyrekin can cast their spells normally in vortex form. A gyrekin can transform from vortex to humanoid (or vice versa) a number of times per hour equal to his level.

Water Skills: Naturally, gyrekin can breathe underwater and are excellent swimmers in their humanoid forms, swimming at 40' base rate and receiving a +1d bonus to underwater skill or ability checks. Additionally, gyrekin can detect the flow of water, including speed and volume, in a range of 50' per level. Thus, a 2nd-level gyrekin can detect the flow of water up to 100' away. Sometimes a gyrekin will take human form and pose as a "water witch" to help a town dig a well. Often they use rods or wish-boned branches to fool onlookers, but these devices are unnecessary.

Languages: At 1st level, a gyrekin automatically knows Common, the Tongue of Waves and Weeping, plus one additional language for every point of Int modifier.

Action dice: A gyrekin's action dice can be used for attacks *or* spell checks at any level.

Level	Attack	Crit Die/ Crit Table	Action Dice	Known Spells	Maximum Spell Level	Reflex	Fortitude	Willpower
1	+1	1d6 / I	1d20	2	1	+1	+1	+1
2	+1	1d6 / I	1d20	3	1	+1	+1	+1
3	+2	1d8 / I	1d20	4	1	+1	+1	+2
4	+2	1d8 / I	1d20	5	2	+2	+2	+2
5	+3	1d10 / I	1d20+1d14	6	2	+2	+2	+3
6	+3	1d10 / I	1d20+1d14	7	2	+2	+2	+4
7	+4	1d12 / I	1d20+1d16	8	3	+3	+3	+4
8	+4	1d12 / I	1d20+1d16	9	3	+3	+3	+5
9	+5	1d14 / I	1d20+1d20	10	3	+3	+3	+5
10	+5	1d14 / I	1d20+1d20	11	4	+4	+4	+6

Old Skule

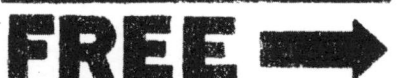

BOOKSTORES OF WONDER

Transport yourself to another world with a visit to your favorite book store. The Skull commands it!

We are not all fortunate enough to live near a great book store, but we meager servants of the Skull are here to help. As part of the Kickstarter to launch this magazine, we asked our backers to tell us about their favorite book stores. Here is their list. You'll notice a few game stores (and other establishments) made it into the list too. Some entries are duplicates. We have deliberately left those duplicates intact, so you can see the varied endorsements and be impressed by multiple recommendations. This is not paid placement – it is word-of-mouth recommendations from other readers of this magazine. In many cases you will see their endorsements.

Would you like to add a local book store this list? E-mail skull@goodman-games.com to tell us!

Country	Region	Details
Brazil	Florianópolis	Dragon's House Hobby Store - Address: Rua Conselheiro Mafra, 246 - Sobreloja - Centro, Florianópolis /SC, zipcode 88010-100, Brazil – The best hobby store in south of Brazil. A great place to buy and gather to play.
Brazil	Rio de Janeiro	Baratos da Ribeiro, R. Paulino Fernandes, 15 - Botafogo, Rio de Janeiro - RJ, 22270-050 – A bookstore that has great out of print collection for very reasonable price!
Canada	Alberta	Books Between Friends, 3434 34 Ave NE #14, Calgary, AB, Canada T1Y 6X3 – Books Between Friends is an entirely not for profit used book store run by Louise Nestrenko. All the money made by the store (after heat, rent and electricity) goes to various charities around the City of Calgary. What makes the store stand out is its massive selection of science fiction and fantasy (at mostly $1-$4 a book), and the passion of its staff for reading and literature.
Canada	Alberta	Sentry Box, 1835 10 Ave SW, Calgary, AB T3C0K2 Sentrybox.com – North America's largest gaming and book store.
Canada	Alberta	Sentry Box, 1835 - 10th Ave SW, Calgary, Alberta, Canada T3C 0K2 – Friendly store with huge selection
Canada	British Columbia	Pulp Fiction Books, 2422 Main St, Vancouver, BC V5T 3E2, www.pulpfictionbooksvancouver.com.
Canada	Ontario	Bakka Phoenix, 84 Harbord Street, Toronto, Ontario M5S 1G5, Canada – Bakka Phoenix is Toronto's premiere science fiction and fantasy bookstore.
Canada	Ontario	BMV Books Toronto - 471 Bloor St. and 10 Edward St. - Used and discounted books (including a wide selection of Appendix N books). Good staff, great shop.
Canada	Ontario	KW Bookstore, Kitchener, ON Canada – Both madness and treasures beyond counting can be found heaped upon its non-euclidean shelves....if you dare.
Canada	Ottawa	Black Squirrel Books - Ottawa, Canada.
Germany	Hamburg	Atlantis - Fantasy & Science Fiction, Güntherstraße 98-100, 22087 Hamburg, Germany – The place in Hamburg to visit for everything from Books to Miniatures, Board- and Roleplaying Games.
Great Britain	East Yorkshire	PS Publishing, Grosvenor House, 1 New Road, Hornsea, East Yorkshire, HU18 1PG, Great Britain – A wonderful selection of beautifully done books at reasonable prices.
Great Britain	Ely	Topping & Company Booksellers of Ely, 9 High Street, Ely, CB7 4LJ, UK – A friendly independent store with a little bit of everything, no matter what your tastes. And they put on a great festival of talks and signings as well!
Great Britain	Leeds	The Travelling Man, Leeds.
Sweden	Stockholm	Science Fiction Book store, Old town Stockholm, Sweden.
USA	Alaska	Title Wave Book Books 1360 W Northern Lights Blvd, Anchorage, AK 99503 – A huge used (and new) book store with almost everything you could want in Anchorage.
USA	Alaska	Hobbies, Crafts & Games; 36254 Kenai Spur Hwy, Soldotna, AK, 99669. HC&G is located in Soldotna and is the only hobby store around. Come by for RPG's, wargaming, MTG, board games, fun for everyone.
USA	Arizona	Book Gallery, 3643 E Indian School Rd, Phoenix, AZ 85018 – They carry first printings of Appendix N literature and original issues of Amazing Stories and Weird Tales magazines.
USA	Arizona	Bookman's at multiple locations in Phoenix AZ - a thorough collection of new & used items of all genres, including paperbacks, magazines, games, video, music, and more.
USA	Arizona	Bookmans 8034 N 19th Ave, Phoenix, AZ 85021. Also a great location in Mesa, AZ.
USA	Arizona	Game Goblins - 1121 S Bowman Rd C7, Little Rock, AR 72211 – Great games and great tournaments. Sponser many tournaments.

USA	Arizona	Zia Record Exchange: 2510 W. Thunderbird Ave. Phoenix, AZ, 85023. I have found more great swords & sorcery and Appendix N fiction here, and at more affordable prices, than anywhere else I have looked!
USA	Arizona	Bookman's, 6230 E. Speedway Blvd. Tucson, AZ 85712 (520) 748-9555.
USA	Arkansas	Dickson Street Bookshop, 325 W Dickson St, Fayetteville, AR 72701 – It keeps good company - https://www.buzzfeed.com/erinlarosa/bookstores-that-will-literally-change-your-life.
USA	California	Book Passage, Corte Madera.
USA	California	Book Shop Santa Cruz, 1520 Pacific Ave, Santa Cruz, CA 95060.
USA	California	Book Soup, 8818 Sunset Blvd, West Hollywood, CA 90069.
USA	California	Bookman, 840 N Tustin St Orange, CA 92867 – They are the only real book store left in the area. Also, they have a huge selection.
USA	California	Copperfield's Books. 3740 Bel Aire Plaza, Napa, CA.
USA	California	Dark Carnival Books, 3086 Claremont Ave Berkeley, California 94705 (510) 654-7323 www.darkcarnival.com https://www.facebook.com/darkcarnivalbooks/ – This bookstore is a Fantasy, Science Fiction, and Mystery lover's dream. They have a ton of books and genre related novelties. It is where I bought my first Tim Powers and Jeffrey Ford books, as well as so many other authors I can't recall. It's a magical place.
USA	California	Dark Carnival Bookstore, 3086 Claremont Ave., Berkeley, CA 94705.
USA	California	Games Empire, Pasadena, Ca.
USA	California	Green Apple Books.
USA	California	Green Apple Books, 506 Clement St, San Francisco, CA 94118 – They are the best new/used book store for spending an hour lost browsing the shelves for all kinds of books
USA	California	Kepler's Books, 1010 El Camino Real, Menlo Park, CA, 94025 – Great selection, great speakers, great service.
USA	California	Logos Books & Records, 1117 Pacific Ave, Santa Cruz, CA 95060 – This multi-floor store is like a hive of books and other great things! The bottom floor is almost like going through a wizards library
USA	California	Pegasus Books, 2349 Shattuck Ave, Berkeley, CA 94704.
USA	California	Tammie's Books, 106 Main Street, Weaverville, CA 96093 – She has a huge selection of books ranging from things published last week to the classic Sci-Fi/Fantasy/S&S from decades ago; you can often find things in her store that you would never find in a modern big-box store and she can order anything you want. Great place to go!
USA	California	The Last Bookstore, downtown Los Angeles.
USA	Colorado	BLACK & READ BOOKS. 7821 Wadsworth Blvd, Arvada, CO 80003 – Extensive collection of out-of-print fantasy from the '60s, '70s, '80s.
USA	Colorado	Park Hill Community Book Store, 4620 E 23rd Ave, Denver, CO 80207 – Awesome co-op with good selection.
USA	Colorado	Tattered Cover - 7301 Santa Fe Drive, Littleton, CO 80120.
USA	Colorado	Tattered Cover Book Store, 2526 East Colfax Avenue, Denver, CO 80206 – They've moved since I went there as a kid, but the memories are real. Size & scope of books was overwhelming. Bought my first book of Greek legends there, as well as so many DragonLance & Forgotten Realms books. Still a great place to browse.
USA	Colorado	The Tattered Cover, 2526 E. Colfax Ave. Denver CO. 80206. A locally owned bookstore with a remarkable selection and fantastic customer service. The Tattered Cover is the premiere bookstore in Denver.
USA	Colorado	Twice Upon A Time Bookshop, 2885 North Ave B, Grand Junction, CO 81501 – They have that great densely packed enviroment of a used bookstore and their selection covers every variety of fiction and a large section of academic history texts.
USA	Florida	Chamblin Bookmine, 4551 Roosevelt Blvd., Jacksonville, FL 32210 – In my opinion, the best bookshop on the east coast from Miami through New York (at least). Incredible selection, great staff.
USA	Florida	Cracker House Books, 236 N. Brevard Ave. Arcadia, FL 34266 - now only open by special appointment. This shop is tucked away from the beaten path, located within a 100+ year old cracker house that is filled to overflowing with great old books.
USA	Florida	Mojo Books & Records, 2540 E Fowler Ave, Tampa, FL 33612.
USA	Florida	The Book Corner, 728 W Lumsden Rd Brandon Fl 33511 – An out of print hardcover bookstore.
USA	Georgia	Corner Bookstore, 43 N. Jackson Street, Winder, GA 30680 – I have purchased many tomes of lore from ages of yore before from this store, and ye shall buy four or more.
USA	Georgia	Heroes and Villains of Warner Robins, 117 Russell Pkwy, Warner Robins, GA 31088, USA.

USA	Georgia	The Book Worm, 4451 Marietta St, Powder Springs, GA 30127, USA – A cozy little used book store that has served the community for years.
USA	Illinois	Anderson's Bookstore, 5112 Main St. Downers Grove, IL.
USA	Illinois	Bookies New and Used Books, 10324 S. Western Chicago, IL 60643.
USA	Illinois	Culture Stock, 43 E Galena Blvd, Aurora, IL 60505.
USA	Illinois	Myopic Books, 1564 N Milwaukee Ave, Chicago, IL 60622 http://www.myopicbookstore.com/ – You may actually get lost.
USA	Illinois	The Book Table, 1045 Lake Street, Oak Park, IL 60301 – Friendly, knowledgeable staff and a great atmosphere.
USA	Illinois	The Gallery Bookstore Ltd. 923 W. Belmont Ave. Chicago, IL 60657.
USA	Illinois	Twice Told Tales, Williams Street, Crystal Lake, IL.
USA	Indiana	Books A Million – They're the only physical Book Store left in the South end of Terre Haute.
USA	Indiana	Caveat Emptor, 112 N Walnut St, Bloomington, IN 47404.
USA	Indiana	Games Inn, 301 Center Street, Hobart, IN 46342.
USA	Indiana	Indy Reads Books, 911 Massachusetts Ave, Indianapolis, IN 46202.
USA	Iowa	Half Price Books, 10201 University Ave, Clive, IA 50325. A great place to find Appendix N fiction!
USA	Iowa	Half Price Books, Clive, 10201 University Ave. Clive IA, 50325.
USA	Kansas	Alas, my favorite book store which sustained me throughout elementary and high school has passed into oblivion. In memoriam, Green Dragon Books of Wichita, KS.
USA	Kentucky	Carmichael's, 1295 Bardstown Road, Louisville, KY 40204.
USA	Kentucky	Joseph-Beth Booksellers, Crestview Hills Town Center, 2791 Town Center Blvd, Crestview Hills, KY 41017, USA.
USA	Massachussetts	Pandemonium Books & Games, 4 Pleasant St, Cambridge, MA 01239, Ph: (617) 547-3721.
USA	Massachussetts	Pandemonium Books and Games 4 Pleasant Street Cambridge MA 02139.
USA	Massachussetts	Pandemonium Books and Games, 4 Pleasant Street Cambridge, MA 02139 – This store has been a friendly source of genre books (and games as well) for decades.
USA	Massachussetts	Three Trolls, 7 Summer St, Chelmsford, MA 01824.
USA	Michigan	Curious Book Shop, 307 East Grand River Ave. East Lansing , MI 48823.
USA	Michigan	Dawn Treader Book Shop, 514 E Liberty St, Ann Arbor, MI 48104.
USA	Michigan	Guild of Blades, Clawson, Mich. 248-430-4980 www.gobretail.com.
USA	Michigan	Nicola's books, 2513 Jackson Ave, Ann Arbor, MI 48103 – A Great independent, locally owned store.
USA	Michigan	Schuler Books & Music, 2660 28th Street SE Grand Rapids, MI 49512.
USA	Michigan	Stadium Cards and Comics, 2061 Golfside Dr. Ypsilanti, MI 48197.
USA	Michigan	Vault of Midnight, 219 S. Main St. Ann Arbor, MI 48104 – Has a generally friendly and welcoming atmosphere, a good selection of comics, and a modest but charmingly eclectic RPG section, that often contains an OSR title or two.
USA	Minnesota	DreamHaven Books at http://dreamhavenbooks.com and 2301 E. 38th St. Minneapolis, MN 55406 (612) 823-6161 – Brilliant, independent book store for the speculative fiction community. New, signed, and vintage books mixed in with graphic novels, comics, and collectibles. Definitely my favorite!
USA	Minnesota	Jimmy Jams. 113 E. 3rd ST Winona MN 55987 – JJ has been a bastion for comics, books, and games for over 20 years. Cool stuff, cool employees, cool owner, cool community!
USA	Minnesota	The Source Comics and Games.
USA	Minnesota	Uncle Hugo's Science Fiction Bookstore, 2864 Chicago Avenue South, Minneapolis, MN 55407 "The best damn collection of Appendix N (and beyond) literature in the Upper Midwest!"
USA	Minnesota	Uncle Hugo's Science Fiction Bookstore/Uncle Edgar's Mystery Bookstore, 2864 Chicago Avenue South, Minneapolis, MN 55407 http://www.unclehugo.com/ – They're the reason I don't have any blank walls or empty bookshelves in my home.
USA	Missouri	Blue and Grey Book Shoppe, 111 N Main #4, Independence, MO 64050 – Best Civil War book store in the area.
USA	Missouri	Inklings' Books & Coffee Shoppe, 1101 W Main St, Blue Springs, MO 64015.
USA	Missouri	Subterranean Books. 6275 Delmar Boulevard, University City, St. Louis, 63130.
USA	Nevada	Amber Unicorn Books, 2101 S Decatur Blvd #14, Las Vegas, NV 89102 – A bibliophile's dream. And that's just the 'open to everyone' section of the store...
USA	Nevada	Grassroots Books, 660 E. Grove St, Reno, NV 89502 – Grassroots Books is Reno's best independent book store. You can find many stories of swords and sorcery in their hallowed walls.

USA	Nevada	The Amber Unicorn, 2101 S Decatur Blvd #14, Las Vegas, NV 89102 – Easily the best used bookstore in Las Vegas.
USA	Nevada	The Amber Unicorn. 2101 S Decatur #14, Las Vegas, NV 89102 – A great used book store deserving of local support. A large genre selection!
USA	New Jersey	Little Shop of Comics, 387 Park Ave, Scotch Plains, NJ 07076.
USA	New Jersey	Second Time Books Inc - 114 Creek Rd, Mt Laurel, NJ 08054 - (856) 234-9335 – Deep and well-stocked shelves of used sci-fi, fantasy, and history. a terrific throwback to the used bookstores of yore.
USA	New Mexico	Coas My Bookstore, 317 North Main Street, Las Cruces, New Mexico 88001 – For all your Appendix N needs! Tell them Trevor sent you!
USA	New York	Fat Cat Comics, 278 Main St, Johnson City, NY 13790.
USA	New York	Iron Crown, 3077 Main St, Buffalo NY 14214.
USA	New York	Strand Book Store, 828 Broadway, New York, NY 10003 – A New York Institution, 18 miles of books!
USA	New York	Strand Bookstore, 828 Broadway, NY, NY 10003.
USA	New York	Strand NYC. Last light left.
USA	New York	The Strand, 828 Broadway, Manhattan, NY 10003-4805 – Sorceries and alchemical tomfoolery abound!
USA	New York	Westsider Rare & Used Books, 2246 Broadway, New York, NY 10024.
USA	North Carolina	Book Buyers, 1306 The Plaza, Charlotte, NC 28205 – As the name suggests, they will purchase the dusty tomes you've pried from skeletal hands. They carry quite the plethora of books to help fill your shelves and, if your lucky, you may meet a few feline friends whilst you shop.
USA	North Carolina	Malaprop's, 55 Haywood Street, Asheville, NC 28801.
USA	North Carolina	Mr. K's Used Books, 800 Fairview Rd. Asheville, NC 28803.
USA	North Carolina	Old Books on Front, 249 N Front St, Wilmington, NC 28401.
USA	North Carolina	Parker, Banner, Kent, and Wayne, 21500 Catawba Ave. Suite A, Cornelius, NC 28031 – Weekly games of playing new roles? What's not to love.
USA	North Carolina	Quail Ridge Books, 4209-100 Lassiter Mill Rd, Raleigh NC 27609.
USA	North Carolina	The Book End Book Store, 119 N Marine Blvd, Jacksonville Onslow NC 28540-6508 – Deals in used books, can find any book you can remember.
USA	North Carolina	Your Local Game Store, 300 East John Street, Suite 110, Matthews, NC 28105 contact@yourlocal-gamestore.com · (704) 729-4547.
USA	Ohio	Bookery Comics & Collectibles, 16 West Main Street, Fairborn OH 45324.
USA	Ohio	Duttenhofer's Books, 214 West McMillan, Cincinnati, OH 45219.
USA	Ohio	Half Price Books Columbus, 1375 W Lane Ave, Columbus, OH 43221.
USA	Ohio	Half-Price Books, 3185 Hamilton Princeton Rd, Hamilton, OH 45011 – Family-owned chain that buys & sells secondhand books as well as movies & music in various formats.
USA	Ohio	The Book Loft, German Village, 631 S 3rd St, Columbus, OH 43206.
USA	Oklahoma	Bibliotech Books and Comics, 123 E Main Street, Shawnee, OK 74804 – Bibliotech is Shawnee's largest used book store and only comic and gaming store. Support your friendly local gaming store.
USA	Oklahoma	Half Price Books. 1159 E. 2nd St. Edmond, OK 73034 (405-359-2934) – Great store, clean, and with a Del Taco across the street!
USA	Oklahoma	Second Chance Books and Comics, 3909 N MacArthur Blvd, Warr Acres Oklahoma 73122 –Because they are awesome!
USA	Oregon	Powell's City of Books, 1005 W Burnside St, Portland, OR 97209 – Aside from the Library of Celaeno gift shop, the finest bookstore I am aware of.
USA	Oregon	Powell's City of Books, 1005 W Burnside St, Portland, OR 97209 – One of the nation's best and largest bookstores, with an entire city block of new & used books, and a large room (the yellow room) dedicated to genre fiction.
USA	Oregon	Powell's City of Books, 1005 W Burnside St., Portland, OR 97209 – Best used books west of the Mississippi.
USA	Oregon	Powell's City of Books, 1005 W.Burnside St. Portland, OR 97209 – A book store occupying an entire city block and housing approximately one million books.
USA	Oregon	Powell's Bookstore, 1005 W Burnside, Portland, OR 97209 "A Cubic Block of Books!"
USA	Oregon	Powell's City of Books, 1005 W Burnside St. Portland, OR 97209 USA "Best and largest bookstore in the entire West."
USA	Pennsylvania	The Archive, 725 West Second Street, Lansdale PA. 19446 – A multi-room, multi-story warehouse of used books and ephemera that any fan of the classics will find rewarding!

USA	Pennsylvania	Comix Connection, 6200 Carlisle Pike, Ste C, Mechanicsburg, PA 17050 – I consume a large part of my Sword & Sorcery diet via graphic novels, and this store has one of the best selections in the area as well as lots of other cool nerd stuff.
USA	Pennsylvania	Thomas Mac slush Used & Rare Books, 130 South Union Street, Kennett Square, PA 19348. – A real gem of a book store. Where else could you find several books written, printed, and annotated by an arthor like Benjamin Franklin that are actually for sale?
USA	Pennsylvania	Caliban Bookshop, 410 South Craig Street, Pittsburgh PA 15213 https://www.calibanbooks.com/ – Caliban has a great selection of books on all topic, but their Paperback Basement is a treasure trove of pulp novels. Added bonus? They're right next door to my favorite gaming store, Phantom of the Attic.
USA	Rhode Island	Cellar Stories Bookstore, 111 Mathewson Street, Providence, RI 02903 – A real treasure, I've gone there for decades now. Enviable display of original Arkham House and other rare editions in the front counter.
USA	Rhode Island	Lovecraft Arts & Sciences, Arcade Providence, Suite 105, 65 Weybosset St. Providence, RI 02903.
USA	South Carolina	Boardwalk, 1175 Woods Crossing Rd, Greenville, SC 29607 – Boardwalk has a great staff. They are very helpful and knowledgeable.
USA	South Carolina	Hub City Writers Project, 186 W. Main St. Spartanburg, SC 29306.
USA	South Dakota	Brookings Book Company (and Comics!), 321 Main Avenue / Brookings, SD 57006 / (605) 692-2665 http://www.brookingsbooks.com/ – Best book & comic joint in eastern South Dakota.
USA	Texas	BookPeople, 603 N. Lamar Blvd, Austin, TX 78703 "Of all the bookstores in all the worlds, you have to walk into this one."
USA	Texas	Dragon's Lair Comics and Fantasy, 7959 Fredricksburg Rd, Suite 129, San Antonio, TX 78229, Ph. #: (210) 615-1229 – They are located just a few blocks from where I live and will order books If I want, and carry lots of nerdy stuff.
USA	Texas	Ettin Games and Hobbies, 241 FM 1960 Bypass Rd East, Humble, TX 77346, www.ettingames.com.
USA	Texas	Half Price Books, 2929 S Lamar Blvd, Austin, TX 78704.
USA	Texas	Heroes and Fantasies 4923 NW Loop 410. San Antonio, TX 78229.
USA	Utah	Weller Book Works l 607 Trolley Square, Salt Lake City, UT 84102, 801-328-2588.
USA	Vermont	Northshire Bookstore, 4869 Main Street, Manchester Center, VT 05255.
USA	Virginia	Mishap Games, 3432 Orange Ave. NE, Roanoke, Va 2401 – With their new(ish) expansion and dedicated gaming room they are a full service gaming hobby store. RPG books, minis, board games, etc., and a friendly, knowledgeable staff makes this a great store.
USA	Virginia	Bender's Books and Cards, 22 S Mallory St, Hampton, VA 23663.
USA	Virginia	Hole in the Wall Books 905 W Broad St, Falls Church, VA 22046.
USA	Virginia	McKay Used Books, 8345 Sudley Rd, Manassas, VA 20109.
USA	Washington	3rd Place Books - Lake Forest Park, 17171 Bothell Way NE, #A101, Lake Forest Park WA 98155 – They have a great selection of role-playing books and materials. They have new and gently used which is great on the pocket book.
USA	Washington	Elliot Bay Book Company, Seattle Washington.
USA	Washington	Golden Age Collectibles, Pike Place Market Seattle WA. – Golden Age is a great spot to find all kinds of stuff and has an enormous selection of graphic novels and art books. The staff is also super friendly and helpful.
USA	Washington	Magus Books, 1408 NE 42nd St, Seattle, WA 98105.
USA	Washington	Main Street Books, Monroe, Washington, This is my local book shop, locally owned and operated. It is tiny and awesome.
USA	Washington	Third Place Books, 17171 Bothell Way NE, Lake Forest Park, WA 98155, This is one of the few book stores that still gives me a sense of wonder. They have a great selection of books and a very helpful staff.
USA	West Virginia	J&Ms Used Book Store, 926 Division Street, Parkersburg, WV 26101 – This store is perfect for special orders, has a classic sci-fi section, a large role playing section, and a sizable board game inventory. They are also incredibly knowledgeable.
USA	Wisconsin	Blue Moon Books – Steven's Point, WI - A great little book store to get lost in. Paperbacks galore!
USA	Wisconsin	Blue Moon Books, 2182 Strongs Ave, Stevens Point, WI 54481 – Many an Appendix N author can be found among the stacks.
USA	Wisconsin	Frugal Muse Books, 235 Junction Rd, Madison, WI 53717 – Many great used tomes change hands here.
USA	Wisconsin	Lake Geneva games 918 s wells lake Geneva WI.
USA	Wisconsin	Renaissance Book Shop, 5300 S Howell Ave; Milwaukee, Wisconsin 53207 – Inside the General Mitchell International Airport, this is the first used bookstore ever located within an airport and has a selection that puts most traditionally located stores to shame.